Production Methods: Behind the Scenes of Virtual Inhabited 3D Worlds

Springer-Verlag London Ltd.

Springer-Verlag London Ltd.

Kim Halskov Madsen (Ed.)

Production Methods

Behind the Scenes of Virtual Inhabited 3D Worlds

Springer

Kim Halskov Madsen
Information and Media Studies, Aarhus University, Aabogade 34,
DK 8200, Åhus, Denmark

British Library Cataloguing in Publication Data
Production methods: behind the scenes of virtual inhabited
3D worlds. - (Human factors and ergonomics series)
 1. Virtual reality 2. Computer programming
 I. Madsen, Kim Halskov
 006
ISBN 978-1-4471-1115-3

British Library Cataloguing in Publication Data
Production methods: behind the scenes of virtual inhabited 3D worlds/Kim Halskov
Madsen (ed.).
     p. cm.
  Includes bibliographical references and index.
  ISBN 978-1-4471-1115-3   ISBN 978-1-4471-0063-8 (eBook)
  DOI 10.1007/978-1-4471-0063-8
  Additional material to this book can be downloaded from http://extras.springer.com
  1. Interactive Multimedia. 2. Virtual reality. I. Madsen, Kim Halskov, 1956–
QA76.76I59 P76 2002
006.7–dc21   2002070459

ISBN 978-1-4471-1115-3

http://www.springer.co.uk

© Springer-Verlag London 2003
Originally published by Springer-Verlag London Berlin Heidelberg in 2003

Typesetting: Gray Publishing, Tunbridge Wells, Kent

34/3830-543210 Printed on acid-free paper SPIN 10877425

Contents

List of Contributors

Jørgen Callesen
The Interactive Institute
Beijerskajen 8
SE-20506 Malmö
Sweden
Email: jorgen.callesen@interactive
institute.se

Ole Caprani
Department of Computer Science
Aabogade 34
DK-8200 Aarhus N
Denmark
Email: oCaprani@daimi.au.dk

Marie Christensen
Playscape Research
Skyggelundsvej 13
2500 Valby
Denmark
Email: marie@playscape.dk

Hanne Dankert
Department of Communication,
Journalism and Computer Science
Roskilde University
Postboks 260
DK-4000 Roskilde
Denmark
Email: hanned@ruc.dk

Lars Bo Eriksen
Visanti ApS
Gugvej 127
9210 Aalborg SØ
Denmark

Jakob Fredslund
BiRC – Bioinformatics Research
Center
Department of Computer Science
University of Aarhus
Ny Munkegade, Building 540
DK-8000 Aarhus C
Denmark
Email: chili@daimi.au.dk

Jørgen Møller Ilsøe
Vigerslevvej 340
DK-2500 Valby
Denmark

Jens Jacobsen
Cotas, Paludan-Möllersvej 82
DK-8200 Aarhus N
Denmark
Email: jens.jacobsen@person.dk

Jesper Kjeldskov
Aalborg University
Department of Computer Science
Fredrik Bajers Vej 7
DK-9220 Aalborg Øst
Denmark
Email:jesper@cs.auc.dk

Torunn Kjølner
Department of Dramaturgy
University of Aarhus
Langelandsgade 139
8000 Aarhus C
Denmark
Email: dratk@hum.au.dk

Søren Kolstrup
Department of Information and
Media Studies
Aabogade 34
DK-8200 Aarhus N
Denmark
Email: skolstr@imv.au.dk

Line Kramhøft
Samsøgade 89
DK-8000 Aarhus C
Denmark
Email: linekramhoeft@hotmail.com

Bettina Lamm
Playscape Research
Valnøddegården 33
2620 Albertslund
Denmark
Email: bettina@playscape.dk

Bjørn Laursen
Department of Communication,
Journalism and Computer Science
Roskilde University
Postboks 260
DK-4000 Roskilde
Denmark
Email: bLaursen@ruc.dk

Morten Lervig
Center for Advanced Visualisation
and Interaction
Aabogade 34
DK-8200 Aarhus N
Denmark
Email: mortenl@intermedia.au.dk

Rasmus B. Lunding
Købmagergade 28A
Gylling
DK-8300 Odder
Denmark
Email: ras.blund@get2.net.dk

Kim Halskov Madsen
Department of Information and
Media Studies
Aabogade 34
DK-8200 Aarhus N
Denmark
Email: halskov@imv.au.dk

Mikael B. Skov
Department of Computer Science
Aalborg University
Fredrik Bajers Vej 7
9220 Aalborg Øst
Denmark
Email: dubois@cs.auc.dk

Jan Stage
Aalborg University
Department of Computer
Science
Fredrik Bajers Vej 7
DK-9220 Aalborg Øst
Denmark
Email: jans@cs.auc.dk

Janek Szatkowski
Department of Dramaturgy
University of Aarhus
Langelandsgade 139
8000 Aarhus C
Denmark
Email: drajsz@hum.au.dk

Mads Wahlberg
Wahlberg Teknik
Jægergårdsgade 152/ 05A
DK-8000 Aarhus C
Denmark
Email: mads@wahlberg.dk

Niels Erik Wille
Department of Communication,
Journalism and Computer
Science
Roskilde University
Postboks 260
DK-4000 Roskilde
Denmark
Email: new@ruc.dk

1

Introduction

Kim Halskov Madsen

Up until a few decades ago, business administration and science were the primary areas in which computers were applied, but terms like *pervasive computing* reflect that interactive computing power is becoming an embedded part of people's everyday environment, not only office buildings and private homes but also art and cultural events. At one of the frontiers of multimedia applications computers are used as part of experimental theatre, puppet theatre, musical performances, museums, entertainment, and learning. In some of these domains, people interact with the computers using a mouse, keyboard and a 17-inch monitor, but present-day interfaces take a variety of forms, including motion-capture technology and displays of up to several metres in height and width.

The trend of applying computer technologies in the domain of art and culture has been one of the pivots of a Danish research project, *Staging of Virtual Inhabited 3D Spaces*. The results of the project are presented in a series of four volumes, of which this book is the last one. The three other publications are: *Virtual Interaction: Interaction in Virtual Inhabited 3D Worlds*; *Virtual Space: The Spatiality of Virtual Inhabited 3D Worlds*; and *3D Applications: Applications with Virtual Inhabited 3D Worlds*.

The present volume, *Behind the Scenes of Virtual Inhabited 3D Worlds*, is about the production processes where digital and physical elements are brought together in virtual inhabited 3D worlds. The chapters of the book are primarily case-oriented and recount the exciting stories of specific production process, focusing on such themes as scriptwriting techniques, interdisciplinary co-operative teams, visualisation of ideas, motivation, prototyping and experimental development. This book brings together a wealth of knowledge from theatre production, film production, design, art and, last but not least, software engineering.

The first two chapters establish a connecting link to computer science. In Chapter 2 Mikael Skov and Lars Bo Eriksen investigate the applicability of an object-oriented analysis approach for the design of interactive narratives focusing on three major activities, namely system choice, problem domain analysis, and application domain analysis. As the test case for the investigation of the applicability of these activities they use Virtual Management®, which is a tool for recruitment consultants during the process of evaluating and assessing job candidates for various job positions. It is a narrative multimedia system, which by using video clips places the job candidates in difficult work situations in a virtual environment. The basic idea is to simulate typical work situations and compel the job candidate to make decisions and manage in these situations. The main conclusion is that there are serious discrepancies between the assumptions behind an object-oriented analysis approach and the situation you are in, when designing interactive narratives. Conventional software engineering approaches need to be adapted to the new situation and methodological knowledge from theatre, film, and so on, needs to be incorporated.

Chapter 3 by Jesper Kjeldskov and Jan Stage takes us from software engineering to human–computer interaction issues by evaluating tools for developing software applications that are targeted at virtual reality display systems like CAVE. The evaluation focuses on the relevance of command language and direct manipulation with graphical representation as the fundamental interaction style of such tools. The basis of the evaluation is an empirical study of two development processes where a tool representing each of the interaction styles was used to develop the same virtual reality application. The development tool that employed a command language was very flexible and facilitated an even distribution of effort and progress over time, but debugging and identification of errors were very difficult. The tool that employed direct manipulation enabled faster implementation of a first prototype but did not facilitate a shorter implementation process as a whole.

The following five chapters bring us into the realm of film, music, paintings, drawings, and theatre.

In Chapter 4, Hanne Dankert and Niels Erik Wille start out with an overview of the variety of forms which scriptwriting techniques may take in film and theatre production. The main focus of the chapter is an exploration of scriptwriting for interactive 3D documentaries, using a work-in-progress on the Nordic Bronze Age as a specific case. Four exhibits, a research summary, a treatment and two outlines, illustrate three alternative interactive approaches to the dissemination of information concerning the Nordic Bronze Age. The first approach is based on the use of a more traditional, screen-oriented digital medium like a stand-alone information kiosk, the Web or a CD-ROM production. The second and third approaches are based on the notion of virtual reality and 3D space: perception space, movement space and body space.

In Chapter 5, Morten Lervig initially observes that, with the spread of new technologies for the production and performance of music, have come new challenges for the visual staging of music. With the advent and increasing utilisation of computers, the inter-relation between what is seen and what is heard is no longer as clear. Morten Lervig provides a comprehensive analysis of a music production aiming at exploring the link between audio and visual elements. The fundamental idea in the production is to take video and motion-captured material of a singer, while she performs one of her songs and then use this material in a virtual 3D world. The focus of the analysis of the production process was the interest in gaining greater insight into, and understanding better, what actually happens in the artistic process when a composer works with 3D.

In Chapter 6, Søren Kolstrup takes us to the world of drawings and paintings in terms of the development of a practical and theoretical tool for the investigation and construction of pictures with an analytical eye. The goal was to supply students and others with a tool that could assist them in answering questions like 'On which basis do we construct pictures?' and 'On which basis do we understand these pictures?' The original conception was based on already existing 2D pictures seen as combinations of set pieces, somehow like the ones that existed in the baroque theatre, and where the idea was to provide the user with the opportunity of combining flat elements which partly overlap each other. The tool ended up being implemented using a 3D tool, which opens up some possibilities and closed others. The *Tool for Picture Analysis*, which is in fact a prototype, covers four aspects: space, light, movement and composition. Each aspect is treated in three sections: (1) a general and systematic introduction, (2) web resources containing a short historical explanation and web addresses, and finally (3) experimental presentations of pictures. The current version of the *Tool for Picture Analysis* is on the CD enclosed in the present book.

In Chapter 7, Bjørn Laursen and Kim Halskov Madsen look into the production of images of Viking ships for the interactive screen of *The Eye of Wodan*, a multimedia installation which tells the story of the life of the Danish Vikings. A central part of the installation is an interactive screen that enables visitors to explore drawings of Viking-age scenes on a canvas larger in size than the screen. The chapter focuses on the complex use of the design materials applied, including scale models, photographs, hand-drawn sketches, and cardboard models. Particular emphasis is placed on the evolution of the raw materials through a series of experiments and transformations, which eventually lead to a new kind of topological image.

In Chapter 8, Torunn Kjølner and Janek Szatkowski explain how *devising* has become a commonly used term for a set of principles for the production of contemporary theatre performances. According to the two authors, devising can be considered to cover a collection of practices that have certain characteristics in common, including focus on collaboration, generation of material, and composition. As opposed to conventional theatre production, which starts out from a text, devised theatre may start out from almost anything, for example a photo, a biography or a location. The particular way of thinking unique to *devising* is illustrated by the production of *Man Power*, which is a performance where a small audience walks and stands inside ten mobile 2 m × 3 m big projections screens. During the performance the position of the screens is changed four times forming different spatial configurations, while the screens were used for projections of slides, live video, 3D animation and shadow work.

The chapter on devising did address the issue of collaboration but the following three chapters have a particularly strong focus on interdisciplinary collaboration.

In Chapter 9, Jørgen Callesen takes us to a new interdisciplinary art form, *performance animation*, which includes the manipulation of a computer-generated image in real time by a performing artist using motion-capture technology. Callesen emphasises that this field is interdisciplinary in its core, since it requires the participation of performers, animators/3D modellers, programmers and system developers. As an illustrative case of performance animation, the chapter tells the story all the way from the initial idea to the final premier of *The Family Factory*, which is a performance in this new genre, bringing people from as diverse areas as puppet theatre, 3D animation and software engineering. Activities covered include scriptwriting, character development, experimenting with puppet animation using motion-capture technology and design of virtual puppets.

In Chapter 10, Ole Caprani and his team take us further into the realm of the mixture of digital and physical materials. An investigation of LEGO robots as a medium for artistic expression has evolved from an initial idea of animal-like robots, to Bugs, and finally to an artificial world, *The Jungle Cube*, inhabited by Bugs. The robots use movements and sounds to express what to an observer seems like emotions, intentions and social behaviour. To enhance the perception of Bug behaviour as aggressive, hungry, afraid, friendly, or hostile, the artificial world has been created for the Bugs, an environment with a soundscape, dynamic lighting and a scenography of biologically inspired elements. The making of *The Jungle Cube* was an *artistic prototyping* process, which took the multidisciplinary effort of a team of software engineers, a composer, a scenographer, and a light designer, who each contributed to the unique experience of *The Jungle Cube*.

In Chapter 11, Morten Lervig and Kim Halskov Madsen provide an analysis of three artistic projects from a virtual studio, which is a video technology that makes it possible to combine videos of physical objects, such as people, with video images generated in real time from digital 3D models. The artistic background includes oil painting, sculpture and concept art, and the production team includes, in addition, people with a background in 3D, scenography and architecture. The experiences from the project are presented in terms of an outline of a pattern-language, identifying important issues and providing guidelines concerning the use of aesthetic materials, the technical and the aesthetic competencies, the co-operative nature of the production process, and so on.

In Chapter 12, Marie Christensen and Bettina Lamm tell the story about how motivation and visual expression have been the focal point in the development of *Morgana*, which is a digital multimedia universe on a CD-ROM. The user can set off on a spiritual and poetic journey into a landscape charged with symbolic meaning and fairytale atmosphere. An essential part of the driving motivation of the development process has been to develop an experience that would appeal to women by introducing emotions and personal growth into the experience of entering the universe.

In its totality the book covers a broad span of methodology issues concerning the application of diverse technologies and addressed from a large number of fields (see Table 1.1).

Table 1.1 Overview of the chapters.

Chapter	Technology	Methodology issue	Tradition
2	PC	Object-oriented analysis	Computer science
3	PC and CAVE	Interaction style of development tool	Computer science
4	PC and projection screens	Scriptwriting	Film
5	Video and motion capture	Transformation from music to visual 3D	Music
6	CD-ROM	2D vs 3D Picture construction	Painting and drawing
7	Projection screens	Design materials	Drawing
8	Motion capture and projection screens	Devising	Theatre
9	Motion capture and projection screens	Inter-disciplinarity	Computer science, puppet theatre and 3D animation
10	RCX controlled robots and light	Artistic co-operative prototyping	Computer science, light design and music
11	Virtual studio, video and Internet	The artistic process	Painting, sculpture and conceptual art
12	PC	Motivation and visual expression	Architecture and visual arts

CD-ROM

This volume includes a CD-ROM with picture and video material from the production cases presented in the book. Furthermore, it contains the *Tool for Picture Analysis* from Chapter 6.

Acknowledgment

This book has been made possible through support from the Danish Research Councils, Grant no 9600869 (*The Staging of Virtual Inhabited 3D Spaces*), which have funded the major part of the work on which the book is based.

2

Evaluating Software Engineering Modelling Concepts for Interactive Narratives Design

Mikael B. Skov and Lars Bo Eriksen

Mikael B. Skov has a background as a computer scientist and has worked with systems development methods for many years. He has recently started to explore the role of systems development methods in interactive narratives design.

Lars Bo Eriksen has a background as a computer scientist and has worked with Internet technologies for several years.

2.1 Introduction

Webb (1996) points out that most multimedia systems are functionally more complex than conventional computer systems and are often used by a wider range of inexperienced or novice users. Also, multimedia systems often incorporate a higher degree of human–computer interaction than more conventional systems. The increased complexity in functionality is often a result of integration of modalities, time variation and navigation. The design and creation of multimedia systems is difficult and challenging (Grosky, 1994). During the last couple of years, with the evolution of hardware technologies, numerous multimedia applications have been the focus for industrial development and research interest (cf. Druin and Solomon, 1996; Plowman and Luckin, 1998; Webb, 1996). The diffusion of multimedia technologies has been so intensive that multimedia systems have emerged and penetrated almost every type of environmental settings. These applications include a wide range of computer-based systems ranging from interactive storytelling for children at a hospital unit (cf. Umaschi Bers et al., 1998), to educational titles for work professionals (cf. Lewis et al., 1998).

The broad variety of multimedia applications makes it difficult to identify and delimit the class of applications. In fact, Eriksen, Skov and Stage (2000) state that it is difficult to identify a unified and accepted definition of the term "multimedia system". McKerlie and Preece (1993) offer a broad definition with an asset perspective saying that a multimedia system is an "umbrella term for the integration of different elements, such as text, graphics, video, still photographs and sound, in a single application". Nemetz and Johnson (1998) expand this definition using an interaction perspective stating that "multimedia systems encompass both input and output media and focus on human–computer interaction rather than on the technological aspects". Skov and Stage (2001) define a multimedia system as "a computer-based system that integrates a multitude of assets to facilitate user immersion and activity in a virtual situation. The assets are representing fragments of a fictitious situation and are based on modalities such as text, graphics, pictures, video, animations, sound, tactile information, and motion." They continue by saying that multimedia systems "involve interaction with objects in the virtual situation and it is limited by certain temporal and spatial structures. A plot usually defines the development of the virtual situation." Webb (1996) argues that multimedia systems are more mediums or theatres than tools, bringing new kinds of complexity into the design of these systems. As shown, more multimedia systems integrate aspects of narrativity or storytelling in creating immerse and entertaining computer-based systems. In the remainder of this chapter, we will refer to a specific class of multimedia systems called "interactive narratives" that enables users to create stories when using the system.

The design of interactive narratives is more difficult and less understood than conventional software design (cf. Grosky, 1994; Sutcliffe and Faraday, 1994). During the development of conventional software, designers are primarily concerned with identification and description of work processes and work tasks (cf. Booch, 1994; Rumbaugh et al., 1991; Jacobson et al., 1992; Mathiassen et al., 1999). However, Webb (1996) stresses that the business metaphor does not apply well for interactive narratives design since many interactive narratives are not intended for supporting work tasks in a traditional sense. Furthermore, Sutcliffe and Faraday (1997) state that research within interactive narratives design shows that contemporary interactive narratives are designed and created primarily by intuition and hence lacking method support and systematic approaches to work practices. Years of research within software engineering shows that improvements in software design processes require systematic work practices that involve well-founded methods (cf. Fairley, 1985; Pressman, 1996; Sommerville, 1992). Furthermore, Eriksen, Skov and Stage (2000) recognise that no methodological approach to interactive narratives design that embodies an established tradition exists.

This chapter investigates the usefulness of software engineering concepts for the design of a typical interactive narrative. This is done by discussing the key concepts and activities of a systems development method in the context of a specific interactive narrative. The chapter is organised as follows: Section 2.2 presents the background of systems development methods and concepts, and the example of an interactive narrative, which will be used for the discussion. Section 2.3 illustrates the applicability of these concepts for interactive narratives design. Finally, Sections 2.4 and 2.5 discuss the results and conclude the work.

2.2 Background

We will investigate the applicability or usefulness of key concepts of an established systems development method for the design of interactive narratives. First, we will introduce the focus and concepts of systems development methods and show how development methods have evolved over time. Second, we will describe a real inter-active narrative, which will be used for the discussion. Finally, we will present the chosen method for this discussion.

2.2.1 Systems Development and Methods

Mathiassen et al. (1999) state that system development involves the adaptation of computerised systems to peoples' needs. That is, during the development of com-puter systems, you are focusing on making the computer system useful and usable for people. As a result of a long tradition, the system development process consists of three activities – analysis, design and programming – where programming is the key activity with its focus on the actual construction (Booch, 1994; Rumbaugh et al., 1991; Jacobson et al., 1992; Mathiassen et al., 1999). Before programming, the system needs to be understood and described. The goal of analysis and design activities of systems development is to create an overview of requirements to the system and establish a basis for implementing the system (Mathiassen et al., 1999). Jacobson et al. (1992) state that since systems development is a relatively young industry, the development of software systems has not reached the level of maturity typically found in traditional branches. Therefore, developed systems often suffer from a lack of the established practices required for their development and exploitation as com-mercial products.

System development methods are attempts to systematise and mature the dev-elopment process by establishing standard notations, guidelines and processes for the development. Booch (1994) defines a system development method as a disciplined process for generating a set of models that describes various aspects of a software system under development using some well-defined notation. Sommerville (1992) continues by arguing that most system development methods can be characterised as either top-down structured design, data-driven design, or object-oriented design. Top-down structured design methods (e.g. Yourdon and Constantine, 1979; Myers, 1978), are characterised by algorithmic decomposition of the problem. Top-down structured design methods have shown their usability for many years and are probably more used than any other methods (Booch, 1994), but do not address issues of data abstraction or information hiding and have problems when modelling extreme complex systems. Data-driven design methods (e.g. Jackson, 1975; Orr, 1971), are characterised by the direct mapping of system inputs and outputs and have been successfully applied in modelling complex domains like information management systems. Object-oriented design methods (e.g. Booch, 1994; Rumbaugh et al., 1991; Jacobson et al., 1992), rely on the fact that one should model software systems as collections of co-operating objects, treating individual objects as instances of a class within a hierarchy of classes. During the 1990s object-oriented design methods became state-of-the-art both within research and industry (cf. Mathiassen et al., 1999) and with the invention of the Unified Modelling Language (UML), this position has been strengthened even more.

Even though system development methods have evolved in response to the growing complexity of software systems (cf. Booch, 1994), the methods are direct symbols of their time. Monarchi and Puhr (1992) argue that most object-oriented analysis methods emphasise modelling the problem domain. The methods are concerned with abstracting relevant objects from the problem domain, defining the structure and behaviour of the objects, and determining the interrelationships of the objects. The goal is to model the semantics of the problem in terms of distinct but related objects. Booch (1994) extends this by saying that object-oriented analysis is a method of analysis that examines requirements from the perspective of the classes and objects found in the vocabulary of the problem domain. Hence, the focus is on analysing and describing the problem domain and on work tasks of future users of the system. Züllighoven (1998) even stresses that the systems of focus are intended to support the work of domain experts of a given problem domain. Typical examples would be administrative systems such as a bank account system, or technical, embedded systems such as a cruise control system for a car.

2.2.2 The System Development Method Case: OOA&D

The chosen development method for this investigation is a Scandinavian systems development method. It is called Object-Oriented Analysis and Design (OOA&D) (cf. Mathiassen et al., 1997, 1999). The motivation for choosing this particular method is straightforward. It combines strengths from a number of well-known system development methods (Booch, 1994; Jackson, 1983; Jacobson et al., 1992; Rumbaugh et al., 1991). In addition, it integrates the Unified Modelling Language (UML) as notation.

We have chosen to include only the analysis part here. The analysis part consists of three major activities, namely system choice, problem domain analysis and application domain analysis. First, in the system choice activity, one has to establish a foundation for the remaining analysis by selecting and describing the overall structure of the future computerised system. Second, in the problem domain analysis, the computerised system must be understood from an information perspective. It contains a model of the relevant elements in the problem domain that enables the users to administrate, monitor or control phenomena in the problem domain. Third, in the application domain analysis, the computerised system should be understood from the user's point of view. One should understand which people, apparatuses and other computerised systems it should interact with and which functions to offer these actors (Mathiassen et al., 1999).

2.2.3 The Interactive Narrative Case: Virtual Management®

Virtual Management® is an interactive narrative developed by a Danish software firm, InterAct ApS. Virtual Management® is an interactive narrative in the sense that it creates or presents stories to the user in order to enhance realism in use. The stories of the system enable users to identify and recognise familiar situations of real life situations.

Virtual Management® can be viewed in two different ways. First, it is a tool for recruitment consultants during the process of evaluating and assessing job candidates for various work positions. Secondly, and for this chapter more importantly, it is a narrative multimedia system placing the job candidates in difficult work situations in a virtual environment. The basic idea is to simulate typical work situations and compel the job candidate to make decisions and manage in these situations. Figure 2.1 shows a typical situation from Virtual Management® where a video sequence from a staff meeting is played.

The job candidate plays a virtual figure in the story (system) and is going to attend a staff meeting as the new manager of the department. The job candidate is to assess the situation of the staff meeting and later make a decision on the situation. The candidate can select from different predefined decisions, leave the meeting, interrupt people talking etc. Often these video sequences reflect conflicts in the organisation forcing the candidate to make both unpleasant and tough decisions. All actions of the job candidate are recorded for later analysis and assessment.

Further aspects of Virtual Management® will be discussed during the evaluation in the following sections. We will not discuss concepts and activities from the actual design process of Virtual Management® in this chapter, the system will merely serve as a concrete example of a typical interactive narrative. Discussion of the design process can be found in Skov and Stage (2001).

Figure 2.1 A scene from Virtual Management®, where video footage from a staff meeting is played.

2.3 Interactive Narratives Analysis

Having established the foundation for this discussion, we will discuss key concepts and aspects of the three activities of the analysis part.

2.3.1 System Choice: Two Kinds of Situations

A computerised system in OOA&D is put into use in a specific use context called the application domain. The purpose of the system is to administrate, control or monitor a problem domain. Users interact with the system, either to feed data into the system about changes in the problem domain, or to get information from the system about the problem domain. These actions make sense in a broader organisational view of a situation. For example, a librarian who uses an information system to register that a book has been loaned by a particular user of the library, or the same librarian uses the information system to check whether a book is available for loan or whether it has been reserved etc. The librarian is in the application domain, administrating the problem domain of books and book loaners. The problem domain and the application domain are part of the same *situation* in which objects, users, structures and processes are causally coupled. An important part of the method is to understand which parts of the situation belong to the problem domain, which parts belong to the application domain, and which parts of the complex reality does not belong in the system development project at all.

Let us look at the Virtual Management® case. The situation for this system would be the environment in which the job candidate takes the test or uses the system. This environment could be any kind of room or office where the job candidate can interact with the system without being disrupted. In fact, the environment could be any kind of room; the job candidate could in fact sit at home doing the test. Therefore, analysis and definition of this situation does not necessarily bring any important information to the development on how the system should be used. On the other hand, one could argue that another kind of situation exists, namely the situation that is depicted by video footage in the system. As illustrated in Figure 2.2, the situation is a staff meeting where the job candidate as the new manager of the department is confronted with a virtual situation.

The video footage depicts a situation where the manager is having a conversation with the employees. This is not the situation presented in OOA&D, however, and one could argue that we need to analyse the situation at different levels. Interactive narratives often require analysis of situations at two levels: the situation which is to be depicted by the interactive narrative (we name it system content situation), and the situation in which the interactive narrative is to be used (we name it system use situation). Whereas administrative, control or monitor systems have a tight coupling between problem and application domain, interactive narratives may have very little. Using the two types of situations mentioned above, the system content situation describes the simulated management environment in which the job candidate reacts, and the system use situation describes the environment, e.g. an office, in which the job candidate takes the test.

Figure 2.2 A scene from Virtual Management® – employees from the department outline the current problems in the department to the new manager (the user).

The consequence of there being no single situation is that we cannot simply look at the future use context to get information about what is to be in the system. We may identify needs or problems in an application context, but these will not necessarily help us in understanding the situation to be depicted by the system. Thereby the principle, "Use the situation of the users as a basis, but be critical towards the task description", does not have the same impact as it has when problem domains and application domains are tightly coupled. Whereas an administrative system development project will gain much information by looking into the everyday situation of future users to learn about processes, structures and objects being managed, the situation of an interactive narrative user will not necessarily inform system developers as to what the system should contain. This is because the system situation is not part of the user situation. We may identify a need of some sort by looking at the user's situation, but when it comes to realising an interactive narrative that fulfils this need, we are left almost blank on whether we are to shoot 35 hours of movie, segment it into a hyper-structure, replicating a multiple choice test, or whether we should produce an interactive book, or something completely different.

2.3.2 Problem Domain Analysis: No One-to-one Relation Between Environment and System

Having separated the situation description into two situations for interactive narratives, the next question arises whether the concepts of problem domain and application domain are still useful for describing interactive narratives in detail. At first glance the definition of problem domain poses problems by the terms with which it is constructed. Interactive narratives are typically not used to *administrate, monitor or control* something. Interactive narratives often convey a story (or plot) and serve as the basis for an experience of some duration. To make the definition more adequate in terms one could extend it to: "...administrated, monitored, controlled *or simulated* by the means of a computer-based system". This extension would allow for a broader range of system, possibly including interactive narratives, to fit into the scope of OOA&D, but at a more fundamental level the definition still is troublesome in its reliance on an environment. Our argument is that there is no environment of relevance, at least not in the terms of OOA&D. The environment referred to in the definition of problem domain must necessarily be the environment of the user. But as argued in the previous section this environment is part of system use situation, and not necessarily system content situation. And the study of the environment of the user does not inform us on how to structure the system.

OOA&D assumes that there will be a one-to-one correspondence between the user environment and a model of that environment within the system – the purpose of user interaction with the system being to either update the model in the system, or to extract data from the system to get information on the real world objects. Since this is not the case for an interactive narrative in which a virtual environment is created, the definition of problem domain leaves the developers using OOA&D with no idea of how to make sense of the problem domain definition in interactive narratives design. The argument for situations which lack one-to-one correspondence between the user environment and the system model creates problems with the definition of an object system. The definition of an object system is reliant on the definition of problem domain, and as we have argued above, the problem domain definition is not valid for many interactive narratives; thus the object system definition is probably not valid either.

Virtual Management® works around a temporal plot or structure. The data in the system is a representation of the segments that make up the story, with functionality that will alter the flow of the story in response to the user's interaction. Figure 2.3 illustrates a general representation of the temporal structure in Virtual Management®, where the boxes represent video clips depicting different work situations, and the arrow-lines represent different choices or selections made available to the user. Each selection made by the user activates a certain video clip to be played thereby making up the entire plot of the system.

Let us return to the situation illustrated in Figure 2.2 as an example of this structure. Here the user is the manager of a department taking part in a staff meeting. Suddenly the phone rings, and the video sequence is stopped. The user is then forced to select one of typically four predefined actions, e.g. answer the phone, or continue talking with staff. Based on the choice of the user the story continues and this pattern is continuous through the entire use of the application. The actions of the user in a temporal plot only moves in one direction: forwards. There may be some diversions on the way, but the nature of a temporal plot is that the experience will progress towards an ending. Virtual Management® has actually integrated an

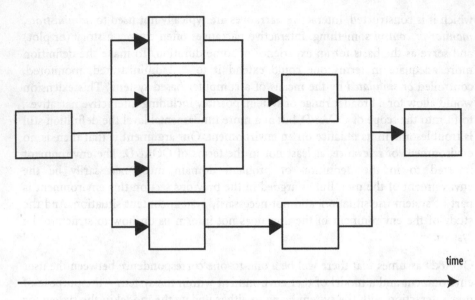

Figure 2.3 Illustration of the temporal structure in Virtual Management®.

explicit representation of the temporal aspect. A clock is shown at all times in the top right-hand corner of each screen picture, indicating the virtual time of the day to the user. From Figure 2.1 to Figure 2.2 you will notice that the time has changed from 9.05 to 9.10.

Whereas Virtual Management® evolves around a temporal structure, other kinds of interactive narratives are built upon spatial structures, e.g. various arcade games, where the user typically orientates and navigates in a 3D virtual environment. Take, for instance, the famous action game "Quake" developed by id Software. Here the user is a virtual figure in a virtual spatial world where the goal is to eliminate other virtual figures.

The two types of system realised from relying on either *temporal* or *spatial* organisation of the plot, rely on very different models. Whereas the spatial plot is represented in a spatial structure in which the user orientates and navigates, the temporal plot is represented in a temporal structure indicating flow of progression. This distinction we believe to be fundamental, in that it is informing at a basic level on how the content of the system will be structured. Both the definitions of object system and model are highly reliable on the definition of the problem domain. Having argued that the definition of problem domain is not applicable when it comes to developing interactive narratives, the consequence is that one of the basic building blocks of OOA&D, the model, in its definition becomes blurred.

2.3.3 Application Domain Analysis: Lack of Focus on Interaction

User actions are related to either feeding information to the system for maintaining the model, or to extracting information from the system with the purpose of getting information on the real world objects, thereby using the system to automate trivial tasks. The applications are sometimes trivial identified for future computer-based interactive narratives. Some interactive narratives are intended for training purposes for specific work tasks. As an example, take a training system for engineers working at a nuclear power plant where the objective is to train engineers in operating a specific part of the main control system. Here you are able to describe the application domain and furthermore identify work tasks of these engineers. However, another type of training system, namely Virtual Management®, does not share the same characteristics. Here you cannot identify the same type of user but the environment may vary from time to time.

Further, OOA&D suggests that aspects of using the system should form the basis when describing the application domain. The focus is on actors and use patterns. Conceptually we question the firmness of the definition of an actor: "[A] role including users ... which has the same use pattern." We find this definition to be somewhat wrong. An actor fulfils a role – an actor is an instance of a human being, the role is the general pattern. For example, many different actors have played the role of Hamlet. OOA&D mixes up the concepts of actor and role into one definition. Secondly, we claim, the concept of *use pattern* is not applicable to the use of interactive narratives. Let us look at the distinction between spatial and temporal structured interactive narratives. First, in spatial structured interactive narratives, the actions of the user are of the type orientation, navigation or general actions. These actions may not necessarily arise from predefined patterns of interaction; they may arise from the history of the interaction, the current state of the system, or the user's intentions. Secondly, in temporal-structured interactive narratives, specifying a progressive plot, the temporal structure of the system is exactly a use pattern. Any user interaction with a temporal structured interactive narrative, will undertake the predefined plot of progression, possibly with some deviations dependent on the sophistication of the plot structure. However, whereas use patterns by definition are relatively small sequences of interaction with the system, a temporal plot structure is a specification of the complete interaction, including a beginning, middle and an end.

Another assumption of OOA&D failing to meet the form and structure of interaction with an interactive narrative is the assumption that there is a strong relationship between real world activities (tasks in the application domain) and what is represented in the system. This assumption does not hold for interactive narratives, rather the situation is the opposite. Interactive narratives at best simulate real world activities, and in case they do, these activities are not necessarily related to tasks in the user's environment. The everlasting principle of "the inseparability of form and content" is the key to the conflicts between method concepts and interactive narrative development. The temporal plot structure is a form for how to present the actual content of an interactive narrative. The observation is that a temporal plot structure is one single use pattern, and that spatial plot structures do not afford specification of use patterns. This leads us to conclude that the concepts of actor and use pattern cannot immediately transcend to interactive narrative development.

2.4 Conclusion

This chapter has illustrated some of the discrepancies between the traditional software engineering concepts for modelling computer systems and requirements for interactive narrative development. Our main critique of the concept applicability in interactive narrative development is on the basic assumption of a single situation comprising a problem domain and an application domain. We have argued by example that this initial view of a situation is not applicable in interactive narrative development. The consequence of this observation is far reaching for applicability of the method, because the conceptual framework of terms created in the method builds on the one situation assumption. As argued in this chapter both the problem domain activity and the application domain activity builds on the one situation perspective, and hence these activities cannot inform interactive narrative developers with the same degree of detail as the method afforded by more traditional systems development.

Future research within the field may show how methodological support can be provided for the development of interactive narratives. The key question could be whether methods are appropriate or applicable in interactive narrative development at all. Some would probably argue that designing interactive narratives is an even more creative activity than designing traditional systems and, hence, one cannot set up activities and guidelines to be followed for this kind of systems development. Webb (1996) argues that interactive narratives are more theatres than software tools and should therefore be treated as such. However, Skov and Stage (2001) found that interactive narratives that have been developed as narratives or movie productions suffer in software quality with respect to performance and stability. This is supported by Sutcliffe and Faraday (1994), saying that most interactive narratives are developed and created by intuition. We believe, however, that more empirical studies of the design process of interactive narratives, such as the one presented in Skov and Stage (2001) are needed.

Acknowledgment

The research behind this chapter has been partially financed by the Danish Research Councils' joint Multimedia Program No. 9600869.

References

Booch, G (1994). *Object-Oriented Analysis and Design with Applications*. Redwood City, CA: Benjamin/Cummings.

Druin, A and Solomon, C (1996). *Designing Multimedia Environments for Children*. New York: John Wiley & Sons.

Eriksen, LB, Skov, MB and Stage J (2000). Multimedia Systems Development Methodologies: Experiences and Requirements. In *Proceedings of the First International Workshop on Narrative and Interactive Learning Environments*, Leeds University, 75-82.

Fairley, RE (1985). *Software Engineering Concepts*. Singapore: McGraw Hill.

Grosky, WI (1994). Multimedia Information Systems. In *IEEE Multimedia*, 1, 12–23.

Jackson, M (1975). *Principles of Program Design*. Orlando: Academic Press.

Jackson, M (1983). *System Development*. Englewood Cliffs, NJ: Prentice-Hall.

Jacobson, I, Christerson, M, Jonsson, P and Övergaard, G (1992). *Object-Oriented Software Engineering*. Wokingham: Addison-Wesley.

Kautz, K, Malmborg, L and Pries-Heje, J (1998). Does University Education Lead to Adoption? In: *Proceedings of the IFIP WG 8.2 and 8.6 Joint Working Conference on Information System: Current Issues and Future Changes*. Helsinki, Finland, 10–13 December.

Lewis, C, Brand, C, Cherry, G, and Raber, C (1998). Adapting User Interface Design Methods to the Design of Educational Activities. In *Proceedings of Human Factors in Computing Systems: CHI98*, April.

Mathiassen, L (1998). Reflective Systems Development. In *Scandinavian Journal of Information Systems*, 10 (1&2), 67–117.

Mathiassen, L, Munk-Madsen, A, Nielsen, PA, and Stage, J (1997). *Object-Oriented Analysis and Design* (in Danish). Aalborg, Denmark: Marko.

Mathiassen, L, Munk-Madsen, A, Nielsen, PA, and Stage, J (1999). *Object-Oriented Analysis and Design*. Aalborg, Denmark: Aalborg University.

McKerlie, D and Preece, J (1993). The Hype and the Media: Issue Concerned with Designing Hypermedia. *Journal of Microcomputer Applications*, 16, 33–47.

Monarchi, DE and Puhr, GI (1992). A Research Topology for Object-Oriented Analysis and Design. In *Communications of the ACM*. September, 35 (9).

Myers, G (1978). *Composite/Structured Design*. New York: Van Nostrand Reinhold.

Nemetz, F and Johnson, P (1998). Developing Multimedia Principles from Design Features. In A Sutcliffe, J Ziegler and P Johnson (eds.), *Proceedings of Designing Effective and Usable Multimedia Systems*. Stuttgart: Kluwer Academic Publishers, 57–71.

Orr, K (1971). *Structured Systems Development*. New York: Yourdon Press.

Plowman, L and Luckin, R (1998) Designing Multimedia for Learning: Narrative Guidance and Narrative Construction. In *Proceedings of Human Factors in Computing Systems: CHI98*, April.

Pressman, RS (1996). *Software Engineering: A Practitioner's Approach*. Singapore: McGraw-Hill.

Rumbaugh, J, Blaha, M, Premerlani, S, Eddy, S and Lorensen, W (1991). *Object-Oriented Modelling and Design*. Englewood Cliffs, NJ: Prentice-Hall.

Skov, M and Stage, J (2001) Experimental Evaluation of an Object-Oriented Modeling Method: Designing a Multimedia System. *Proceedings of the 6th CAiSE/IFIP8.1 International Workshop on Evaluation of Modeling Methods in Systems Analysis and Design (EMMSAD'01)*, Sintef, Oslo, pp. XVIII-1–XVIII-12.

Sommerville, I (1992). *Software Engineering*. 4th edition. Wokingham: Addison-Wesley.

Sutcliffe, AG and Faraday, P (1994). Designing Presentation in Multimedia Interfaces. In B Adelson, S Dumais, and J Olson (eds.), *Proceedings of Computer-Human Interaction Conference '94*. 92–98.

Sutcliffe, AG and Faraday, P (1997). Designing Effective Multimedia Presentations. In C Ware and D Wixon (eds.), *Proceedings of Computer-Human Interaction Conference '97*.

Umaschi Bers, M, Ackermann, E, Cassell, J, Donegan, B, Gonzales-Heydrich, J, DeMaso, DR, Strohecker, C, Lualdi, S, Bromley, D and Karlin, J (1998). Interactive Storytelling Environments: Coping with Cardiac Illness at Boston's Children's Hospital. In *Proceedings of Human Factors in Computing Systems: CHI98*, April.

Webb, BR (1996). The Role of Users in Interactive Systems Design: When Computers are Theatre, Do We Want the Audience to Write the Script? *Behaviour and Information Technology*, 15(2), 76–83.

Yourdon, E and Constantine, L (1979). *Structured Design*. Englewood Cliffs, NJ: Prentice-Hall.

Züllighoven H (1998). Das Objektorientierte Konstruktionshandbuch nach dem Werkzeug & Material-Ansatz. Heidelberg, Germany: dpunkt.verlag.

3

Interaction Styles in Development Tools for Virtual Reality Applications

Jesper Kjeldskov and Jan Stage

Jesper Kjeldskov has a background in the humanities with a Master's degree in humanistic computer science. He is currently a PhD student working with human–computer interaction for virtual reality and mobile computers.

Jan Stage is associate professor in computer science. He holds a PhD degree in computer science. His research interests are usability testing, HCI design, and software engineering.

3.1 Introduction

Methods and guidelines for user interface design embody certain computer technologies. This also applies to interaction styles. Interaction based on a command language was a relevant solution with the character-based display. Direct manipulation emerged from the potentials of the graphical workstation and personal computer. This inherent relation between interface design and computer technology implies that our established guidelines and experiences are challenged when new technologies emerge.

Virtual reality display systems are used to create and visualise virtual three-dimensional (3D) worlds. This technology is emerging, and practically relevant applications are being developed for a broad range of domains. As the use of the technology is increasing, there is an increasing demand for tools for developing applications.

The purpose of this chapter is to compare and discuss the relevance of classical interaction styles for tools that are used to develop virtual reality applications. The focus is on the process of developing actual virtual reality applications. More specifically, we compare the potentials of a development tool based on a command language with one that is based on direct manipulation. The discussion is structured in the following way. First we review selected literature on command language and direct manipulation as classical interaction styles. We then describe the virtual reality display technology in order to specify the target platform we are aiming at. The comparison of the two classical interaction styles is based on a development experiment. After that we describe the design of that experiment, and emphasise the relevant results. The empirical findings are then related to the authors' experiences with a successful tool for developing traditional 2D multimedia applications. Finally, we conclude the discussion and point out avenues for further work.

3.2 Interaction Styles for Development Tools

The interaction style is a key determinant of the design of the user interface. Many discussions on the advantage or disadvantage of a certain design relate to this characteristic. The options available for design of this characteristic have been denoted as: command language, menu selection, form filling, and direct manipulation (Shneiderman, 1998). Below, we will refer to these as the classical interaction styles.

The development of a virtual reality application includes an essential task of constructing the 3D world that will be visualised by the application. The fundamental interaction style of existing tools that support this task is either direct manipulation or command language. Menu selection and form filling are also employed but only for secondary interactions that deal with limited issues, e.g. the specification of properties of a certain object that is manipulated directly on an overall level. Based on these priorities, the discussion below deals only with command language and direct manipulation.

Shneiderman (1998) provides a general definition of direct manipulation and command language. Direct manipulation is an interaction style where the user experiences a representation that can be manipulated directly. Thus the key challenges in designing systems based on this interaction style is to find an appropriate representation and to provide simple ways of manipulating the representation. Command language is an interaction style where the user issues commands in a formalised language and the system responds by carrying out these commands. A typical example of this interaction style is an operating system where the user provides commands line by line and the operating system responds by executing the commands one by one. Yet command language is also used to denote systems with facilities for constructing and executing larger collections of commands such as macros and programs. Many development tools are characterised by an interaction style where the user develops a collection of programs and macros that are executed by the system. We will consider such systems as employing the command language interaction style.

The literature on human–computer interaction includes numerous attempts to answer the question whether direct manipulation is superior to command languages. Much of this is description of advantages whereas the amount of empirical evidence is very limited (Benbasat and Todd, 1993). An early contribution compared file manipulation commands in MS-DOS with Macintosh direct manipulation. This study concluded that the Macintosh users could perform the manipulations faster, with fewer errors, and they were more satisfied with the interface (Margono and Shneiderman, 1987). A similar study where command line and direct manipulation was compared concluded that the users of direct manipulation made only half as many errors and were more satisfied. In this study, the time to perform the tasks turned out to be comparable (Morgan et al., 1991).

The limited number of reports from empirical studies of command language and direct manipulation seem to indicate an advantage in terms of error rate and user satisfaction. When it comes to time to complete a task, the conclusions are more varied. Our intention in this article is to examine these expectations in relation to tools for developing virtual reality applications. The examination is based on an empirical study of an application development process.

3.3 Virtual Reality Applications

A virtual reality application that visualises a 3D world consists of a number of mathematically defined 3D models that are covered with colours or textures, e.g. pictures or video images. The 3D models are spatially distributed in a 3D co-ordinate system that the user can experience as a 3D world by viewing the 3D models from a given point in the co-ordinate system. The correct perspective is rendered real-time by a graphics computer and projected by means of a display system as illustrated in Figure 3.1.

Navigation or motion in the virtual world is accomplished by means of position tracking or a specialised interaction device. Tracking the position of a user's head has the additional advantage of ensuring that the correct visual perspective is calculated. Interaction with objects in the virtual world is typically supported by techniques for selecting and modifying 3D objects by simply "grabbing" them just like one would do in the real world. The 3D experience requires shutter glasses worn by the user allowing separate images to be projected to the user's left and right eye and thereby creating an illusion of 3D.

A virtual reality application may use a multitude of display systems to visualise the virtual 3D world. Examples of display systems are traditional desktop monitors, head-mounted displays, holobenches, large wall-mounted displays or caves with different numbers of sides. These display types represent the array of technologies for creating immersive experiences that range from "looking at" a virtual 3D world to "being in" that virtual world (Shneiderman, 1998).

The six-sided CAVE (Cave Automatic Virtual Environment) is currently the display system that offers the greatest level of immersion into a virtual 3D world. The user is placed in a small cubic room, measuring approximately 3 m on all sides, in which the computer-generated images are back-projected on all four walls, the floor and the ceiling (see Figures 3.2 and 3.3).

Figure 3.1 A virtual 3D world.

Figure 3.2 Outside the six-sided cave.

Figure 3.3 Inside the six-sided cave.

The benefits of the six-sided cave for exploration of virtual 3D worlds originate from the vividness of the virtual environment projected and the very high degree of immersion. This is caused by the freedom of movement that is possible inside the cave and the large horizontal and vertical field of view covered with images. Exploration of the virtual world is much more natural in a six-sided cave compared to any other display system because the user can move around physically and look in any direction without breaking the illusion of being in a computer-generated world. The primary downside is that physical objects and the user's body itself may occlude the images, thus locally breaking the visual illusion (cf. Kjeldskov, 2001).

Virtual reality applications displayed in a cave are very different from many traditional computer applications. First, the user interface is completely surrounding the user and is presented in 3D as opposed to conventional 2D interfaces covering only a fraction of the user's physical surroundings. Second, the types of applications running in a cave are typically offering a complete virtual 3D world for exploration as opposed to traditional tools for office or home use. Third, applications running in a cave are by default both highly graphical and interactive.

3.4 Two Categories of Development Tools

Virtual 3D worlds are usually developed on ordinary – yet powerful – desktop computers with traditional 2D displays. Although virtual reality applications are fundamentally different from typical applications, they are not developed *in* the cave itself. The existing tools for developing virtual reality applications fall into two different categories.

The first category can be characterised as a command language approach, since the creation and manipulation of the virtual world and the objects in it are specified in a formalised command language. Within this approach, special libraries for creating cave applications are available for C and C++. One of the most widely used binary libraries for developing virtual 3D worlds is CaveLib. This library enables development of highly immersive 3D interfaces for projection in a cave, or any other virtual reality display system, as well as implementation of interaction techniques for 3D interaction devices. For preview purposes, CaveLib offers a simple tool for representing the cave display and simulating simple 3D interaction (see Figure 3.4).

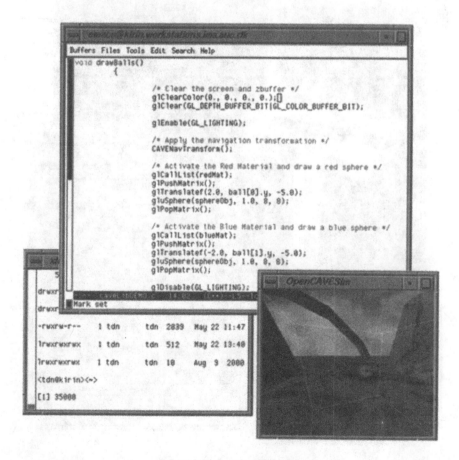

Figure 3.4 Development with CaveLib.

Using CaveLib to develop an application is not very different from developing any other graphical application in a typical programming language. With CaveLib, the developer constructs a program code consisting of commands that point at a number of geometry files and specify the layout of a virtual 3D space as well as the functionality of the application. The commands are constructed in a simple text-editor and they are typically collected in a number of script files. To see if the code is working properly, the developer has to compile all the scripts and run the application either in the cave itself or in a preview tool. If the code contains errors or otherwise needs to be modified, the developer returns to the text-editor.

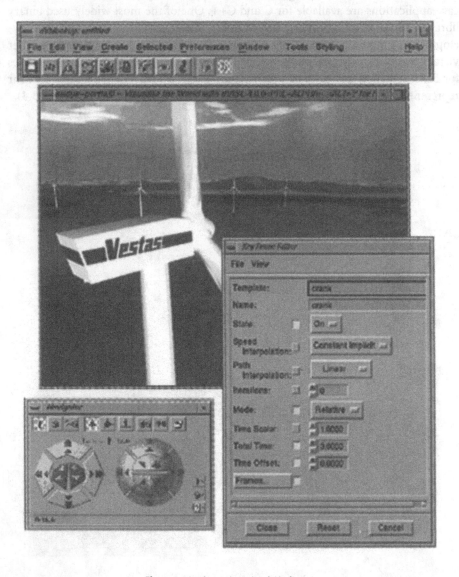

Figure 3.5 Implementing using dvMockup.

The second category of tools for developing virtual reality applications can be characterised as a direct manipulation approach. One of the few professional tools in this category is dvMockup.

This tool enables the developer to create an application by directly manipulating the objects of the virtual 3D world within the preview window along with the use of menu selections and fill-in forms (see Figure 3.5). Using dvMockup, implementing an application for the cave is achieved without doing any actual programming.

When developing a virtual reality application using a direct manipulation tool like dvMockup, the developer imports a number of geometry files and locates them in the virtual 3D space of the application. This is done either by direct manipulation in a workspace window or by specifying data in forms. The functionality of the application is created and modified by selecting 3D objects and applying behaviours through menu selection. Through the workspace window, the developer can continuously see if the application is working properly.

3.5 Experimental Design

A development experiment was conducted to inquire into the research question that was raised in Section 3.1. This section describes the design of that experiment.

3.5.1 Tools

We briefly surveyed potentially relevant tools for implementing virtual reality applications and related them to the fundamental aim of comparing direct manipulation tools with command language tools. Based on the survey and the facilities available, we selected two established tools: dvMockup, a direct manipulation tool that enables people without programming experience to create a virtual reality application, and CaveLib, an advanced development tool that facilitates development of virtual reality applications characterised by high performance and flexibility. In addition, we selected a new and promising programming tool, VR Juggler, which extends CaveLib with a more flexible and modular structure and open source architecture. The first two tools were already installed, configured, and used extensively by other developers and researchers who could be consulted when technical problems arose. The third tool, VR Juggler, was acquired right before the beginning of the experiment and there were no experiences with it.

3.5.2 Participants

A development team of three persons and the two authors of this chapter planned and designed the experiment, and the development team conducted the implementation phase. The three developers had recently completed a master's degree in computer science/computer engineering. Thereby, they had considerable experience and knowledge about programming in general. In addition, they had previously taken a one-semester course on computer vision and virtual reality and worked with projects within that subject. They received a one-day introduction to the tools used in the experiment but had no experience with them.

3.5.3 Overall Task

The comparison of the three tools was based on solving the same overall task. The overall task was to develop a virtual reality application that visualised a maze in which a user could move an avatar around by means of an interaction device. This task was specified in detail by dividing it into 14 milestones. Thus, the overall task was solved when all of these milestones were met. The specific milestones involved tool and cave set-up (milestones 1 and 2), implementation of a simple application (milestones 3 and 4), implementation of the application visualising the maze (milestones 5 to 8), implementation of interaction techniques to facilitate motion of the avatar (milestones 9 to 12), and adjustment (milestones 13 and 14).

3.5.4 Hypothesis

Based on the literature on interaction styles reviewed in Section 3.2 above, we developed the following hypothesis:

> The direct manipulation tool is superior to the programming tools in terms of the efforts required to implement the virtual reality application that is specified by the overall task.

3.5.5 Experimental Procedure

When the planning phase of the experiment was complete, the implementation phase started. This phase was planned to last three weeks but was extended by a couple of days because of technical problems. Each member of the development team was assigned one of the three tools to produce the best possible solution to the overall task. During the implementation phase, they were not supposed to communicate with each other about their work, problems and solutions.

3.5.6 Data Collection

The primary means for data collection were private diaries written by each developer (Jepsen et al., 1989; Naur, 1983). After a day of work on the implementation, each developer used about an hour to describe the work done and its relation to the 14 milestones, the problems faced, and the time spent on tasks related to each of the milestones. A checklist that emphasised the points that should be touched upon supported the daily writing of the diary. One week into the implementation phase, the diary entries produced so far were reviewed in order to enforce the use of the check-list and increase consistency. The three diaries amount to a total of 45 pages (Hougaard et al., 2001).

3.5.7 Data Analysis

The primary dependent variables were work practice and development effort but we focus here only on development effort. Based on the diaries, we have calculated and compared the efforts spent on completing the different milestones of the overall task. The results of this are presented in Section 3.6.

3.5.8 Limitations

The design of this experiment imposes certain limitations on our results. First, the members of the development team were not highly experienced in implementing virtual reality applications. Secondly, the overall task defined a specific application that should be implemented. These limitations imply that the results primarily facil-itate relative as opposed to absolute conclusions about efforts. Thirdly, the diaries of the three developers were different. In order to handle this they were reviewed after one week of work. The fourth limitation was that two of the tools were established on the development platform whereas the third was not even configured and there was no experience with its use. The developer who worked with this tool ended up spend-ing a considerable amount of effort on issues related to installation and execution. Therefore, we ignore this part of the experiment in our comparison below.

3.6 Findings

In this section, we present and discuss the findings from the experiment with CaveLib and dvMockup. The developer who used CaveLib was able to meet all mile-stones, but the navigation technique specified was changed due to usability issues. The developer who used dvMockup was not as successful, since collision detection could not be implemented satisfactory. However, the final solution was acceptable. The development time spent using CaveLib amounted to 42.3 hours, whereas the time spent using dvMockup amounted to 37.8 hours. The total time spent on devel-opment with the two tools thus differs by only 12 per cent. The distribution of time spent on each milestone does, however, reveal significant differences between the programming and direct manipulation approaches. This distribution is shown in Figure 3.6. Below we will highlight interesting points from this distribution.

Setting up the development tools and the cave (milestones 1 and 2) amounted to a total of 12 hours spent on CaveLib whereas only 3.75 hours was spent on this with dvMockup. Thus the developer who used dvMockup only needed about 30 per cent of the time spent using CaveLib. Setting up CaveLib demanded a series of separate tools to be configured for individual tasks, e.g. scripting, compiling and previewing,

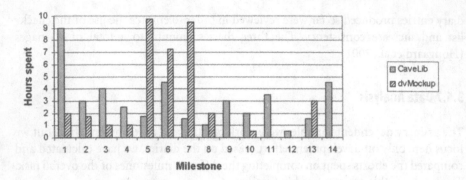

Figure 3.6 Development time spent using CaveLib and dvMockup.

as well as creation of a number of configuration files on both the workstation used for development and the graphics computer that was executing the display system for the cave. With dvMockup only one tool had to be set up, and when an application was running on the workstation, only a few scripts were needed before it was also operational in the cave.

Implementing a preliminary application with the purpose of testing the development and target platform and the connection between them (milestones 3 and 4) took 6.5 hours using CaveLib but only 2 hours with dvMockup. Again, for dvMockup this is only about 30 per cent of the time spent using CaveLib. Thus up to milestone 4 it is clear that the direct manipulation approach supports a faster kick-off in the development process.

Implementation of the primary application, which was the maze specified in the overall task (milestones 5 to 8), was done in 10.3 hours using CaveLib. With dvMockup the same milestones required 27.5 hours. So here we see the same pattern where one tool requires only 30 per cent of the time spent with the other tool. Yet this time the roles are reversed, as CaveLib is the favoured tool. Thus the programming approach seems to facilitate a more effective process in this part of the implementation. The major reason for the considerable amount of time spent with dvMockup is that the tool provides no direct support in a situation where making and running a simple set of commands might avoid numerous repetitions of simple operations. For example, the developer using dvMockup faced the task of *manually* inserting 800 identical cubic objects into the virtual 3D world, whereas the developer using CaveLib could perform the same task simply by writing a small piece of code. This limitation becomes even more serious when we take the question of scale into consideration. If we compare a small application to a large one, the difference in amount of work will occur precisely on milestones 5 to 8 whereas the remaining milestones will largely be unaffected. Therefore, the difference between the two tools on these milestones will even be more significant if we expand the scale of the application being developed.

Implementation of interaction techniques (milestones 9 to 12) took 7.5 hours with CaveLib but only 2.5 hours using dvMockup. This is a 30 per cent reduction in favour of dvMockup. The time spent implementing interaction techniques with dvMockup is, however, influenced by the availability of supporting software. In a related project, a considerable amount of time had recently been spent developing "off-the-shelf support" for implementing interaction in dvMockup in order to facilitate a general reduction of development effort (Kjeldskov, 2001). Had this support not been available, the time spent on these milestones would definitely have increased, but we will not attempt to estimate by how much.

In CaveLib, all interaction techniques were implemented from scratch. This had the advantage, however, that the interaction technique specified in the overall task was actually implemented. With dvMockup it was necessary to modify the task specification by selecting one of the available techniques, which did not fulfil the specification completely. If the implementation in dvMockup should have fulfilled the requirements completely, additional programming at the device driver level would have been necessary.

Final adjustments of the applications (milestones 13 and 14) took 6 hours for CaveLib while only 3 hours was spent with dvMockup. The larger amount of adjustments of the CaveLib application primarily consisted of correcting errors with the scaling of 3D objects. This was necessary in order to make the objects fit properly for projections in the cave. This kind of error was absent in the application developed with dvMockup.

3.7 A Successful Direct Manipulation Tool

The findings described above raises a number of questions. What caused the direct manipulation approach to be outperformed by a command language approach? Is it really fair to conclude that direct manipulation is simply not a well-suited interaction style when developing virtual reality applications? Or what exactly were the limitations of dvMockup? In order to address this question we will take a closer look at a widely used tool for developing interactive multimedia successfully employing direct-manipulation and compare a number of central characteristics of this tool with the corresponding characteristics of dvMockup.

For several years Macromedia Director has been considered state of the art within development tools for interactive multimedia targeted at traditional desktop computers. Much like dvMockup, the interaction style in Director is primarily direct manipulation and fill-in forms but with additional facilities for scripting/ programming. Director is based on a film/theatre metaphor putting the designer/developer in the "director's chair". The end-user's screen is represented as a rectangular surface (the stage) on which the designer/developer can place and directly manipulate the different elements: graphics, video, sound etc. (the cast) of the application using the mouse and the keyboard. The functionality of an application being developed is defined on a central timeline (the score) and in a number of accompanying scripts and behaviours linked to he appropriate elements on the screen.

Around the stage there is a number of tools and fill-in forms for manipulating the elements of the application. Further tools are available through menus or buttons at the top of the screen. The application being developed can rapidly be previewed directly and accurately on the workstation used for development, because display and interaction devices used by the designer/developer are comparable to those of the end-user.

Based on our experiences from teaching Macromedia Director to university students and industrial software developers over the last four years, we have observed that the direct manipulation interaction style employed in Director performs very well and fits with the developers' needs during the different phases of the system development process. But why is it that direct manipulation is apparently a successful interaction style when developing desktop multimedia using Macromedia Director but is outperformed by command language when developing virtual reality applications?

At first sight Director and dvMockup may seem very much alike. Systematically comparing the two tools, however, reveals a number of fundamental differences.

3.7.1 Creating a Simple Application

Applications developed in Director or dvMockup typically consist of a large number of different elements such as graphics, 3D objects, sound/video files and scripts/behaviours. When creating a simple application these elements are put together to form a coherent whole, which is then presented to the end-user. Director and dvMockup both provide means for organising and putting together application elements for this purpose. The approaches enforced in the two tools are, however, fundamentally different in relation to both interface design and support for interaction.

In Director, direct manipulation is used extensively when creating and modifying an application. Every element of the application (e.g. images or video) are represented graphically in the cast window (see Figure 3.7) and can be used anywhere in the application by simply dragging them from the cast window on to the preview window (stage). This action creates a local instance of the element at that given point of the application. These instances can be modified (e.g. scaled or rotated) either in the preview window using direct manipulation or in the timeline (score) window using fill-in forms. In this way, multiple independent instances can be created and modified at multiple points of the application simply by using the mouse. In the timeline (score) window the dynamic state of the application over time is represented graphically (see Figure 3.7). The developer can interact with this representation and modify its properties using direct manipulation (dragging, dropping and scaling) or fill-in forms.

All phases of creating and modifying a simple application in Director are thus supported by various and coherent direct manipulation interaction styles. Furthermore, the separation between cast and score allows the developer to concentrate only on the elements in use at one particular point of the application and ignore the rest.

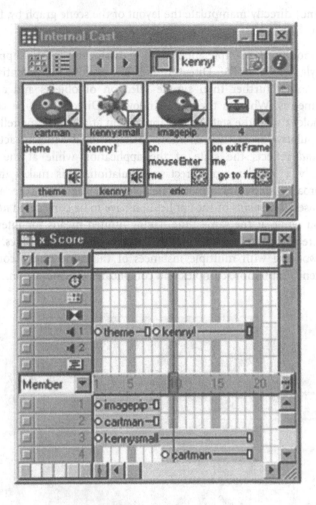

Figure 3.7 The cast and score windows.

In dvMockup, direct manipulation is not used as extensively during the creation and modification of a simple application as in Director. The elements of an application developed in dvMockup are grouped hierarchically within a "scene graph", which can be accessed through the assembly manager (see Figure 3.8). The structure of the scene graph can be compared to the structure of the file system on a computer. Every entry in the assembly manager corresponds to a unique element in the application with unique parameters. If the same 3D object is used twice in the application, it will, contrary to Director's cast window, appear twice in the assembly manager. The scene graph facilitates manipulating whole "branches" of, for example, virtual 3D objects without affecting the mutual spatial relationship between the sub-objects in the branch. This is very helpful when working with virtual 3D worlds, which can easily consist of more than a thousand 3D objects. Manipulating the scene graph (e.g. moving an element from one branch to another or turning the visibility of an element on or off) is done by menu selection. The developer cannot directly manipulate the layout of the scene graph by, for example, drag and drop.

Creating and modifying a simple application in dvMockup is thus supported by an interaction style, which, unlike Director, does not explore the potentials of direct manipulation much further than simple selection of objects and activation of buttons and menus. Whereas the cast window in Director can be considered a central placeholder with the state of the application at a given time reflected in the directly manipulative score, the assembly manager in dvMockup acts *both* as a placeholder *and* reflects the state of the application while at the same time supporting only a low level of direct manipulation. This makes the assembly manager approach in dvMockup less flexible than the cast/score approach in Director because *all elements* of the application have to be considered *at all times* of the application while at the same time having limited means for interaction as a developer. Moreover, there is no distinction between objects and classes. This lack of support for working with multiple instances of the same object contributes to making the scene graph more complex and complicates the interaction.

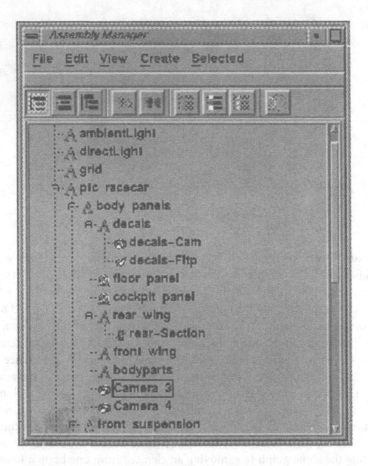

Figure 3.8 The assembly manager.

3.7.2 Previewing an Application

There are two fundamental differences between applications developed in Director and dvMockup: (1) applications developed in Director are targeted at desktop 2D displays while applications developed in dvMockup are targeted at immersive 3D displays; (2) applications developed in Director are *typically* explored screen-by-screen while applications developed in dvMockup constitute 3D worlds, which the user can explore freely. These differences affect the previewing of the application as well as the potential for direct manipulation in the preview window offered by the two tools.

In Director, the developer is *constantly* faced with a preview that *exactly* matches what the user will be presented with at a given time of the application (see Figure 3.9). This makes previewing and directly manipulating the elements of the

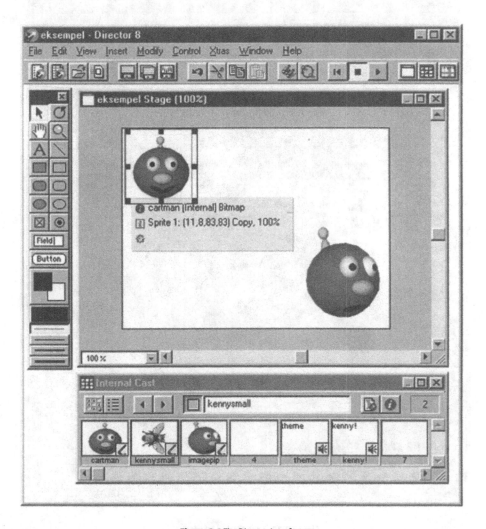

Figure 3.9 The Director interface.

application accurate and non-problematic. In the preview of dvMockup, however, the developer can choose to see the virtual 3D world from *any* perspective wished, without relation to the perspective chosen by the end-user in the cave (see Figure 3.10). Moreover, the preview in Director matches the number of dimensions used when displaying the final application on a computer monitor while the 2D preview in dvMockup *does not match the 3D displaying of the virtual world in the cave*. The developer is thus left to *imagine* how the end-user may explore the application. This introduces a difference between previewing and the user's experience of the final application

Interaction with the preview constitutes yet another difference between the two tools. Whereas interaction with the preview in Director using mouse and keyboard

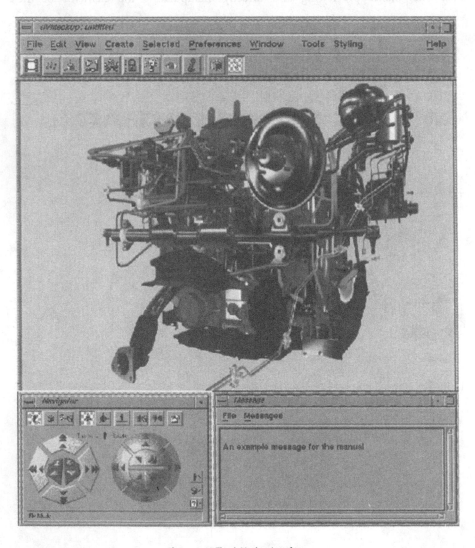

Figure 3.10 The dvMockup interface.

matches the interaction with the final application, interacting with the preview of dvMockup does not. In the cave, interaction is primarily a question of navigating in a virtual world as well as selecting and manipulating virtual objects. This is typically supported using motion tracking and other 3D interaction devices. In the preview of dvMockup, however, the developer cannot interact as if being in the cave, but is limited to the use of the mouse and keyboard or dedicated control panels in the interface to which the end user will not have access. This further extends the gap between the preview in dvMockup and the user experience of the final application, and it makes manipulation of the elements in the preview window less direct.

3.7.3 Programming Functionality and Interaction

Multimedia and virtual reality applications typically have complex functionality and supports complex interaction. Tools for developing applications must therefore support programming of such functionality and interaction. In dvMockup, the user can create simple behaviours consisting of predefined events and actions and relate these to objects in the virtual 3D world. This is done by the use of menu selection and fill-in forms (see Figure 3.11). It is, however, not possible to extend the functionality of the predefined events and actions in dvMockup by doing "real programming". If additional functionality is desired, the application has to be hooked up to external executables programmed in, for example, C or C++.

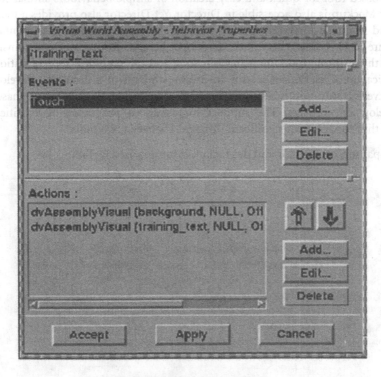

Figure 3.11 Behaviour tool in dvMockup.

Figure 3.12 Scripting tool in Director.

A menu-based tool for quick and easy creation of simple behaviours similar to the one in dvMockup is also accessible in Director. Yet Director also provides a tool for command language interaction using high level scripting and object-orientation (see Figure 3.12). Using Director, the developer benefits from a seamless transition between the scripting tool, the behaviour tool, and the graphical representation of the application. Observing Director in use by students and industrial developers clearly reveals a continuous iteration between these three tools at different phases of the development process. The support for advanced programming facilities in Director thus constitutes a significant difference between two tools.

The comparison of Director and dvMockup is summarised in Table 3.1.

Table 3.1 Comparison of Director and dvMockup.

	Director	dvMockup
Creating a simple application	The elements of the application are *separated* from the state of the application at a given time.	The elements of the application *reflect* the state of the application at a given time.
Previewing an application	Previewing *matches* the end-user experience of and interaction with the application.	Previewing *does not match* the end-user experience and interaction.
Programming functionality and interaction	Use of both predefined events, actions, *and* object-oriented programming.	Only use of predefined events and actions. No direct support for programming.

3.8 Conclusions

We have conducted a qualitative empirical study showing that implementing a virtual reality application using a command language tool and a direct manipulation tool required efforts in terms of time that are comparable. The command language tool, however, resulted in faster implementation during the most essential phases of the implementation process and will outperform the direct manipulation tool on larger scale applications. The direct manipulation tool, on the other hand, resulted in fewer errors when creating a virtual world.

The empirical results suggest that the command language interaction style is superior to direct manipulation when developing virtual reality applications. By focusing on application development for a six-sided cave using tools running on desktop computers we have, of course, taken things to the edge. There is a continuum of virtual reality displays for which the distance between development tool and target platform may be less significant than for the six-sided cave.

A comparison of the direct manipulation tool, dvMockup, with Macromedia Director, which successfully employs direct manipulation, reveals a number of more specific issues, which may have negatively influenced the performance of dvMockup. These include: (1) the extent to which the potentials of direct manipulation has been exploited; (2) the distance between development platform and target platform; and (3) the support for combining direct manipulation and collections of commands in a programming language.

A central question arises from this conclusion. Can direct manipulation be further exploited in tools for developing virtual reality applications? One thing is improving the user interface of development tools and further exploiting the potentials of direct manipulation with applications like Macromedia Director as role models, but how can we overcome the problem of distance between development and target platform? A relevant solution might be making direct manipulation more direct as discussed in Beaudouin-Lafon (2000) and Schkolne et al. (2001). Developing virtual reality applications *in* the cave could be an interesting path for further exploration.

Acknowledgments

The authors would like to thank the development team: Mike H. Hougaard, Nikolaj Kolbe and Flemming N. Larsen. We also thank VR-MediaLab (www.vrmedialab.dk) for access to virtual reality installations and development tools.

References

Beaudouin-Lafon, M (2000). Instrumental Interaction: An Interaction Model for Designing Post-WIMP User Interfaces, *CHI Letters* 3(1), 446–53.
Benbasat, I and Todd, P (1993). An Experimental Investigation of Interface Design Alternatives: Icon vs. Text and Direct Manipulation vs. Menus. *International Journal of Man-Machine Studies* 38, 369–402.

Hougaard, MH, Kolbe, N and Larsen, FN (2001). *Comparison of Tools for Developing Virtual Reality Application* (in Danish), Aalborg Denmark: Aalborg University.

Jepsen LO, Mathiassen L, Nielsen PA (1989). Back to Thinking Mode: Diaries for the Management of Information System Development Projects. *Behaviour and Information Technology* 8(3), 207–17.

Kjeldskov, J (2001). Combining Interaction Techniques and Display Types for Virtual Reality. In W Smith, R Thomas and M Apperley (eds.) *Proceedings of OzCHI 2001*, Churchlands, Australia: Edith Cowan University Press, 77–83.

Margono, S and Shneiderman, B (1987). A Study of File Manipulation by Novices Using Commands vs. Direct Manipulation. In: *Proceedings of the 26th Annual Technical Symposium*, Washington: ACM, 57–62.

Morgan, K, Morris, RL and Gibbs, S (1991). When Does a Mouse Become a Rat? or … Comparing the Performance and Preferences in Direct Manipulation and Command Line Environment. *Computer Journal* 34, 265–71.

Naur, P (1983). Program Development Studies Based on Diaries. In: TR Green et al. (eds.) *Psychology of Computer Use*. London: Academic Press, 159–70.

Schkolne, S, Pruett, M and Schröder, P (2001). Surface Drawing: Creating Organic 3D Shapes with the Hand and Tangible Tools. *CHI Letters* 2(1), 261–68.

Shneiderman, B (1998). *Designing the User Interface: Strategies for Effective Human-Computer Interaction*. Reading, MA: Addison Wesley, Longman.

4

In the Mists of Prehistory: Scriptwriting for Interactive 3D Documentaries on the Nordic Bronze Age

Hanne Dankert and Niels Erik Wille

Hanne Dankert originally trained as a commercial artist and has been a student of the Danish Film School. She holds a master's degree in film and television studies and a PhD in Media Studies.

Niels Erik Wille has a broad academic background in philosophy, linguistics, semiotics, text theory and communication. He has worked for several years with various types of electronic works, primarily as vehicles for information to the general public.

4.1 Introduction

The focus of this chapter is the early stages of scriptwriting for interactive 3D documentaries (the term is discussed in Dankert and Wille, 2001). The specific case is a work in progress on the Nordic Bronze Age and the chapter includes four exhibits – a research summary, a treatment and two outlines (or synopses) – taken from this work.

A *script* in this sense is a document used to describe a complex work in such a way that decision makers, planners and producers are able to grasp what kind of work is intended, and also to provide their own specific contributions to the process. The word *script* is used by programmers and system developers in a related but different sense – a special type of programming instructions – and the two concepts should not be confused.

Figure 4.1 Rock carving from Engelstrup, Zealand in Denmark.

Scripts come in many varieties and flavours, many with their own names and nicknames. In the theatre the traditional script is the *play*, written by the *playwright*. The play contains primarily the dialogue (the lines to be read by the actors) with normally very sparse stage directions. This reflects a division of labour between the playwright on the one side and the producer/director, the stage designer, the costume designer and all the actors on the other side. They realise the play by filling in details and making the play come alive on the stage. In the process of the actual staging of the play, a copy of the script provided by the playwright is supplemented with notes by the people involved, in order to function as a shared reference for the production and performance of the play. This script is known as the *prompt book* and it is only valid for a specific production of the play.

Less literary forms of the theatre rely on another form of script, the *scenario*. A scenario is an outline of the plot and the action, but without any specification of the words the actors have to say or details of their actions. This is left to the actual performers, who either rely on well-established routines and conventions, or improvise over the structure provided by the scenario. This is typical of the *Commedia dell'Arte* of the 17th and 18th century, and the later *pantomimes*.

The arrival of film and radio, and later television, gave rise to further development of scripting techniques on the basis of the theatrical *play*. For film and television the term became the *screenplay*. But the highly complex and costly production processes of the film industry gave rise to a whole series of scripts, each adapted to a specific phase of the production cycle. This has been systematised and codified by the film industry, with Hollywood as a trend setting force.

Philip Parker, in *The Art and Science of Screenwriting* (Parker, 1998) lists the following sequence that a prospective screenwriter (the modern age playwright) will have to know and master:

- *The proposal* (*idea* or *premise*). This is a short, one to three sentence statement, that encapsulates the essential elements of the proposed film. The aim of the proposal is to convince the receiver that there is a genuine screen potential, that it has a proper balance of familiar and original elements, and the "premise" or problem has enough substance to carry a full-length narrative.

- *The outline.* The outline is also known as a *synopsis* or a *treatment*. What is meant is a short prose version of the screen narrative. It is normally told in the present tense and presents the *story* of the film while suggesting the style of the presentation (the discourse) (Dankert and Wille, 2001; Chatman, 1978). For a full-length feature film about four pages seem to be expected.

- *The treatment.* This is more or less just a longer version of the outline (which is also known as a treatment; treatments therefore occur in condensed and more elaborated varieties.). The treatment is closer to the actual film presentation than the story outline. It describes the dramatic structure of the proposed film; it is semi-dramatised and told in the present tense. It concentrates on the main stories, leaving out story information that is not needed to understand the motivations of the main characters, the story line and the most important themes. This version of the treatment is often the crucial one, since this is normally required for raising the initial funding of the project or the go-ahead signal of the customer.

- *The step outline.* The step outline is a further step towards the screenplay. It gives a step-by-step presentation of the individual scenes, in short terse paragraphs. There is still no dialogue, and the scene is not broken down into shots. It is more like a series of stage directions than a play. The step outline makes a good basis for writing the actual screenplay, and could in fact be written by somebody who is good at visualising a filmplay and putting this into words, but not good at writing dialogue. So the next step could be to pass the job onto another type of screenwriter.

- *The screenplay.* The screenplay is traditionally very much like the traditional stage play: A dialogue supplemented with suggestive stage directions. These provide enough information to follow the action, without restricting the creative efforts of the producer/director or the various designers too much.

In the actual production other types of scripts are used, but they are not produced by the screenwriter and so are outside the scope of Philip Parker's book. The most important one is the *shooting script*, a detailed description of the filmed sequences that has to be produced in the studio or on location. The shooting script does not have to follow the planned sequence of the film. A more practical approach is to organise it according to the sequences that have to be produced on a certain day, at a certain place (the *set*) and with certain actors, specialists, props etc. available.

The scripts of the film industry have been mimicked and adopted by the multi-media industry, as demonstrated by several textbooks aimed at prospective script-writers (for example, Samsel and Wimberley, 1996, 1998; Garrand, 1997, 2001). The strong focus on dialogue of the screenplay creates obvious problems with the new interactive media, and seems primarily suited for certain types of interactive fiction and computer games. And the implicit structure where the author controls the flow of action, also conflicts with basic presentational demands of the new interactive media.

Animated films have developed other types of scripts than live-action films, and one invention of the producers of animated films has turned out to be an interesting tool for multimedia productions: the *storyboard*. It was originally a strictly linear presentation of the planned film through a sequence of drawn sketches of the screen image but it turned out to be easily adapted to a multilinear format and also useful for text oriented works like Web presentations. Good introductions to animation scripting techniques are Halas and Manwell (1971), Halas (1976), Halas (ed.) (1976) and Hayward (1977).

For obvious reasons documentary film-makers cannot organise their work around a dialogue script. As demonstrated by Baddeley (1975, pp. 12-32) many different techniques are used, from no script at all, to a detailed *shooting script* describing what sequences the director wants the film crew to produce. In many cases a script emerges from the sequences shot on location, rather than the other way round. But these practices have very little value in a production where all the images have to be produced in the computer and not with a camera in the field. A variation on the shooting script adapted to multilinear presentations is possible and seems to go well with the storyboard technique.

Other approaches to documentary film scripts are discussed in Swain and Swain (1988, pp. 7–74) and Rosenthal (1996).

3D installations like the CAVE and other types of spatial projections may have limited use for a storyboard type of script. Perhaps a digital simulation may take its place. But it is certainly an area that will demand entirely new types of scripts.

But for this discussion we are not going into any details about scripts needed and useful for the later stages of an interactive 3D production. We want to concentrate on the early stages of the pre-production phase, the stage where the focus is on development of ideas and preliminary presentations of the prospect.

We want to explore the possibilities that the well-established film *treatment* offer in the world of multimedia. And what problems, if any, are encountered in the process of adapting this primarily verbal form of early script.

Since a treatment does not presuppose any kind of actual programming or other forms of production, it is possible to sketch out several possible productions in order to assess the feasibility and desirability of the alternatives. The treatment format forces the developers to make their ideas explicit to each other and to other members of the prospective production team, and so invites contributions and constructive criticism. Another important aspect at this stage is that the treatment can be a fairly concrete basis for decisions on the part of the people who may fund the production. In fact, this last part is the main function of the treatment in the film and television industry as indicated above.

To write a good treatment is probably a skill that demands a certain kind of talent, a "way-with-words", and so not something that all members of the production team will be expected to master. But both the creative leader of the team and any scriptwriter involved should be able to do this.

In order to focus the attention on words, even as image-evoking devices, we have left out all graphical illustrations, which would of course normally be included in even early scripts.

4.2 The Research Phase

As stated above this chapter is about the early stages of the pre-production phase. A documentary that aims at communicating the results of academic research and similar types of complicated knowledge will normally include some extensive research into the existing knowledge in the field. This has a dual purpose: (1) to brief the people on the team who are not subject specialists about the knowledge available; and (2) to create a platform for the discussion of possible ways to realise the project at hand, given the sort of material available.

This in practice means extensive reading of various presentations and summaries; examination of objects, stories, images etc. that may be included in the production, or form the inspiration for graphical styles, illustrations by sound effects or music, colour schemes etc.; visits to sites and exhibitions; and analysing other examples of communicating the same material in order to discover the communicative potentials and pitfalls.

The main findings of this phase should then be condensed into a *research summary*, supplemented typically with a notice board full of scraps, sketches and copies of pictures (this aspect has, for reasons stated above, been left out in the present chapter).

For this project the following research summary was produced. The sources for this research summary are found in a separate section at the end of the reference list.

The Challenge of Prehistory

The Nordic Bronze Age belongs to prehistory. No written records tell us about people or events, and no oral tradition has survived (as far as we know).

The period designated by the term "Bronze Age" has varying extensions, depending on the part of Europe taken into account. In the eastern Mediterranean and the Middle East it starts about

2500 BC and ends about 500 BC with the widespread use of iron for weapons and utensils. In the northern part of Europe the beginning is variously dated, some sources say 1800 BC, others 1700 BC and others again 1500 BC, with all agreeing that it ends about 500 BC. The term itself was actually coined by the Danish scholar C.J. Thomsen in 1836, based on a periodisation of the archaeological specimens in the collections of the Danish king, the later National Museum of Denmark. He divided the prehistory into three periods, Stone Age, Bronze Age and Iron Age, according to the materials utilised for weapons, utensils and ritual objects.

Perhaps a better description would be that the division is based on the level of knowledge of metallurgy demonstrated by the findings: Stone Age – no knowledge of how to produce things by metals; Bronze Age – knowledge about preparation of gold, silver and bronze (a mixture of copper and tin); Iron Age – knowledge of iron smithing. Two different methods of working metal were known: hammering cold metal into the wanted shape, which is the oldest, and melting the metal and casting the desired object in a form. Since bronze is an alloy, a mixture of two or more metals, the Bronze Age represents a fairly high level of metallurgical knowledge and skills.

The knowledge of bronze casting originated in the Middle East and the Mediterranean (with a parallel development in China) and arrived in the Nordic area after a delay of about a 1000 years. The last phase of the Stone Age (late neolithic) saw a slow flow of metal objects into the area, while the knowledge needed to produce objects "at home" heralded the true Nordic Bronze age. The raw material, copper and tin, still had to be imported, but the objects produced take on a distinct Nordic style.

The Nordic Bronze Age coexists with the emerging high cultures of Egypt, the Middle East (a.o. the kingdoms of Solomon and David, known from the Bible) and the early Greek Kingdoms (Crete, Mycene) and the Greek societies of the Balkan peninsula and the mainland of Minor Asia (now Turkey). The Homeric epics and the Bible are the spectacular heritage of a rich oral literature, later fixed through the exciting new technology of writing.

But the Nordic societies were very different from the high cultures of the period, that is obvious from the archaeological findings. So we cannot infer anything about life and beliefs in the Nordic Bronze Age from the findings and literary sources handed down to us from the high cultures.

Our knowledge about the Nordic Bronze Age includes: the climate and the landscape, including flora and fauna; the typical dwellings, farms and villages; clothing, specially of families in power; utensils, weapons and jewellery; burials (again of the families in power); and, last but not least, an impressive selections of objects meant for ritual and religious purposes– the sun chariot from Trundholm, the lures and spectacular horned helmets, huge bronze axes unfit for anything but ceremonial use, and a plethora of rock carvings (helleristninger) with inscrutable pictures of people, ships and variations of circular signs.

We know from the rock carvings and other depictions that the Bronze Age knew of ships, probably even quite large ships fit for both trade and war, but we have no archaeological evidence of this before the advent of the Iron Age (only some smaller boats have been found).

Some small sculptures of humans are known, in all probability connected with religious rites, but whether they represent god-like beings or human worshippers is not known.

We can infer quite a lot about conditions of daily life in the period, but since we have no record or tradition about characters or characteristic events, a narrative reconstruction would have to be modelled on the contemporary sources from the high cultures, or on the later rich heritage of Germanic and Nordic Iron Age heroic legends and epics. The last solution will probably give the least unsatisfactory results, but none of them seem very good.

Narrative reconstructions have been attempted, such as historical novels aimed at young people, and with an obvious didactic purpose, like the Norwegian Johannes Heggland's *Folket i de hvide både* (1964) [The People of the White Boats] and *Bronzesværdet* (1965) [The Bronze Sword]. But the amount of necessary fictional filling in of details like names, social structure, motivations, function and construction of the boats and so on, almost defies the purpose.

In a sense we know more about the ritual and religious aspects of life in the Bronze Age, but only from the objects and depictions left to us. What kind of world view and pantheon of gods were involved, and the rituals enacted to make them come to life, are irrevocably lost. And nothing indicates any relationship to the mythological structures that we have some knowledge of from the time of the Vikings (known as the Nordic Mythology). Again we have to infer some rather abstract and generic ideas and experiences, like a cult of the sun, fertility rites, burial rites implying some sort of afterlife etc.

The solution chosen in the Danish film reconstruction from the 1950s (*Bronzealderen*, 1958), was an episodic presentation of probable situations like bronze casting in the smithy, a burial scene, a non-specific meeting of people to demonstrate clothing, and a sun ceremony involving fires, blowing the lures to call forward the sun and similar semi-dramatic staging of Bronze Age life. The overall structure of the documentary is an expository presentation.

4.3 The Scripts

This section demonstrates the results of further considerations and reflections regarding the planning of three alternative interactive approaches to the dissemination of information concerning the Nordic Bronze Age.

The first approach is based on the use of a more traditional, screen-oriented digital medium like a stand-alone information kiosk, the Web or a CD-ROM production. And the discussions involved representation; storytelling; how to (re)construct history; the mediated transformation of a bygone historical period into the twenty-first century; as well as considerations about scriptwriting and design; the role of the user; interactivity; and context. A fully worked out treatment is presented below.

The second and third approaches are based on the notion of virtual reality and 3D space(s) – perception space, movement space and body space – and the discussion regarding these installations included reflections on convergence, in this particular connection, between factual information, entertainment and art; organising information in an interactive 3D space; non-objective as opposed to representational; interactivity and virtuality; sound as an important narrative and atmosphere creating element; as well as considerations about the user, the design and the context. For this, two outlines are exhibited.

4.3.1 The Treatment

The treatment concerns a production that is targeted at users who want information, but who don't want ready made, too absolute statements. They want to explore the available material, and to play an active role as amateur scholars or "detectives". So we had to ask ourselves questions like: "How do we present the different aspects of the Bronze Age that we know of at this particular time and place?"; "How is 'the Bronze Age' perceived by an adult audience of the twenty-first century interested in history and art – or art history?"; and "What kind of 'storytelling' is conceived to be 'in accordance' with the subject?"

The medium, a screen-based, single-user application, supports an individualistic approach where the user concentrates on exploring the material offered in his or her own rhythm.

History is a kind of storytelling that necessarily reflects contemporary beliefs – value systems, convictions, a way of life, etc. – when depicting the past. In this case Bronze Age customs, rituals, patterns of life and the mythological scheme of things, and so on. We want the application to explicitly emphasise this point of departure, which means that the presentation will have to contain a certain level of self-reflexivity on behalf of the subject matter.

The reflexive and self-reflective mode (Nichols, 1991; Dankert and Wille, 2001) seemed evident and in accordance with the overall objective of the project that deals with symbols, myths and the cult and invites the user to explore the varied material with a certain amount of freedom. In the context of film documentary, the reflexive mode is the most self-aware of the four modes: the expository, observational, interactive and reflexive. Reflexive texts are self-conscious not only about form and style, but also about strategy, structure, conventions, expectations and effects (Nichols, 1991). This mode directly challenges the impression of reality; and draws the viewer's attention to the device as well as the effect. It presents and provides the viewer (user) with meta-reflexions about the mediated truth or representations of reality. And thus it "demands" a certain degree of self-reflectivity on behalf of the user (viewer). In accordance with the reflexive mode the individual user (viewer) is encouraged to deduct his or her own truth from the given material and to form his or her own opinion about the subject matter.

However, in order to establish a kind of continuity or maybe rather build a bridge between the different sub-themes, facilitating the movement from one to the other and/or establishing a sort of structural, formal connection, we might have to consider the support of the expository mode. And again we refer directly to one of the classical modes within the film documentary tradition. The expository mode establishes a firm structure in order to deal with a coherent historical world.

"The expository text addresses the viewer directly, with titles or voices, that advance an argument about the historical world", as Nichols (1991, p. 34) puts it. The expository mode emphasises the impression of objectivity and of well-substantiated judgment.

In an attempt to present some of the established scholarly findings about the Bronze Age the expository mode thus seems most suitable. At the same time this mode seems appropriate, guiding the user around the hypertext structure in a more traditional, linear storytelling fashion. In this particular case, first and foremost the expository mode will be used as a tool for introducing each (new) theme/sub-theme.

The coherent world view and the well-structured organisation of the presented material with an anchoring voice-over give a great deal of credibility to the presented facts and smoothen the navigation. And this approach most likely appeals to an audience occupied with fact finding on a more traditional or straightforward information-based level.

On the other hand it might not appeal to a user group which regards this as a tool for a more playful reflexive exploration. In any case, the linear introduction to each theme and sub-theme should be seen as a choice that the user is free to skip at any time.

It is self-evident, though, that the reflexive mode applied for the bulk of the multimedia text enhances the principle of non-linear thought. And this principle is embedded in interactivity, which works in a non-linear way. Because "thought is not a linear process, it's a multiplane, multidimensional process" (Samsel and Wimberley, 1998, p. 6).

Nevertheless, the fact is that the coherent linear narrative fashion, embedded in the expository mode, is in no way obsolete when it comes to structuring principles. And we have to deal dramaturgically and designwise with a fruitful blend or shift between the two modes of (re)presentation.

The various interpretations of myths, symbols and objects reflect certain specific (ideological) positions, idiosyncrasies and thought patterns, etc.; and thus in particular or peculiar ways, for instance, the 1950s, 1970s and 1990s, respectively are somehow mirrored in the different (re)presentations of the Bronze Age. It will be up to the individual user to examine, detect and form opinions about the material presented, interacting in an explorative fashion. And hopefully along his or her journey the user is going to discover new ways of combining various issues, information and material, which leads to new and unexpected answers and questions.

So how would we describe the world we are in thematically and designwise? First and foremost it is a world of symbols and cult objects. It is a mythological universe with an overriding worship of the sun, situated within the imagined landscapes of the Nordic Bronze Age. If Bronze Age people are represented, acting out some rituals, they primarily appear in a few video clips. Otherwise it is an informational and at the same time lyrically perceived, poetic and artistic journey into a mythological universe filled with various interpretations and representations of how the people of the Bronze Age envisaged life and death and the powers and cycles of life and nature. Thus, it is not a database containing scientific information about the Nordic Bronze Age.

In order to embrace this sort of approach, it is necessary to be consistent in the use of an overall style, when it comes to colours, icons and metaphors. Dealing with the Bronze Age and the worshipping of the sun, it seems obvious that the consistent colour has to be of a golden, bronze-like character. And since the sea, the soil and the harvest are fundamental elements in the life and spiritual beliefs of the Bronze Age people, naturally blue, green, brown and yellow will be preferred as additional colours.

The design of icons and metaphors will have to reflect the patterns and design of the various symbols and cult objects. The rich ornamentation found on swords, axes and jewellery, for instance, will be the backbone of the consistent style of the application.

As noted earlier, the bulk of the application is meant to be interactive, with an emphasis on the reflexive, explorative, non-linear and "self-paced". Within the structure, however, there will be provisions for an additional linear introduction to each sub-theme, which could be considered as a kind of expository documentary based mainly on film/video aesthetics and devices.

The text used in this treatment (outline) builds primarily on Brøndsted (1977), but it should be seen as no more than an example of plausible explanations and interpretations to be presented in the final product.

Nordic Bronze Age: In the Mist of Prehistoric Time (Treatment)

Point of Departure

In order to establish the theme of the presentation, the expository mode of representation is employed.

The title and credits are seen like reflected in water and a musical "leitmotif" for lure-players are heard. The following text:

> A symbol for the Bronze Age? We choose the ship! On the bronze sword from Rørby, Zealand – a rare treasure – the artist has engraved his drawing of the long, magnificent vessel. Well manned with 35 rowers, there it is lying in the water, built at the same time with care, consideration and self-assurance.

is displayed on the backdrop of water (in close up). Simultaneously a voice-over declamation of the text is heard. During the passage, beginning with "the long, magnificent vessel" we hear the sound of water splashing, the stroke of oars and the sounds of the ship. At the end the text dissolves in the streaming water and superimposed imagery of a stem gliding through the glittering water emerges.

A short montage of different shots of the ship and the oars in the water (as well as reflected in the water) follows: transition from beautifully lit and filmed, photo-realistic rendering to a more graphic, abstract and symbolic representation and finally to the depiction of ships in rock engravings.

A voice-over declamation of the following passage is heard:

The ship is the most beloved and depicted object through literally the whole of the Bronze Age; and already by the beginning of the period, year 1500 BC, there exist in Denmark these kind of advanced and perfect ships like the one you find depicted on the Rørby Sword.

During the last passage of this text a visual transition from the rock engraving imagery to the depiction of the ship on the so-called Rørby Sword is taking place by means of "double exposure" or morphing.

The voice-over declamation continues after a short break, in which the sounds of stroking oars, vessel and water are replaced by the lures, which are then faded out.

The ship, the symbol we have chosen for this strange period, the Bronze Age. Let this vessel thus be specified as a skin construction fully manned, ready for a long voyage.

And let us follow this sign straight in to the noisy, crowded and motley world of the Nordic rock engravings. Once we have seen it, presumably we'll feel more inclined to take a deeper look into the picture-book of the Bronze Age.

During this passage superimposition or morphing from the sign of the ship on the sword to the "picture-book" universe of the rock engravings is applied. And here the thoroughly structured expository mode of (re)presentation ends for this part of the web-presentation and a more reflexive, explorative and user-interactive mode takes over.

The user is, of course, at any time free to skip this opening and the other, linear expository sequences within the application.

The picture world of the rock engravings is at first supported by the following written text shown on the right side of the screen:

Among scholars there is a common agreement about the interpretation of the rock engravings of the Bronze Age as these are seen as documents of a religious-magic nature.

These rock engravings are found in the Nordic regions, where the principal occupation had to do with agriculture and cattle breeding, and are seen as an expression of the peasantry's attitude towards the strong and determining powers of existence.

During the following voice-over passage, the transition takes place, and the symbolic world of the rock engravings open up to the exploring user:

What a noisy crowd and what a commotion! You are surrounded by swarming life. There is so much to look at! Ships; two or four-wheeled carts; cattle; hunting and fishing; men with enormous weapons; men dressed like birds; wedding couples; trees; single combat; spirals; bowl signs; large foot-prints; vessel-carrying men; lots of sun images; axes; swords; spears; archers; gods; horses; deer; dogs; serpents; axe-carrying men with bird-heads on wheels; large-hand figures with bristly fingers; giants with thick calves; lure players; women (rare); birds in trees – and that is not all!

Imagery

The user is introduced to multiple choices exploring the "picture book" world of the rock engravings. A 3D universe is constructed, in which computer animations bring alive the swarming (teeming) life described above. The free floating figures, signs and symbols by means of computer graphics establishes an organic coherence.

The accompanying sound is an electronic sampled montage of different effects associated in a more abstract way with the imagery.

It is possible to focus on each individual figure, sign and symbol. When the user clicks on one of these, the chosen object fills the screen. Every single click on different parts of the object will produce an enlargement of a particular, selected detail, shown in split screen. One, smaller part of the screen shows the full object; and enlarged fragments and details fill the other, main part of the screen.

Different interpretations of the symbolic world of this "picture book" and of each singular figure and sign will be activated by a click on the line indicating various time periods in the bottom of the screen.

These various interpretations may at times contradict each other and definitely help ask questions like: "Who is seeing and saying what, with what reason, and on the basis of what kind of 'factual' or actual knowledge?"

Among the illustrative pictorial examples, the user will find some artistic imaginations and representations, as the ones made by the Danish COBRA painter, Asger Jorn.

With the point of departure in the magic picture universe of the Bronze Age rock engraving it is possible to elaborate an exploration of the following themes: (1) sun-worshipping: *the ship* and *the chariot*, both objects connected to the *sun cult;* and (2) sword, spear and axe as cult objects. Only one of these options is developed in the following, namely sun-worshipping.

When entering this menu point the user will be provided with an expository mode introduction to the subject matter in the tradition of documentary film where a well-structured, coherent view of the presented world, including a voice-over commentary goes hand in hand with poetic perspectives (like in the former introduction). Again, however, it is the free choice of the user to make use of this linear introduction.

The introduction begins with the following text:

> *Sun-worshipping. Sun, rain and fertility were needed for agriculture, which was closely tied to the changing seasons*

Voice-over speak:

> *Many depictions of the sun cult exists, and they group themselves in four categories:*
> 1. *Where the sun disc is depicted in connection with carriage or horses/draught-animals or both,*
> 2. *Where the sun disc is seen in connection with worshipping people,*
> 3. *Where the sun disc is placed on a stand, and finally,*
> 4. *Where the sun disc is depicted in relation to a ship.*

These four categories will be illustrated by means of different material: drawings and paintings.

When the user activates the icons representing the ship and the chariot, respectively, text fragments from the research sources appear:

The Ship: The most impressive and prominent single object in the rock engravings is the ship.

The ship has infinite significance as far as the well-being and trade of the Bronze Age society go, and in the religious and spiritual life as vessel of the sun and the scene of ritualistic games, processions and ceremonies.

The Sun Chariot: The Chariot of the Sun has to be seen as a rendering of the real, big cult carriage, as this looked on its journey with the divine cargo.

When the sun with its draught-animal, the horse was presented to the people at the sun-celebrations and – equally important – was taken around the fields to help fertilise the soil, it was done by placing the big sun disc and the real horse, the whole divine apparatus on wheels. Which then was transported by other live horses or priests during the walk round processions. Thus the primary thing here is the sun and the horse, and the secondary, the chariot.

While the user scrolls through these quotations and others on the same issue – placed on the right-hand side of the screen – the pictorial illustrations change with the various explanations and interpretations.

An animated 3D sequence shows the scenery described above. It is possible for the user to freeze the motion at any given point and concentrate on one object at a time.

For example, the user might be interested in exploring the role of the horse within the sun cult and the spiritual life as such. It should be made possible to investigate the different depictions of the horse and its transformation throughout the Bronze Age and the explanations ascribable.

Similarly the sword, spear and axe will be presented visually in various ways including 3D computer animations showing scenes of spiritual rituals involving these cult objects.

The magnificent weapons of the ruling class – sword, spear and axe – all aim at divinity.

The fact that the sun worshipping is a superior theme seen from a Bronze Age perspective as well as in the context of the application, there will be cross references to various couplings of other objects and images, signs and symbols of the sun cult. For example:

On razors the blade is like a picture-book, where the celebration of the sun is the main theme. The big, glittering sun-vessel is still lying in the water, lit by the sun, and in its centre the double-axe is towering.

Incidentally, the eternal motif of razor ornamentation is the ship. Ships over and again, the whole ship, parts of ships, bow and stern!

Themes and sub-themes should be made accessible for exploration, each in their own right. But at the same time they should be presented as interwoven. And the gradual changing of the various symbols throughout the whole period known as the Bronze Age, is open field for playful interaction.

If we use the axe as an example, the change or transformation could be described roughly as follows:

> The golden years of the axe of splendour were not ever lasting: in the beginning of the period it was a divinity in itself, and then the cult axe of the gods; a weapon in the hands of the new gods, no longer a god itself.

One way of dealing interactively with the gradual changes of the individual object is to supply the user with a multiple layered fabric of pictorial information.

One of the options for the user is to activate particular elements in a collage of various representations of objects and symbols and changes in the use of these throughout the period. The changes will show visually, and a "pop-up" text will contain information about the changes in short. Details, for example regarding ornamentation, will appear and disappear, with a click. For the user who wants more information, there will be additional written material available, and maybe a voice-over speak as well.

At the bottom of the screen a line indication of time (from 1500 to 400 BC) is made available for activation by a click of the mouse on either the line itself or the chosen object. Activating the indication of time simultaneously means that the changes in details will appear in the visuals above.

If necessary, each of the main objects in question throughout the application should be provided with separate indications of time by way of "pop-up" icons representing the changes along the time line.

Possibly, the individual object will be added a specific sound – when activated – in order to make fast distinctions and provide for a certain kind of clarity.

(Meta)Reflections on the Making of History

On this last plane different interpretations and conceptions of the so-called Bronze Age will be brought into focus.

A collage of images consisting of six separate pictures – drawings, photographs or paintings – illustrates four different times.

The first collage, a row of pictures, will show representations of life in the Bronze Age seen from a 1930s' perspective; the second from a 1950s' perspective; the third from a 1970s', and the fourth from a 1990s' one. When activated, some of these images will turn into small narratives about different aspects of life in the Bronze Age. These will consist of animations and video clips, original and (re)constructed material.

Each of these four types of representation are connected to a variety of text material – oral and written – that all reflects the particular time in which they were conceived, in one way or the other.

Voice-over speak will display the tone and atmosphere of the day, whether we talk about the 1930s, 1950s, 1970s or 1990s. Preferably, the material will be the original one, collected partly from archives of different sorts.

There will be provided for playful interaction with choices of oral presentations – dramatisations, declamatory/recitations, neutral speak (as in the National Radio and Television), and personal, enthusiastic, vivid narratives.

In addition a supply of pieces of music and sound effects used in, for example, radio and television programmes through the years in relation to the subject will be made available.

The six images are supposed to be interrelated in more or less subtle ways, so that the activation of one picture releases some changes in the composition as a whole in terms of themes, narration, style or mode of (re)presentation.

4.3.2 Outline I and II

The two outlines are concerned with prospective productions that are aimed at target groups that do not prefer a factual- and information-oriented approach, but rather a more entertaining and event oriented. They do not find it important to investigate various possible interpretations in peace and quiet, undisturbed and in an individual pace, but prefer a presentation with a strong sensory appeal and the feeling of being immersed in a universe, and for whom a 3D space seems the ultimate experience.

The two approaches also aim at groups of users who share the interactive experience, and who interact in order to influence this experience. In order to accommodate multiple choices and appeal to more senses the projects include the construction of 3D worlds within a physical space, for instance inside a museum.

Among the inspirational sources, when it comes to method considerations, are the works of Maurice Benayoun, the French multimedia artist and his staff; of the American, Vibeke Sørensen; and the Spaniard, Agueda Simo. (All of them exhibited in connection with the *World Art* event in Aalborg, Denmark, in the autumn of 2000).

In Maurice Benayoun's interactive 3D installations, "Is the Devil curved" I and II, he works with "spheres" that interact with the audience/users and kind of react to user interest. To put it bluntly; the more interest the user shows, the more he or she gets from the installation. The complex sensoric system, so to speak, detects the amount of interest and acts upon it. The five spheres show up, get bigger and closer, fuse, or diminish and eventually disappear, while the sound functions simultaneously in accordance with the reaction of the spheres. The more user interest the more intense the sound effects and vice versa. The installation points to the overlap from reality to hyper-reality or virtual reality. Maurice Benayoun talks of "Infra Realism", which is not synonymous with "super realism", but connected to "the deep realism behind the surface". The spheres of "Is the Devil curved" do not look like the real world, but behave like it.

One of the main principles behind the system is the attempt to work with a "non-declarative" (as opposed to "declarative") response from the audience/user towards the installation. Mouse, push buttons and icons are abandoned in favour of a complex sensoric system, which "reads" the actions and reactions of the user and responds to the reading.

In projects like "The Atlantic Tunnel" and "Le Tunnel des Voyages", Benayoun and his team worked with four-sided cubes in a virtual tunnel using a "non-declarative" principle in providing the user with multiple choices.

In the first project the cubes represented layers of archaeology, so to speak, and the virtual travel through the tunnel (from Paris to Montreal) on one plane was a travel through several hundred years of European art history. The cubes showed glimpses of artwork throughout centuries, and digging through the tunnel the user would show more or less interest in each image. When the user stopped to concentrate on a particular image the sensoric system would register this behaviour; and after following more registrations of each move of the user, the system (ZAProfile) would select an individual user profile, based on the choices he or she had made so far.

In line with this "non-declarative, dynamic profiling" principle the individual user is met in a particular interest in or fascination with a subject, theme, style, etc.. From the database, images and sound which comply with the displayed interest or fascination would be selected.

The same principle is at work in the latter project, where the user was travelling through a virtual tunnel filled with sound and visual representations of sand beaches with palm trees, mountain scenery and New York/Manhattan. Sensors were registering user interest and the system worked out a "behaviour analysis", which led to a "dynamic profiling" that follows the "non-declarative" principle of desire or pleasure. The individual user thus would see his or her immediate fascination reflected in the supply of sound and images.

In connection with "The Atlantic Tunnel" installation it should be noted that it was constructed to accommodate two users at a time, one at each end of the virtual tunnel (in fact one in real Paris and one in real Montreal). Thus an interaction took place between users on each side. In the case of the other installation more users simultaneously were able to interact, in the sense that different "profiles" to a certain degree were able to merge and create a mix between the different types of land- and city-scapes. (Benayoun's Master Class, World Art 2000).

Vibeke Sørensen's interactive installation, "Morocco Memory II" combines the virtual with a concrete physical space, material objects and the deployment of multiple senses. Six wooden boxes filled with different spices are placed on a real table, surrounded by real chairs or cushions in the construction of a representation of a Bedouin tent. Sensors are built into the boxes containing the spices. Whenever the user opens a lid of one of the boxes, it releases a signal to one of the dias projectors, which then projects images on one of the walls of the "tent". The images are based on poster material, photos and pages with texts from literary works and diaries. And the sounds that are activated consist of voice-over readings of extracts from these different visually presented texts as well as various pieces of music to create a certain atmosphere. If simultaneously more lids are opened more projections get started and eventually a many-layered fabric will be displayed on the walls.

The users on chairs or cushions in this physical concrete tent construction are encouraged to meditate or contemplate in peace and to reflect on their own personal memories, sentiments and travel experiences. The installation is a sort of an invitation to a mental journey involving more senses.

The 3D installation, "Microworlds, Sirens and Agronauts" by Agueda Simo is about beauty and seduction. The user gets entangled and immersed in a floating oceanic world filled with sea creatures, which now and then lure the spectator or lash out at her or him. The user-controlled navigation device makes feasible a certain variation in the interactive encounter with the different individual organism. It is possible to get inside some of the sea organisms and to view them from various perspectives and distances, and enlarge or diminish these organisms. The moves and actions are underscored by electronic sounds and music. The installation is displayed in a space with a panoramic screen with room for more spectators at a time, all of which are wearing 3D glasses. One of the spectators is provided with the steering gadget and thus becomes the interactive user. The combination of randomness and a certain amount of control means that the user either enjoys the trip and gives in to the beauty and allure of this oceanic world or (as a control-freak) gets a bit frustrated after a while, because of the lack of total control. (But maybe this is true for most interactive 3D installations so far!)

If we look at some of the salient features of these various projects and inspirational sources, we may extract some useful methodological considerations referring to the Bronze Age projects described in Outline I and II.

The concepts of "non-declarative" and "dynamic profiling" provides interesting fuel for thought as well as the use of physical space, material objects, tactility and the notion of beauty, seduction or fascination.

Nordic Bronze Age: Symbols, Mythology and Rites (Outline I)

The interactive 3D installation – situated in a museum – is located in a physical space with a panorama screen and room for 20–25 people, seated. The code word for the concept is "infotainment". The audience is supposed to be entertained and learn something at the same time.

The theme deals with mythology, cult, and the symbolic world of the Bronze Age.

The "establishing shot" (in film terms) shows a summer-like marsh landscape. The images are constructed on the basis of paintings, photos and video recordings of actual landscapes, which are then digitally manipulated in order to create a richness in substance, structure, texture and density. We do not aim at a photo realistic rendering of landscapes or any other scenery. However, the represented cult or ceremonial objects shown in 3D in oversize will be reproduced in a realistic fashion, imitating the actual material used. This is in line with the idea of providing the audience with some information founded on facts.

It is early in the morning and the mist is rising from the still water. We hear the sounds from the surrounding landscape corresponding to the time of day: frogs, birds, cows, goats and sheep. But in the very beginning we only hear the frogs.

When the steering gadget is activated the sunlight gradually will increase and so will the "sound-scape". This controlling device is either in the hands of a guide or somebody in the audience. If controlled by a guide the narrative structure will be emphasised. Besides, for an audience with no prior experiences with interactive 3D systems, a skilled guide will assure that the usual frustrations with the steering and navigation is avoided.

But in order to maintain the idea of user interactivity the audience should be accommodated in their respective interests as far as possible, which means that an "official" guide needs to be sensitive to the wishes of members of the audience and react accordingly. In the end, however, the audience will be given the choice to attend a guided "show" or to try it out on their own. There will be fixed times for "guided tours".

The narrative is partly structured by means of a narrator. This narrator is a storyteller, who tells of the spiritual beliefs and the mythological world of the Bronze Age people.

Of course, no written accounts from the days of the Bronze Age exist, only more or less substantiated conceptions or imaginative speculations about the time and its people. But then again, quite a number of artefacts, objects and symbols do in fact exist, on the basis of which the tales of this narrative are told.

On the next level the narrative thus takes it point of departure in the cult objects raising from the ground mist of the marsh; swords, axes, jewels, vessels. When the guide/user tracks an object and focuses, it enlarges and "swallows" the user/the audience or rather makes a passage for an opening into a mythical world filled with symbolic images, referring to that particular cult object.

The artefacts will be placed in a wider context, dealing primarily with sun worshipping and the cult of fertility. Landscapes, the different elements of nature, the different seasons, diurnal rhythm and diurnal circle will be the backdrop of the symbolic images of different rites in order to visualise the spiritual connectedness of all things.

Sampled sound effects, including lure playing, will form the backdrop of the narrator (voice-over) from time to time, and otherwise create a condensed and imaginative acoustically atmosphere.

Nordic Bronze Age: Symbols and Mythology – The Spiritual Universe (Outline II)

The space is a concrete, physical construction representing a Bronze Age burial mound (in a museum context). The inner walls of the cupola structure, including the ceiling, function as screens for both 2D and 3D projections. Inside this representation of a burial mound there are imitations of three cult artefacts – a sword, an axe and a circular belt buckle. These objects made of suitable material for this particular purpose contain built-in sensors, which are connected to the projection system.

The actual 3D projection is dependent on characteristics of the particular artefact and the "mode of touch". The theme of the installation is focusing on the spiritual world of the Bronze Age and the approach is built on the notion of "seduction", fascination, aesthetics and experience.

The projected 3D images consist of a variety of material – photos, video recordings, graphic illustrations, drawings, paintings, as well as pure computer-created and generated scenery and objects – and the aim is to produce a rich multi-layered texture and structure of pictorial presentations and imaginative interpretations of the theme, dealing with a symbolic universe and the spiritual beliefs of the Bronze Age people. It is an attempt to create a universe by means of lyric and poetic elements, which convey a mental mind-set, in which the sun and cult of fertility reign. The more tactile aspects of this spiritual universe will be represented by the cult objects only. User interaction with the axe will release certain images related to the role of this object in connection with rites and spiritual celebrations and the same goes for the sword. The circular belt buckle symbolises the sun, and when touched the sensor signal will provide from the database a multi-layered depiction of the worship of the sun in its different forms.

When two, or maximum three, users simultaneously interact with the artefacts, the projection will reflect the fact that two or all of the three cult objects are activated. By merely slightly touching an object the sensory system will respond by releasing only a limited signal projected on a very small part of the wall or ceiling. The space around the projection will be kept in darkness. However, sounds will fill the room: sounds of nature and forces of nature, such as rain, thunder, and ocean waves; computer manipulated and sampled, synthesizer sounds; sounds in varying degrees, tone, pitch and interval.

The sounds may correspond with the picture signal, which means that a slight touch releases a single sound effect or a very brittle one, whereas a more robust handling of an object corresponds with a more satiated, powerful surround sound. In certain passages there may be an interplay between picture and sound, which is based on the principle of counter-point. It means that if the picture signal is reduced, the sound density will be heightened and vice versa.

These strategies are employed in order to create a more artistic, poetic, sensuous and fascinating presentation of the diverse material and the theme.

Dramaturgically speaking, the point of departure is a circular spiral model, a non-Aristotelian model, which seems to correspond nicely with the theme, and figurative is visualised in the various sun symbols. The installation thus is a non-linear, non-narrative (in the Aristotelian sense) presentation based on strategies concerned with fascination and poetry in motion. The inspiration for the dramaturgic point of departure is the work of Ulla Ryum, a Danish writer and playwright, who proposed a refined spiral model, which among other things make it possible to deal with time and space in another dimension – in opposition to the Aristotelian catharsis model.

4.4 Concluding Remarks

Hopefully the four exhibits and the comments have demonstrated that verbal communication in the form of outlines and treatments is a highly flexible and useful tool for sketching complex multimedia productions, and even for works including virtual and physical 3D installations. They are easy to produce and revise, and they make it possible to "visualise" the preliminary plans in order to have a shared platform for further work.

But of course more work and practical elaboration is needed in order to test suitable formats for different types of productions. The material provided here should not be taken as more than examples of how to go about it.

We have to stress the fact that we are talking about verbal sketches, suitable for the early stages of the planning process. There is still a long way to go and a lot of decisions to be made before we arrive at fully worked out scripts (or specifications) for the productions. But we find that first and tentative sketches in a comparatively cheap medium (words on paper or a computer screen) are very useful tools indeed.

References

Baddeley, WH (1975). *The Technique of Documentary Film Production*, revised edn, London and New York: Focal Press.

Chatman, S (1978). *Story and Discourse: Narrative Structure in Fiction and Film*, Ithaca, NY: Cornell University Press.

Dankert, H and Wille, NE (2001). Constructing the Concept of the "Interactive 3D Documentary": Film, Drama, Narrative or Simulation? In L Quortrup (ed.) *Virtual Interaction: Interaction in Virtual Inhabited 3D Worlds*, London: Springer, 345–70.

Garrand, T (1997). *Writing for Multimedia, Entertainment, Education, Training, Advertising, World Wide Web*, New York and London: Focal Press.

Garrand, T (2001). *Writing for Multimedia and the Web*, 2nd edn, New York: Focal Press.

Halas, J (1976). *Film Animation: A Simplified Approach* (Monographs in Communication Technology and Utilization, 2), Paris: UNESCO.

Halas, J (ed.) (1976). *Visual Scripting*, in collaboration with S Hayward, D Vukotic, J Brdecka et al. (The Library of Animation Technology), London: Hastings House.

Halas, J and Manwell, R (1971). *The Technique of Film Animation* (Communication Arts Books), New York: Hastings House.

Hayward, S (1977). *Script Writing for Animation*, London: Focal Press.

Nichols, B (1991). *Representing Reality: Issues and Concepts in Documentary*, Bloomington and Indianapolis: Indiana University Press.

Parker, P (1998). *The Art and Science of Screen Writing*, Oxford: Intellect.

Rosenthal, A (1996). *Writing, Directing, and Producing Documentary Films and Videos*, revised edn, Carbondale and Edwardsville: Southern Illinois University Press.

Samsel, J and Wimberley, D (1996). *The Interactive Writer's Handbook*, Los Angeles and San Francisco: Carronade Press.

Samsel, J and Wimberley, D (1998). *Writing for Interactive Media: The Complete Guide*, New York: Allworth Press.

Swain, DV and Swain, JR (1988). *Film Script Writing: A Practical Manual*, London and New York: Focal Press.

Historical and Archaeological Sources

Bronzealderen (1958). Director: Carl Otto Petersen; Production: Dansk Kulturfilm in collaboration with a.o. Nationalmuseet. Copenhagen. (7 min). [Documentary film. Historical reconstruction of the Bronze Age in Denmark.]

Brøndsted, J (1938). *Bronzealderens soldyrkelse* [Sun Worship in the Bronze Age] (Nationalmuseets Gule Bøger) Copenhagen: Gyldendal.

Brøndsted, J (1941). Et fjernt Danmark. Bronzealder, in J Brøndsted and P Nørlund (eds.) *Seks tværsnit af Danmarks Historie* [A Far-off Denmark, the Bronze Age], Copenhagen: Gyldendal.

Brøndsted, J (1977). *De ældste tider – Danmark indtil år 600* [The Earliest Times – Denmark till Year 600.] (Politikens Danmarkshistorie). Copenhagen: Politiken [1962].

Gods and Heroes of the Bronze Age. Europe at the Time of Ulysses. National Museum of Denmark. 25th Council of Europe Art Exhibition. [and others]. Copenhagen, Bonn, Paris, Athens. 1999. [Exhibition catalogue.]

Guder og Grave. En præsentation af dansk bronzealder på baggrund af Nationalmuseets tekst- og billeddatabaser. National Museum of Denmark. 1998 <http://www.natmus.dk/kulturnet/index.htm> [Gods and Graves. A Web-presentation of the Danish Bronze Age with text and pictures from the databases of the National Museum of Denmark.]

Heggland, J (1964). *Folket i de hvide både* [The People of the White Boats] Copenhagen: Høsts Forlag.

Heggland, J (1965). *Bronzesværdet* [The Bronze Sword] Copenhagen: Høsts Forlag.

Hvass, L (2000). *Egtvedpigen* [The Egtved Girl], 2nd edn, Copenhagen: Sesam.

Jensen, J (1979a). *Bronzealderen 1. Skovlandets folk* [The Danish Bronze Age 1. The People of the Woodlands] with illustrations by F Bau (Danmarkshistorien. Oldtiden), Copenhagen: Sesam.

Jensen, J (1979b). *Bronzealderen 2. Guder og mennesker* [The Danish Bronze Age 2. Gods and Man] with illustrations by F Bau (Danmarkshistorien. Oldtiden), Copenhagen: Sesam.

Jensen, J (1988). "Bronzealderen" [The Danish Bronze Age] in *I Begyndelsen til år 200 f.Kr.* (Gyldendals og Politikens Danmarkshistorie. Bd. 1. Redaktion Olaf Olsen). Copenhagen: Poltiken & Gyldendal.

Jensen, J (1998). *Manden i kisten. Hvad bronzealderens gravhøje gemte* [The Man in the Coffin: What Was Hidden in the Bronze Age Burial Mounds], Copenhagen: Gyldendal.

Kiviksgraven (Svenska Kulturminnen 1) [The late Bronze Age burial Mound at Kivik in Southern Sweden], Stockholm: Riksantikvarieämbetet, 1998.

Laursen, B (1991). *Topologiske Bronzealder-Hypoteser* (VENUS Report no. 13) [Topological Bronze Age Hypotheses: Proposal for a Multimedia Presentation], Institut for Informations- og Medievidenskab, Århus Universitet: Århus.

Rieck, F and Crumlin-Pedersen, O (1988). *Både fra Danmarks oldtid* [Boats from the Danish Prehistory], Roskilde: Vikingeskibshallen.

Tanderup, R and Ebbesen, K (1979). *Forhistoriens historie. Med vor ældste udgravningsberetning* [The History of the Danish Prehistory: With the Oldest Excavation Report], Højbjerg: Wormianum.

5

From Music to 3D Scenography and Back Again

Morten Constantin Lervig

Morten Constantin Lervig is a composer and has held the position of musical director for a range of major multimedia events. A primary focus in his work has been the use of music as an element in holistic performances. In addition, he has published a large and varied collection of works.

5.1 Introduction

For the production of works that use music as a scenic form of expression, experiments that examine the relationship between the visual and auditive centres are needed. With the spread of new technologies for the production and performance of music have come new challenges for the visual staging of concerts. Previously, the scenic presentation was anchored in the physical form of the instruments and the musicians who played them. Today, however, with the advent and increasing utilisation of computers in the context of concerts, the inter-relation between what is seen and what is heard is no longer as clear. It therefore appears appropriate to analyse the new technological opportunities for establishing a link between the auditive and visual elements. Persona 3D is such a project, where experiments aimed at creating a link of this kind are being carried out on the basis of the auditive material.

This chapter examines the process behind this production – a production which, using a clear and operative idea, tests the opportunities in a link of this kind between music and the living images presented in a concert context.

The fundamental idea in the production is to take video and motion-capture material of Maria Christensen, the singer, while she performs one of the songs from the Persona project repertoire (Lervig et al., 1998), and then use this material in a virtual 3D world which, in turn, is subsequently to be used in a concert context. The collection of material for the Persona 3D production involved fitting Maria Christensen, the singer from the Persona orchestra, with motion capture equipment. In all, seven sensors were placed on Maria's upper body – two on her hands, two on her elbows, two on her shoulders and two on her neck.

A small black and white (B/W) monitoring camera was suspended from a bracket on each of Maria's hands, and these cameras continuously monitored the backs of her hands from a distance of approximately 20 cm. Finally, Maria's face was filmed on a blue background. The music was played, and Maria sang playback to this while motion capture data were taken along with video footage of her hands and face.

The result of this material collection phase consisted of: video footage of Maria's face on a blue background, two B/W videotapes of Maria's hands, and a motion-capture data set comprising the position and rotation of seven different points. Maria's singing was added to this material to complete the basis for the production.

When this material is implemented into a digital virtual 3D world, a virtual world is created that in time has clear and precise references to the physical world. This must be understood in two ways: first, there is the actual registration of motion-capture data and video recordings and the fact that these are used synchronously in the work; and secondly, there is the aesthetic reference in that the fact that video is used of the singer singing the song in the work establishes a direct reference from this to the situation that the singer is actually singing the song in the physical world. The production strives to make use of these conditions, as they provide a broad scope of opportunity to use the finished production in a concert context.

In the digital virtual world, which is the space of the work and stretches over the length of the piece – i.e. approximately 3 minutes – only the following rules apply: The music is present in its entirety, and is represented by a stereo signal. The video and motion-capture material is used in full synchronisation, and the motion-capture material is applied in the development process to experiment with different options with the aim of finding a use that adds a dimension of experience which could not have been created – or would at least have been very difficult to create – in any other way.

This chapter demonstrates the application of process-analytical tools, as described by Donald Schön, on the artistic process. The analysis is particularly interested in how a single individual artist deals with situations where his knowledge is limited, and tries with this focus to uncover strategies for approaching new technology.

The fundamental motivation of the analysis of this project was the desire to gain a greater insight into and a better understanding of what actually happens in the artistic process. The central process analysis in this chapter concentrates on the initial and most important stage of the production process on the basis of the range of versions of the product, in that an analysis model developed in the second part of the chapter is used to take hold of the material before terminating in a conclusion of how the analysis has provided insight into the artistic process.

5.2 Central Technologies

5.2.1 Motion Capture

Motion-capture equipment is equipment which can measure and register the position of objects and people with the assistance of different technologies, and, as the name implies, primarily concentrates on the recording of movement over time, which is achieved by registering series of positions.

There are several technologies that can be used for this, many of which have been developed for specific areas of use. The most common are: mechanical units attached to objects or the body; electromagnetic units that position themselves in relation to a magnetic field; acoustic units that use microphones or loudspeakers to pinpoint a position; and finally, optical systems that use one or more cameras to calculate the position of an object, a process which is also known as optical tracking. This last type is called passive motion capture, as it is exclusively based on the observation of objects through one or more cameras, possibly helped by visual markings on the objects – in the form of points of reflective material, for example. These observations are then distilled through calculations to present information about the spatial location of the objects. The other types are called active motion capture. Motion capture technology has been described in more detail by Thomas Moeslund (2001).

In this production, an active system – the Motion Star Wireless Capture System from Ascension Technology Corporation (http://www.ascension.com) – was used. This is an electromagnetic system consisting of a set of sensors and a field generator. The field generator emits an electromagnetic field that pulsates at a fixed rate. The sensors are small coils that are influenced by this field and, through the medium of a radio transmitter, send these data to a computer, which uses them to calculate the position and rotation of the sensors, using six different parameters for each of the sensors.

5.2.2 3D Modelling and Animation Tools

A 3D modelling and animation tool is software that allows the user to create and process his own digital 3D models on a computer to give them texture, that is, to add surfaces and light to the models and animate them over time. The 3D modelling and animation tool used in this case is Maya, a product made by Alias Wavefront (http://www.alias-wavefront.co.jp/). It is one of the most comprehensive programs of its kind and is widely used in the production of 3D cartoons and in the post-production of films.

In addition to an almost overwhelming number of interaction options involving models and animations, it also features a scripting language that makes it possible to create self-defined functions. The 3D model created using this tool has to be rendered in 2D to draw out the images that constitute the individual components in the final product, that is, the video sequence. Rendering a 3D model requires positioning a virtual camera in the 3D model and defining the specifications of the 2D image. These specifications include resolution, reflections and the like. Rendering can be a time-consuming process. In the current production, the calculation time for each image was between 5 and 10 minutes. This appreciably influences the production process, as a total of 5,300 images have to be produced to encompass the full extent of the song.

5.3 Analysis Model

Donald Schön (1983) analyses design processes and in his work, *Educating The Reflective Practitioner* (Schön, 1991, pp. 41 ff.) he presents a range of examples of the different disciplines that make up a design process. Here, Schön categorises the artistic process as a design process: "Artists make things and are, in this sense, designers" (Schön, 1991 p. 42). The basis for creating an analysis model for use on the Persona 3D production was drawn from Donald Schön's process analysis.

As an explanation of why he uses an architectural design process as a prototype for introducing central concepts of his analytical method, Donald Schön states that: "designing, broadly conceived, is the process fundamental to the exercise of artistry in all professions ... I see designing as a kind of making" (Schön, 1991, pp. 41 ff.). In the following section, he explains his opinion that designers put things together and create new things in a process involving numerous variables as well as a range of obligations and limitations; that almost anything a designer does involves consequences that far exceed those expected, and that a design process is a process which has no unique concrete solution. He also states that he sees a designer as someone who changes an indefinite situation into a definite one through a reflexive conversation with the material of the situation.

In this way, Schön positions the artistic process in the field in which his analysis operates. It was this, combined with my own personal observation of the fact that Schön's concepts could encompass the artistic process in Persona 3D that encouraged me to use a method derived from Schön's work for the project in question.

In the following sections I will pursue the thread through Schön's case study of the previously mentioned architectural design process (Schön, 1991, pp. 44 ff) – a process that Schön uses as a prototype example of a design process, which he then applies to illuminate his own concepts and method.

Pages 56 ff. of *Educating the Reflective Practitioner* present the analysis of the architectural process, where Schön uses the first section to demonstrate how the student has difficulty in starting work – she cannot make the buildings in her project fit in with the background available. The teacher, therefore, so to speak moves the framework for the design of the work by telling the student to start somewhere else with an arbitrary detail and then work cyclically between the individual parts and the whole. Every stage of this process is an experiment in which saying "What if ..." entails consequences for the next process. Some things are impossible to do, for example, a classroom must have a certain size, and the landscape looks the way it does. The teacher thus demonstrates an operative way out of a situation where there is no development. In other words, he *reframes* the situation.

Schön then derives three other dimensions – which he considers particularly important – from the process he observes:

1. Linguistic domains, where the designer describes and accepts the consequences of his actions,
2. The consequences for the process that the designer discovers and pursues,
3. The designer's changing perspectives in relation to the situation in which he finds himself.

Schön groups the linguistic domains in the conversation. In this design process, these linguistic units comprise: names of elements, qualities, innate conditions, actions and norms for dealing with problems, consequences and difficulties.

In dealing with the consequences of the process, Schön states that a professional discipline is constituted by the relationship between the norms that exist for areas such as place, layout, geometry and structure: situations arise that can be defined by thoughts along the lines of "what if … then we would have to do this or that …" In fact, you are faced with a problem for which you attempt to imagine a solution – this solutions opens up a range of new solutions and consequences, and so on. As the designer reflects on the moves he has made previously, branches of problems begin to appear, along with possible consequences and options, all based on the current situation. The virtuosity of the teacher is displayed (Schön, 1991, p. 62) in his ability to maintain an overview of large areas of these branches, but even though he is very skilled, he must eventually move on from the *what if* position and take a decision, which then becomes a design point with obligations and consequences for the future development of the design process.

The point of view of the teacher in relation to the design undergoes multiple changes as the process continues. He changes from viewing something that *could happen* and *might happen* to something that *should happen* or *must happen*. There are series of *must happen* actions that relatively simply uncover new branches between which choices can be made freely, and it is demonstrated that, so to speak, *the whole* is constantly on the line. As the work progresses via iterative movements, the teacher's perspective changes from sketching and testing as he makes every group of actions the object of evaluation in relation to the design domains he commands, to the final obligation. This change eases the situation, thus simplifying the branches and making it possible to deal with the situation.

On the basis of this, Schön asks himself the following questions:

1. When, as a practitioner, you are working on a unique project in a unique situation, how can you make use of your experience?
2. The reflective method, Schön observes, is a kind of experimental method, but practical situations – like the design situation described in the example – are notoriously bad environments for experimentation in the scientific sense. So what is the actual form of the experimentation that takes place?

Schön concludes on the basis of his analysis that even though the architect has probably found himself in similar situations – working on a difficult building site and facing some of the same problems – he has never been in exactly the same situation before. Schön's suggestion for understanding how the architect can put himself in a fruitful situation from this basis is that the architect, the experienced player, has built up a repertoire of examples, images, understandings and actions through his previous work. In this case, the repertoire stretches across all the design domains that his profession comprises. When a practical worker is faced with a unique situation – that is, a situation he has never encountered before – he sees it as something that already forms a part of his repertoire. His problem-solving behaviour thus becomes a variation on the problem-solving behaviour he has displayed in similar situations. Schön defines these as *seeing-as* and *doing-as*, and states that these processes take place without the conscious awareness of the person doing them.

The second question is the question about experimentation, which Schön presents as the classic scientific method of understanding this concept. Schön divides experimentation in the practice of design into three main areas. Schön calls the process of acting simply to see what the result will be, *exploratory experimentation*. This is reminiscent of the way in which children gain experience about the world. Exploratory experimentation is a game with the world, and it succeeds when it results in something being changed. Schön calls another way we act to achieve change, *move-testing*. This has to do with situations where we know what we want to achieve, and we therefore experiment in an attempt to reach this goal. The carpenter adds an extra plank to his scaffolding to stabilise it, the chess player moves a piece to protect his queen, parents give their children sweets to stop them crying. Schön says that in simple cases, such moves are either confirmed (the move chosen solved the problem) or negated (the move did not solve the problem as expected). It is seldom this easy, hoewver, and the result of such experimentation is often more complex. The move may have been confirmed, but an unexpected result was also produced. Schön therefore expands the answer from: *did you achieve what you wanted?* to *do you like what you achieved?* Confirmation is thus expanded to encompass all these consequences and applies when you can say that you like all these consequences – which is not the case if your move has been negated. A third way of experimenting is to test a hypothesis, which is how the world of science defines experimentation. A hypothesis A is confirmed if its predictions match the observations resulting from the experiment and if the predictions of an alternative hypothesis B are refuted by the experiment. The reality of the practitioner is different to that of the researcher. The practitioner wishes to change the situation to something he prefers. He is also interested in understanding the situation, but only as a tool for changing the situation for the better. When a practitioner acts and reflects and acts again in a situation he perceives as unique – conscious of the phenomenon, skating over his intuitive understanding of it – his experiments can simultaneously be *explorative, move testing* and *hypothesis testing*. These three methods can be incorporated in the same action, and it is this that defines the particular character of the practitioner's experiments.

The practitioner, in this case the design teacher, operates in a virtual world (Schön, 1991, p. 75). In this virtual world, the practitioner can try some of the experiments that are so difficult to perform in reality. It is therefore of crucial importance for the ability to experiment and create virtually that the practitioner can construct and manipulate virtual worlds. The teacher and the student use a sketch pad to mediate their work in the virtual world. They move components, change access, talk about and with the things. Limitations that would exist in the real world are drastically reduced. Drawing is a quick, spontaneous technique that leaves clear tracks of the process that has taken place.

The conditions in the virtual world are unique. Forward drive can be varied – you can work quickly, and make large, violent changes that would take a long time in the real world. In a drawing, such changes take just moments to make. The process is reversible to a certain extent, and you can experiment with something, reject the idea and return to the starting point. However, the actual strength of the virtual world thus created from drawings is wholly dependent on the extent to which it can be transformed or translated to the real world. Here, it is the experience from the practice of the profession that is crucial for the successful use of the virtual worlds.

5.4 Analysis

Schön looks at the process that takes place when a skilled professional works on a process within his field. He has access to the process from looking at a teaching situation in which the student and teacher talk to one another – a situation in which he can record what is actually happening in this process. However, in the Persona 3D project, there is no communication to record between the parties involved, so what does that mean? The difference lies in the fact that in a communicative situation, the practitioner will have a tendency to choose moves which he can support with verbal arguments, or which, in translating them to linguistic expression, he will describe in a certain way. The question is, does the same thing happen in a non-verbal process in all situations? In the Persona 3D production, the communication is not translated into language in the process itself, as it does not take place in a linguistic interpersonal space but only in my mind, and the act of delimiting the linguistic domains within it – which I subsequently have done – becomes only an approximation, as I initially had to translate it into language, and this translation is influenced by the context in which it takes place.

To take this train of thought further, it is worth noting that while some processes, such as architectural design, have clearly defined professional and linguistic domains – partly because these are essential in the communicative union this discipline shares with other professional areas – the situation is very different for modern art production. In this area, the artist is often alone in uncharted territory as regards professional disciplines. Linguistically, the artist will often be required to take up or adopt new domains in relation to the professional disciplines within or with which he is working. With these reservations, this analysis will reveal whether Schön's concepts will prove operative in the present context. Another reservation is the fact that Schön works with the process of the trained practitioner. An important element of the present production is the acquisition of new skills during the process itself. Schön's method of understanding the design process does, however, also involve a considerable degree of acquiring experience through practical work.

5.4.1 Examination of the Material

I carried out the work with the raw video, motion capture data, sound and 3D model in the production by modelling and animating a version to a point at which I wished to evaluate the result. The 3D modelling environment does not provide particularly comprehensive feedback within the process, more especially, it does not support the screening of a video feed –that is, using a video film as the surface of an object – while the modelling is taking place. Instead, what is displayed is a blurred fixed image positioned somewhere around the place where the video will be shown. During the process, it is necessary to render individual pictures so as to see whether the positioning in question is correct. If you want feedback on the entire animation, however, you have to render entire sequences of individual pictures and then splice them together to create a film in a post-production process.

The empirical material consists of nine renderings of video film (RT0–RT8). These all last 1–3 minutes and represent situations in which I have chosen to make a version of the production for more detailed evaluation for myself. I have written comments on each of these versions, in which I formulate what takes place in the version in question and how it is related to the previous versions. This is followed by a reflection on the basis of the material and my memory, as in only a few cases did I make notes linked to the separate versions. These reflections should be seen as a counterpart to the communication which Schön registers as taking place between the teacher and the student, and as my own chronological observation of the process: which elements stand out in the individual sequences, where do the changes from sequence to sequence occur? What do I consider interesting? Noteworthy? Strange? And what is the basis for the changes that take place? Both the descriptive comments and the reflections were written subsequent to the completion of the production.

The following presents a single example of the processing of a video version (RT1) of this kind to illustrate the method I employed (Figure 5.1). First comes the description of the version (RT1) and then Table 5.1 shows, in a systematic way, my analysis of the material.

The length of RT1 is 3:23, full length. You see, as in RT0, a figure with a green-yellow-blue woven texture. Video of Maria's face is projected onto this figure (see Figure 5.1). In this way, the figure forms a kind of body, with Maria's face as its head. In addition, video film of Maria's face is displayed at the bottom of the screen, centre right, as a 4:3 format video image. This has moved free from "the body". Moreover, there are two objects with a greyish video texture that are moving around "the body". These are the two deformed planes that carry the projections of the B/W video film from the original recording session. The altered camera angle makes "the body" taper off towards the bottom, inwards into the space.

Figure 5.1 Version RT1.

5.4.2 Overview of the Process

This section provides a summary of the entire production process, which describes the important developments and changes in the individual versions. In RT0, the focus is largely on the technical side, the linguistic domain of the 3D tool is dominant, and this is the tool in which I have experimented. The fact that the aesthetic linguistic domain is represented at all is due to the fact that I have been forced to take a stance as regards texture and choice of colour, and this is done with an aesthetic consciousness. There are consequences of the sum of actions, which, together, have influenced me to implement my production concept. I see that the way in which the material has been collected is of crucial importance to the result.

When I see the effect of the video film of the hands, they appear in poor quality B/W, and their effect is neither that intended, nor particularly appreciated.

In RT1, I imagine for the first time the two different angles on the production: am I making material for inclusion in a larger context, or am I making a complete film or video? At this early stage, conditions are beginning to suggest this change in obligations in relation to the product.

Table 5.1 Analysis of RT1.

My own observation	Reflection	Concepts in play
It was very important for me to see the process in its entirety.	Perspective examining the entire process.	Perspectives.
This is actually opposed to my sustained claim that I did not want to make a film or a video, but material for a stage performance. Nevertheless, it is implicit in some of the circumstances that to a limited, modest extent, I am also making a video.	Still examining, but on the way to obligation as the material supports one perspective while the other has been dropped in the starting concept.	Perspectives.
I have not taken as my basis a concept for a major performance, I do not have a set task in relation to which this production is to fulfil requirements. In fact, in one way or another, it must create its own meaning. I have consciously chosen video and motion capture material from a single song (whereas I could have chosen bites from several). Finally, it would not be too terrible to be able to have a video to present in various Persona contexts.	I am trying different positions in my mind, my virtual world.	Virtual worlds.
It is difficult for me to avoid working with the progression of the product, as it is second nature to me as a composer to work with it.	Change to a perspective of near obligation in relation to the aesthetics.	The aesthetic domain.
I prefer my own camera angle.	Evaluation of the experiment.	Consequence of acting in the aesthetic domain.
Because I am getting some associations to a nightclub singer wearing the type of dress that only allows tiny steps as it tapers in towards the feet. This feeling is reinforced by the fact that I only have motion capture links to the upper body.	Associations to film aesthetics.	The aesthetic domain.
This version makes it clear to me that while I personally have a clear feeling for and perception of the spatial figure – because I can move it around and change it on my screen in the 3D software – I must show consideration for the audience and generate a movie with a moving camera.	I examine the effect of the figure standing still, and discover that it must be changed.	The first move in a move-test experiment.
I prefer my own camera angle in this version.	My attempt to move the camera succeeds.	The aesthetic domain. Consequence of the move-test experiment.
The viewer does not have much chance to scan the spatial properties of objects that do not directly call to mind something in the spatial dimension of the real world.	It is important to me to make the spatial properties understood.	A perceptual observation in the aesthetic domain.
The two film planes that represent the hands do not really work in this context, I will have to decide whether the rest of the production should be tailored to accommodate them, or whether they should be cut.	Using these was a part of the original concept.	My observations now impose obligations on my perspective.

This is happening because I am changing my perspective from seeing a small section limited by time, to forcing myself to look at the song in its entirety. This change is identified from the aesthetic linguistic domain, where I have skills as a composer in maintaining an overall view of aesthetic progressions over time.

In RT2, I work in the virtual world in an aesthetic linguistic domain, I imagine a camera usage with or without objects other than the central one. My method of collecting material – the videos of the hands – has resulted in the need to cut these elements, as their aesthetic expression collides too violently with the other material, the other idea. I reflect on the audience perspective with regard to the spatial reading of the objects that is made possible by the movement of the camera, and the perspective has changed in some way, from the interest in the atomic part – the individual image – to an interest in both the individual part and the whole. At present, there is conflict between these perspectives, as each results in completely different processing of the material.

In RT3, a major reframing has taken place – the fundamental object has been replaced by a plane made up of a wealth of repeated video images. This reframing is the framework for an experiment concerning how far it is possible to stretch the use of motion capture data in an abstract direction, without them, in an undesirable manner, losing their referentiality to the movements that have created them – in this case, Maria's movements while she sang. Observations are made from an aesthetic linguistic domain and the conclusion is that here, the use of these data has become

Figure 5.2 Version RT3.

too far removed from their starting point, so far in fact that I no longer believe them to be making a desirable contribution.

In RT4, I work in the aesthetic domain stretching the reference between the body from which the motion-capture data set was recorded to the figure to which I link this data set, without it snapping. From RT3, I have learned that there is a limit beyond which meaning is no longer emitted from the referentiality. The referentiality has something to do with the organic, the fact that all the materials are inter-related in the form of a kind of shared origin, generated in the same situation. The way in which I have linked the motion-capture data set to the central object in my 3D model behaves in an unexpected manner; it hacks and creates some severely angled polygons. I am forced to move into the language of the 3D tool by a realisation in the aesthetic domain that there are some things that do not behave the way I want them to.

In RT5, I pursue this goal: it must be organic and it must be possible to see that while the goal is identified in the aesthetic domain, it is now also being pursued in the 3D domain, and in the specific domain of film aesthetics, not only must shapes and their movements be organic, but the camera work must provide the impression of stemming from a hand-held camera.

In RT6, the different linguistic domains, film aesthetics, aesthetics and 3D work together towards the goal of making the result appear natural, and the experiments I conduct are measured against this goal.

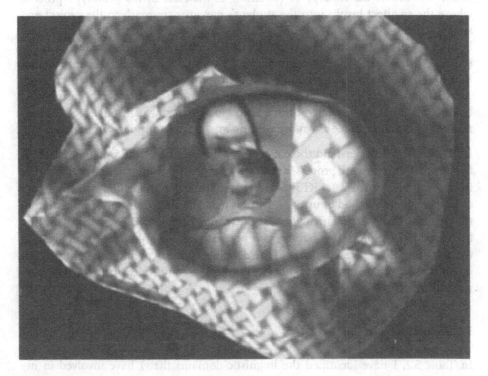

Figure 5.3 Version RT4.

The reframing jostling for attention as early as RT1 appears to have reached completion in RT7. The primary goal has now become to create a complete film, and the secondary goal has become preparing material for a stage performance. I identify this by a conscious and concrete change, namely working to ensure that for the first time the introduction pursues a direct goal of film aesthetics: the creation of a good plot within the production. I carry out a range of experiments described in the area of film aesthetics. I do not experience this reframing, as I can sense the fruitfulness of adopting the point of view that I am working with the creation of a complete film. This approach does not limit the options for using the material in a concert context.

In RT8, I have allowed myself to experiment more freely, I have achieved a little more awareness in relation to the act of creating a complete film. I conduct experiments with camera movement, which, unsurprisingly, are described in the domain of film aesthetics, and this unexpectedly produces the result that the camera sees the face that is projected onto a cylinder, which immediately leads to focus on this aesthetic phenomenon.

5.5 Observation of Schön's Concepts in the Production Process

5.5.1 Reframing

Schön introduces his concept of reframing at the start of his prototype process, where the architect breaks into the student's previous approach to the project and suggests the imposition of a new element on the project. The architect simply takes hold of the current situation, in which the student does not experience taking a subsequent design step, and moves a building with a kindergarten. This is immediately followed by additional design options "...then you might carry the gallery through ..." (Schön 1991, p. 45). This is thus a move of the *what if you did this* type, followed by pursuit of the design-related consequences to a point at which you decide that this move is or is not desirable any more – doing what Schön considers a reframing.

In this context, I understand the concept as a description of the situation in which the approach to the work process is radically changed – possibly on a factual plane, as in the move from RT2 to RT3, where perception and modelling of objects are changed and the method of using textures is radically altered. In my examination of the material, I have experimentally used the term *reframing* to label my act of cutting the video footage of Maria's hands from my material. My argument for doing so is the fact that this material is a part of the described starting point of the process, but it could also be claimed that it is simply a consequence of the way in which the material was collected.

5.5.2 The Linguistic Domains

In Table 5.2, I have identified the linguistic domains that I have involved in my description of the process.

Table 5.2 Linguistic domains.

Domain	Definition	Examples
The function of the work	The purpose of the work The context in which the work is placed.	The discussion about whether the work is a film in itself or material for a performance.
The Virtual World	The mental space in which the production takes place via sketched and imaginary design steps and their consequences.	In RT2, I imagine a camera usage, but decide that this can only happen if something specific is fulfilled. I thus sketch something and reach a point where I know what is needed in order to make this happen.
The aesthetic	The area where aesthetic means are processed.	In RT0, I describe the colour and patterns of the dress.
The film aesthetic	The area where film aesthetic means are processed.	In RT7, I describe the first experiments that resemble film clips.
The positioning of the eye	The positioning of the camera in relation to the objects.	In RT2, I describe the perspective for the movement of the eye through the sponge.
Spatial organisation	The spatial extent of individual objects, and their inter-relationship.	In RT7, the spatial properties of the central object are introduced via the choice of a camera usage that makes them understandable.
3D modelling language	Processing elements in the 3D software	In RT3, I am not satisfied with the effect of linking motion-capture data to the object, as it looks wrong. Making this change requires design work using the 3D modelling tool.
Other elements	Representation of elements from other domains outside the production.	In RT0, I use dance terminology to describe Maria's movements.

These domains reflect how problems are dealt with. For example, for much of the process, I allow the organisation of the eye, and thus the movements of the camera, to be the domain in which I work with the perception of the film entirety, and this excludes me from a whole range of film concepts, such as cutting techniques.

5.5.3 Consequences of Actions

An important element in a production process is made up of what Schön terms *design points*, that is, points in the progress of the process at which binding decisions have been made concerning what is to happen, and which therefore lay the foundations for the subsequent stages of the design process. For example, I took a decision about which colour was to be used for the background for Maria's face on the video. Immediately this decision had been taken, it produced consequences of which the consequences would be felt throughout the rest of the production process. In this case, it was instrumental in the choices of the other colours – and although the most important choice of colour was changed (the alteration of the colour of the principal object from RT7 to RT8), a part of the colours chosen remained in the lighting that survived from the starting point in this background colour.

5.5.4 Change of Perspective

An examinatory approach is used to adopt an attitude to the problems posed in the project – for example, the crucial problem surrounding the two video films of Maria's hands. As early as the first analysis of these films, it is clear that what attracts the attention of the eye is the movement taking place behind the hands, and not, as was expected, the movement of the hands themselves. The approach to this situation is examinatory. Will this unexpected development produce some form of benefit? In the first version, this examinatory perspective is retained, even though it has to be admitted that the material does not function in the manner envisaged. Later on, the perspective changes to the obligatory – if this does not work, reaction is required through action. In this case, the reaction was to remove these video sequences from the production.

5.5.5 The Unique Situation

In this production, the whole overall situation is a unique situation. A high level of skills from other professional domains, such as the composition of music and film aesthetics, come into play. This confirms Schön's observation that in unique situations, people refer to other unique situations – *seeing-as* and *doing-as*. For example, this occurs when, in RT7, experience is transferred from the way in which the progression of a work is dealt with in a musical context.

5.5.6 The Exploratory Experiment, Move-test and Hypothesis Test

Examination of the material proves that a good deal of experimentation takes place in the production process. Taking the change from RT1 to RT2 as an example, it can be said that a hypothesis has been put forward stating that a good effect will be achieved if the seeing eye passes through an object in the introduction to the production. This hypothesis is tested and confirmed here. In versions RT0 and RT1, it is my other tests which have been refuted on this point. At the same time, it can be asked why this object looks as it does: in relation to what has passed before, it must surely be hollow so that the camera can pass through it, but otherwise …? But in other regards, it is an exploratory experiment at shape level. And is there another reason for introducing yet another object? Yes – it is necessary to give the audience more information about the spatial organisation, and for that reason it seems to be necessary to introduce another object, that is, a move-test which is simultaneously carried out and confirmed.

5.5.7 The Virtual World

It is important to stress that two virtual worlds are involved in this production: the virtual digital 3D world built up in the 3D software, and the virtual world in the Schönic sense, where design ideas can be tested. This section deals with the latter category of virtual world, and it is important to take care, as occasionally these two meanings of the expression converge in that the virtual digital 3D world becomes the medium used to sketch future stages of the design.

En route from idea to product, the production process includes several virtual worlds in the Schönic sense. This in itself is surely not surprising, as it could be argued that the same applies to an architectural process, where, for example, the first sketches are made on a sketch pad; these are followed by scale drawings, then a model is constructed, and finally the technical drawings are prepared. All these are mediating different virtual worlds, or, if you prefer, different aspects of the same, increasingly detailed and concretised virtual world. In Persona 3D, the first representation of the virtual world is presented in the model and animation constructed in the 3D program. Models and animations can be sketched here, but as mentioned previously, the program does not provide instant detailed feedback. This requires rendering – either of individual images if you want detailed information that can be observed from such, or of series of images spliced together to form a video film – this is the next representation of virtual worlds – and finally, when all decisions have been taken, rendering of the finished product.

In contrast to an architectural process, however, this process is reversible from idea to product, in that versions and logs of the changes that occur can be stored, and as long as these are maintained, it can be said that the product is also a representation of a virtual world in the same way as if the architect considered his sketches as his products. It is not until the product is placed into a context, for example by being published as a video or used as video material at a concert, that it leaves the virtual world and enters the physical world. Even in this situation it is possible to think of examples to illustrate that it is not that simple. For example, if the material is used interactively in a stage performance and can still be changed, then it is still subject to conditions that resemble those of the virtual world.

Reversibility seems to be a central element in the dividing line between the virtual and physical worlds, and here, digital technology supports a very high level of reversibility when the subject of the work is digital art.

5.6 Conclusion

As explained above, Schön's method is perfectly suited to gaining insight into the present artistic process, which is taking place via the use of a range of different media and introduces a new use of materials in a new combination of technologies. This is true even though Schön himself limits his method to dealing with processes that take place in clearly defined professional domains, in which professional practitioners dominate.

It is most in the definition of the linguistic domains that the model shows a degree of limitation, because while an architectural process clearly takes place in well-defined and strictly delineated linguistic domains that can be identified at an objective level, the linguistic domains involved in the work process of a novice working in unexplored territory are primarily based on the novice's other, well-grounded professional domains. This in itself is fair enough, but the problem is that although this starting point naturally has a major influence on the process, this part of the analysis unavoidably becomes very personal and difficult to use in a broader context. In addition, it has occasionally seemed that there were so many Schönic concepts in play at once, that it was difficult to decide whether there was any point in attempting to separate and identify them.

The ambition behind this process analysis was to gain insight into what takes place in the artistic process, what drives it forward, and to which mechanics it is subject. Schön's method has demonstrated a range of action options and the background for these, and as projects in the field of digital art often involve new and untested domains, this understanding provides deeper insight into the motives for the actions that make up the progressive design process.

I have identified a number of points which have been uncovered by the analysis.

1. The experimentation in a design process – and therefore also in an artistic process – has the primary purpose of placing me in a situation which I would rather be in than in the present situation, i.e. changing the situation for the better.

2. There is a link between the linguistic domains in which I describe the process and the options to act which are open to me. Some problems can only be identified in specific linguistic domains, and, correspondingly, some experiments can only be carried out within some domains. The linguistic domains that come into play in an artistic process that involves the use of new technology stem from the artist's other spheres of experience until new linguistic domains have been constituted.

3. Within a process of this kind, there are specific concepts that can provoke a development – what Schön calls *reframing*.

4. The fundamental material you take with you into an artistic process – in this case, the three videos, the motion capture data set and the music – can influence the process to such an extent that it can be necessary to deviate from the goal you originally set yourself. Put another way: the approach is crucial to the result.

5. Unexpected side effects of experiments or attempts to solve problems are a large, constant source of development in the artistic process.

References

Lervig, M et al. (1998). Persona, phonogram. Aarhus: Intermusic.
Moeslund, T (2001). Interacting with a Virtual World through Motion Capture. In L. Qvortrup (ed.) *Virtual Interaction,* London: Springer-Verlag, 221–34.
Schön, D (1983). *The Reflective Practitioner.* New York: Basic Books.
Schön, D (1991). *Educating the Reflective Practitioner.* San Francisco: Jossey-Bass.

6

The Making of a Pedagogical Tool for Picture Analysis and Picture Construction

Søren Kolstrup

Søren Kolstrup has a background as a media researcher. He has especially studied visual communication using 2D pictures.

6.1 The Original Project

This chapter presents a project that was initiated in 1996 as an attempt to investigate the possible use of the computer as a pedagogical tool for a production-oriented approach to academic picture analysis. The 1996 version of the project was a purely theoretical plan that was implemented to some extent during the following years. It was based on the rather frustrating realisation that university students may be good at making semiotic analysis of pictures, but they do not have the sense of pictures as production processes, whereas students of photo-journalism have this sense but are not concerned about the meaning of the pictures or about how the viewer constructs meaning of newspaper photos. It should be stressed that this text is only concerned about communicative pictures: the production of visual meaning, the transmission of visual meaning and the reception of visual meaning. These communicative pictures may or may not be art.

The aim of the project was to provide students with a practical and theoretical tool, a grammar, to understand or analyse pictures as a construction and to construct or create pictures with an analytical eye. Construction and analysis were seen as mutually dependent. The learning process was seen accordingly as the reciprocal activity of analysis and creation, and of learner and learning material. We wanted the construction work to precede the analytical reflection. The basis of this concept was the fact that the computer has made it possible to make practical work with pictures precede theoretical work, to deduce systematisation from concrete practice.

The visual grammar should thus contain not only analytical tools but also give the students insight into practical construction principles without being a simple hands-on course or a creative course in drawing or painting. The course was not intended to be an introduction to semiotic or psychological conceptions. The goal was intended to enable students to perform analysis and construction in one and the same operation.

Such a concept of an interactive grammar needs a basic theoretical framework in order to answer the fundamental questions: "On which basis do we construct pictures?", and "On which basis do we understand these pictures?". Different aspects of the Gestalt theories and of social semiotics have contributed. For more details see Section 6.5.

The original project was only concerned about flat, still pictures giving you a 3D illusion. This focus on classic, still pictures and photos was fundamental and had later on some unforeseen consequences.

The general goals of the grammar of visual language could be split into more specific and explicit goals:

- theoretical and practical insight into the construction of space and depth, light and shadow, direction, speed and movement, colour, texture, composition and construction;
- insight into the relations between construction and meaning;
- insight into the fact that with a restricted number of elemental principles you can create a huge number of pictures, that is, the principles seen metaphorically as a generative grammar;
- insight into the ways picture construction and social use of the pictures are related, that is, the picture as part of a narrative, an argumentation, etc.

The original project had some secondary goals. The first was to sharpen the visual attention or awareness of the students. The second was to make students aware that many of the production principles of pictures are not new inventions; that some of these principles (devices or cues) go back to cave paintings, others go back to a remote mediaeval epoch, while others may be newer.

6.2 Thinking in 2D and 3D: The Original Plans for Picture Construction and Picture Analysis

The original conception was based on already existing 2D pictures. These pictures were seen as combinations of set pieces, somehow like the ones that existed in the baroque theatre. This means that the picture was seen as a combination of flat elements partly overlapping each other. The totality of the picture was seen as an interplay of completely visible elements and of partly occluded elements. Figure 6.1 presents the isolated elements and Figure 6.2 presents two possible combinations.

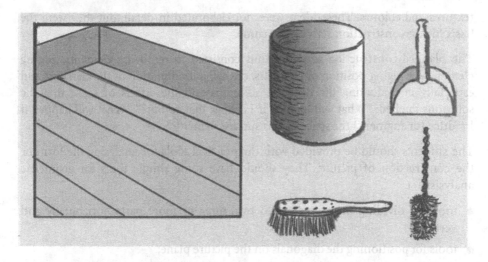

Figure 6.1 The isolated set pieces.

This interplay of occluded and overt parts of the elements constituted the first parameter and not only as a simple assembly of foreground, mid-ground and background. There were plans of more complex assembly work, for instance one based on a still life made by Hans Mertens, a German artist working in the 1920s. Each element of the painting, house-cleaning tools, was laid free, the occluded parts were reconstructed, in order that the student should try to make an ironical and poetic picture in the spirit of Mertens. The main point is that it was possible to omit elements and to fix elements in different places. So, of course, even if Mertens had made one unique solution, the student still had a huge, if not unlimited, number of options.

The position of elements was not the only parameter, however. Each element could and should be submitted to different types and directions of light or to different

Figure 6.2 Combinations of the set pieces.

textures and colours. These ideas were not elaborated in detail, but they were the basis for the construction activities to come.

The planned construction activities thus consisted in removing elements, adding elements, changing position of elements, changing illumination of the elements and especially in evaluating the different solutions and the effects of sense that the solutions implied: "What will happen if I change that colour?", "What will happen if I reduce (or augment) the space of this surface element?".

The students should be provided with the practical tools for analysing the form or the construction of picture. They should have some simple tools for geometric analysis:

- tools for dividing the pictures into two, three or more parts horizontally and vertically;
- tools for positioning the diagonals on the picture plane;
- tools for finding the golden section;
- tools for inscribing the picture elements of the picture plane in circular, triangular, conical, or other geometrical shapes.

We thought and still believe that comparisons of different stages of a picture are an invaluable source of information and basis for analysis: from sketch or first version to final state or last version. It was extremely desirable that the students should be able to systemise observation of a painter's work. Why did Géricault add a new person on his *Le radeau de la Méduse* (1827) in its final state? What were the reasons for and the effects of the changes Rembrandt made in many of his etchings? Some of them exist in more than three versions. Think of his *The Three Crosses* from 1653 that has at least three stages: the first version shows a multitude of persons beneath the crosses and the light is shed over the whole scenery, whereas in the last version there is only a battle of light and shadow around the crosses. What are the effects of this dramatic implosion of light for the meaning of the etching?

If we move to communicative pictures today, we see the enormous importance of the study of different versions of the same subject. Why does the press photographer choose this particular negative out of the 12 or 15 shots? Is it chosen for aesthetic reasons or for communicative reasons?

6.3 Thinking in 2D, Realisation in 3D

During the years 1996–2000 parts of the project were realised; theoretical texts were produced and some of the construction ideas were realised in PhotoShop. It seemed as if all that was needed was to create a system of "free" layers. It should be a system where the student could not change the elements, but was merely able to decide the position and the layer of the element: "Which element should form the foreground, which elements should be placed in the middle and in what order?", "How high on the plane should it be placed?", etc.

In the summer of 2001 the first steps towards creating the experimental prototype "Tool for Picture Analysis" (TPA) included on the CD-ROM were taken. It turned out that no 2D program was efficient to support the ideas of the original project. There was no generalising possibility in the 2D programs available and it would be impossible to create light effects. As for working with space and perspective, obviously a 3D program would be better. The experimental reconstruction work had to be made in some kind of 3D program.

The goals and the target groups have also changed. It consists now of media students, multimedia students and similar groups. In both cases, some knowledge of how pictures are produced, how pictures produce meaning today and how they have produced meaning during history is necessary.

With the introduction of 3D programming there was no real space for the set piece model with its reconstruction of existing pictures. At least this was the conclusion for the moment. Then there were other considerations; for example, the set piece model with its assembly work could be seen more as some kind of advanced jigsaw puzzle than as a true construction work. The interactive experiments had therefore to be placed at a more fundamental level of picture construction. With the new situation the basic paradigms of painting came into focus. The construction work had to do with the following fundamentals: light, colour, depth, texture, movement.

One of the advantages of the use of 3D seemed to be that it would be very easy to change parameters. Let us imagine that we have constructed a picture in the manner of Goya or Caravaggio. It will not be a naturalistic one, and we see an interior, some kind of prison or at least a dark room with some light sources. We see some simplified persons more or less resembling dolls. Table 6.1 lists different light sources, each source being able to project soft or sharp light with different contrast, different brightness and covering smaller or bigger areas, etc. We should even be able to change the position and the number of dolls. In this way each light source has an enormous range of possibilities and the whole scene could be turned into a huge number of pictures. So the grammar could show that a restricted number of rules (light parameters, positions) can generate a large number of sentences (= actual pictures). This is Chomsky at a picture plane.

Table 6.1 Theoretical diagram showing the combinations of light sources, brightness and contrast of the light, soft or sharp light and size of illuminated area.

Light source position	Soft light	Sharp light	High contrast	Low contrast	Narrow area	Large area
Position 1						
Position 2						
Position 3						
Position 4						

Figure 6.3 Group of persons submitted to strong light.

Figure 6.4 The same group of persons submitted to feeble light from a different source.

Here the loss of the set piece model would have turned out to be an invaluable advantage. I have to write "would have" because unfortunately users will not have the same possibilities as the designer. If users were able to manipulate a huge number of possible combinations this would imply that they had the same software as the designer, which is rarely the case.

In fact, users are not able to choose a large and free number of combinations – they only have the choice between pre-formed combinations, and a rather limited number of these. In a way, the 3D construction work loses its raison d'être when you cannot obtain an infinite number of states or versions in real time, but even then, much solid information on the variation of light may be obtained. This appears clearly at Figures 6.3 and 6.4.

The original plan was that the construction of pictures should precede the theoretical learning. As long as the work was seen as manipulation of existing pictures, this procedure was the only reasonable way. With the new (and restricted) role given to the picture reconstruction, the work will follow more classic or traditional ways:

Theoretical and historical introduction → picture manipulation → return to reflection.

As a whole there will be more reflection than creation.

The practical analysis consists of inscribing the elements of the picture's surface in geometric figures like triangles or squares. For example, Goya's picador on his horse

Figure 6.5 The incoherent use of central perspective features and other features on the picture plane.

Figure 6.6 The incoherent use of central perspective on the picture plane.

forms the top of the triangle and the legs of the horse the two other angles. This procedure has been given more importance, but as a whole there are no changes in the original project. The project has kept the idea of creating a geometric tool for picture analysis: division of the pictures plane into zones, marking of the golden section, and defining circular, triangular shapes on the picture plane. Every one who has worked in this field knows that finding the diagonals is no problem, and that dividing the picture into two, both horizontally and vertically, is rather easy too. Dividing the picture into more than two begins to be quite laborious and finding the golden section is boring and often a waste of time. So any automation of these procedures would be a great advance.

The number of analytical procedures has increased. The final stage contains not only procedures for finding deviant features on the picture plane and for sharpening the user's visual awareness, but also tools for geometric analysis. Figures 6.5 and 6.6 are examples of pictures using false features of central perspective.

6.4 The General Use of Web Galleries

The original project was based on the idea that the authors should get the permission to use pictures from the National Danish Art Gallery (Statens Museum for Kunst). In the meantime, access on the Internet to an almost unlimited number of pictures has become possible, such as European art from the 12th to the 18th century and good resources for the last two centuries, as well as Asian arts, and in many cases with a better quality than you find in a textbook. Even the best use of the National Gallery would never yield a pedagogical treasure comparable to the Internet.

Furthermore, the search functions in some databases make it possible to group pictures by themes or in other systematic ways. If you want to know how the problem of grouping characters on the picture plane has been solved or not during the history of art, for instance, you ask the search tool to find all the pictures of *The Last Supper*. If you want to find out if the left-right division of the picture has any importance for the scenes or meaning of the picture, you should ask for all the paintings representing *The Annunciation*. Only in the case of photography are there some shortcomings, since you are far from being sure to find even famous photos on the net.

Some of the chapters of the original project have therefore been extended with a section "Web Resources". These sections contain about ten or more links to sites for pictures which illustrate the specific issue treated in the printed text and in the experimental presentations. In these sections the text is put in a historical perspective: for example, "How did the painters begin to create the illusion of depth, how did they change or develop the illusion of light over the seven hundred years that Western European painting has represented light?". There is no doubt that, at a future stage and with the increasing quality of the picture databases, the students will be even more encouraged freely to use the immense resources of the Web galleries.

6.5 The Actual Stage: Concluding Remarks

The actual experimental prototype, "Tool for Picture Analysis", which is, in fact, a demo, is for the time being based on a written text divided into six chapters: the picture plane, space and depth, light, movement, composition, meaning. The experimental prototype contains four of these chapters: space, light, movement and composition. Each chapter is divided into three sections: (1) a general and systematic introduction; (2) Web resources containing a short historical explanation and Web addresses; and finally (3) experimental presentations of pictures.

The four presentations are all introduced by a very short introduction about what to do. They are of a different nature within each of the four sections. But mostly the experimental presentations consist in changing different parameters ("What happens if I change this parameter?"), such as, point of view or angle and distance, texture, light, etc.

The chapter on space and depth is focused on the different depth cues: the ways the eye is fooled in order to perceive depth on a flat plane surface. Central perspective is only one singular depth cue in spite of what we might think when we know that 3D programming relies on central perspective. This is why this chapter underlines the importance of the different types of gradients. Four researchers are central in this context. Paul Messaris has systemised the presentation of the depth cues in his *Visual "Literacy"* (1994), Rudolf Arnheim has a very broad and detailed approach to space in his classical *Art and Visual Perception* (1974). The gradients (surface gradients or texture gradients), that are fundamental to our perception of depth and space in pictures and in our environment, have been explored by James J. Gibson in several works. Here I rely especially on his book, *The Ecological Approach to Visual Perception* (1986). Central perspective has an (unduly) immense importance in people's mind, not so much because of 3D programming but because the elaboration of the rules of central perspective is a major epistemological achievement of the Renaissance. This is why Hubert Damisch's magnificent *L'origine de la perspective* (1987) has been a source of inspiration. As East Asian art has been able to obtain depth illusions in ways that are analogous to European art except for central perspective, some attention is paid to Chinese and Japanese art in the Web resources.

The second chapter, "Light and Shadow", is focused on two issues. The first issue is the fact that the illusion of light on the picture plane can be obtained by procedures that are far from being realistic, only some kind of differentiation of dark and light colours is necessary. The second issue is the importance of light/shadow for our perception of volume and space. This is very clearly illustrated in the interactive work. Again Rudolf Arnheim is an important source and once more the evolution of Italian art and of North European art is important for the understanding of this phenomenon.

The chapter on movement is especially focused on the representation of the moving body, be it human or animal, and the movement of natural phenomena like the storm, the clouds, drifting objects. This chapter only treats the rhythm of abstract elements very marginally. Arnheim has treated the subject in *Art and Visual Perception* but especially the disciples of Gibson, for example, Friedman and Stevenson (1980), have treated this subject which remains very underestimated in art history and in picture theory.

The chapter relies much on the historical presentation of the movement cues which have remained practically unchanged up until photography became important about 1880.

A systematic description of picture construction must necessarily contain a chapter on composition. However, the subject is overwhelmingly extensive. Every person involved in research in art history and in picture analysis knows that a résumé of picture composition must necessarily be selective. This is why the chapter on composition is focused on three issues: (1) some few general composition principles; (2) the geometrical construction principles of Western art; and (3) the problems of showing groups of persons in interaction. Arnheim remains the most important source of inspiration but the writings of Gunther Kress and Theo van Leeuwen are equally important (1996).

The interactive work is not very developed in Chapter 4 of the demo, but the understanding of composition principles is promoted by the Web resources that

	Printed part			Electronic part	
Number and title of chapter	Systematic section	Historical section	Intro	Web resources	Experiments
1. Construction principles of the picture plane	+	+	+	+	
2. Space and depth	+	+	+	+	+
3. Light	+	+	+	+	+
4. Colour	+	+	+	+	+
5. Texture	+	+	+	+	+
6. Movement	+	+	+	+	+
7. Composition	+	+	+	+	+
8. Picture and meaning	+	+	+	+	

Table 6.2 Overview of the final pedagogical system.

invite the students to explore the ways in which well-known subjects or themes are treated throughout art history – especially *The Last Supper*.

At a final stage the totality of the material will have the shape shown in Table 6.2.

There are gains and losses when the project passes from 2D to 3D. In fact both are necessary. The continuous changing of parameters in real time is easier in 3D, whereas 2D tools would be better for the treatment of existing 2D pictures. In the present case the potential of 3D tools has not been fully exploited.

From an aesthetic point of view 3D and 2D tools have each of them advantages and disadvantages. 3D can give you a very naturalistic presentation of objects and surfaces, but often with a bloodless attempt to create photo-realism. Here a 2D program like PhotoShop gives you a better tool for creating pictures, but unfortunately you have to possess at least some rudiments of a very old-fashioned skill, or in other words, you have to be good at drawing.

The 2D set piece model has, despite any prejudice against jigsaw puzzles, some advantages. First of all, 2D should give us the possibility of changing existing pictures, as if these pictures were not a closed system but something open for an ever on-going experimentation. If there is no tool able to support this work, we must use simpler procedures like the introduction of pre-formed solutions. As an example we can take the experiments with landscapes and light. Here there is a small number of elements that can produce 16 solutions with additional possibilities of producing 32 or even 64 combinations: a foreground, a mid-ground, a background and a sky, each of which has a dark version and an illuminated version. The user need not see all combinations in order to get an idea about the relationship between light and the perception of depth. However, it is not an experimentation in the real time of the material presented. It is a walk through pre-formed solutions. The student cannot produce any kind of surprising solutions unforeseen by the author.

Figure 6.7 Low angle perspective.

The different ways of using 3D construction can be seen in Figures 6.7 and 6.8: two different perspectives of the same landscape.

Figure 6.8 High angle perspective.

Figure 6.9 Daylight.

The different ways of using 2D construction can be seen in Figures 6.9 and 6.10: two very different solutions of light at the same landscape.

Figure 6.10 Dark night with an illuminated mountain.

The project foresees three ways of working: theoretical learning; studies of pictures at the different web galleries; and construction and practical analysis. What is the outcome of this new distribution as compared to the initial project?

The reflection on pictures through a thorough sampling has received more importance. With a fixed number of solutions, the experiments have become more or less an element for reflection and not a true investigation method, they have to some extent become a support for the reflection on the visual problems presented by the pictures from the Web galleries.

Nevertheless the combination of experiments taking the shape of systemised presentations and presentations of pictures on the Web galleries seems to indicate that the students realise that pictures are practical solutions to communicative and aesthetic tasks and that pictures can be interpreted on the basis of this knowledge of practicalities.

The production of the "Tool for Picture Analysis" points out that a large number of competencies are at stake in the process:

- the designer's competence in programming and his or her visual creativity;
- the resource person's knowledge of the subject matter(s). In the present case, knowledge of visual arts, of photography of any kind, of visual communication and culture and of visual perception; and
- the designer's and/or the resource person's abilities in drawing and other practical skills in picture production.

The possession of a double or triple competence at various degrees would be an ideal solution for all the persons involved in the production, but we know that this is hardly ever the case. The resource person knows of no limits at the brainstorming level or at the concept level, but is later crushed, or at least feels crushed, by the hard realities. Frankly, the programs have their limits and restrictions. It is no wonder that they are finally perceived by the author or resource person as barriers and irritating limits.

But let us here for a brief moment at the end turn to a very distant area: media theory. Philippe Marion, professor of media and communication at the University of Louvain-la-Neuve, Belgium, has advanced the, at first glance, paradoxical theory that the communicative limitations of each media are in fact a strength. The limitations are specific to each media. 3D and 2D programs each have limitations and strengths. 2D has in spite of all deficiencies something that 3D cannot provide. The problem is that in order to take advantage of both you have to know them equally well, in order to be able to turn weakness into strength and to keep their strength strong.

Acknowledgments

The first versions of the project were written in collaboration with Bjørn Laursen, Associate Professor at the University of Roskilde. The 3D pictures and the CD-ROM prototype have been made by Bo Degn, designer at the Centre for Advanced Visual Interactivity at the University of Aarhus (www.CAVI.dk). The present chapter is indebted to both for their creative imagination.

References

Arnheim, R (1974). *Art and Visual Perception*. Berkeley, CA: University of California Press [1954].

Damisch, H (1987). *L'origine de la perspective*. Paris: Flammarion.

Friedman, SL and Stevenson, MB (1980). The Perception of Movement in Pictures. In M Hagen, *The Perception of Pictures*. New York: Academic Press.

Gibson, JJ (1986). *The Ecological Approach to Visual Perception*. Hillsdale, NJ: Houghton Mifflin.

Kress, G and van Leuwen, T (1996). *Reading Images*. London: Routledge.

Marion, P (1997). Narratologie médiatique et médiagénie des récits, *Recherches en communication* 7, Louvain-la-Neuve.

Messaris, P (1994). *Visual "Literacy"*. Boulder, CO: Westview.

7

From Archaeological Findings over Scale Models and Pencil Drawings to Digital Images

Bjørn Laursen and Kim Halskov Madsen

Bjørn Laursen holds a PhD degree in visualisation and rhetoric in multimedia and his research interest are studies in artistic processes and human–computer interaction. B. Laursen is a visual artist.

Kim Halskov Madsen holds a PhD degree in computer science and his research interests are design studies and human–computer interaction.

7.1 Introduction

The "Eye of Wodan" is a multimedia installation at Ribe Museum, Denmark, which tells the story of the life of the Danish Vikings in the period 720–980 AD. A central part of the installation is an interactive screen, which enables visitors to explore drawings of Viking age scenes on a canvas larger in size than the screen.

The screen is an integral part of a room (see Figure 7.1), where the various elements of the room, including four 5–7 ft high wooden figures (Figure 7.2), lighting, the room layout, the painting on the floor, wall and ceiling, all contribute to an experience of the mythological life during the Viking age. As a visitor you are permitted to move around to explore the installations and use your hand to interact with the screen. B. Laursen originally designed the room and made the sculptures together with drawings on the interactive screen.

In this chapter we look into the production of images of ships for the interactive screen. Part of B. Laursen's background for developing these images of ships is his sailing hobby in the first half of the 1980s, when on his occasional sailing trips in his

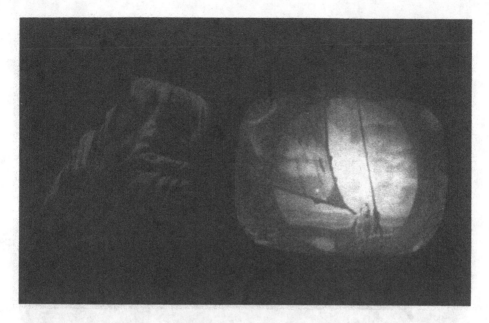

Figure 7.1 The interactive screen.

small boat, he spent time making drawings on Roskilde Fiord. The self-portrait drawn in 1984, Figure 7.3, illustrates some of the preliminary experiments with perspective and spatial complexity which eventually led to the images of ships for the interactive screen (Laursen, 1988, p. 71).

The images presented in this chapter are 2D drawings with some of the qualities of 3D visualisations. Laursen and Andersen (1993) have named his type of visualisation *a topology*. Figure 7.4 shows an example of such a drawing, a reconstruction of the famous Viking ship *Skuldelev 3*, which is a Scandinavian merchant ship found at the bottom of Roskilde Fiord. This drawing actually does look quite strange because the perspective is quite different from the one we usually are familiar with. Why and how was such a picture produced? You will find the answer on the following pages.

On the 150 × 120 cm sized screen in the installation you will see only a minor part of the picture through a frame, which is in this case a circle. In Figure 7.5 you see an example of how the topology appears on the display as only a circular detail of the topology. You are free to move the circle around on the topology, so that you can see every part of it, but just one small part at a time. Figure 7.6 shows the selection in Figure 7.5 within the whole drawing.

When people move around on the topology, seeing only a limited part of the image, they seem not to notice that something is wrong with the perspective.

The use of this new and strange perspective seems to seduce people into experiencing, to some extent, an in-between 2D and 3D experience of being onboard a Viking ship.

Figure 7.2 The sculptures were cut out from old broad chestnut trees.

Figure 7.3 Preliminary experiments with perspective and spatial complexity.

Figure 7.4 A topological image of the Viking ship *Skuldelev 3*.

Figure 7.5 The topology as it appears on the display.

7.2 Theoretical Point of Departure

As the theoretical point of departure for our analysis of the production of images for the interactive screen, we take the design theory of Schön (1983), which focuses on design materials used, including photographs, hand-drawn sketches and scale models. In addition, we use B. Laursen's (1990) three-layer model of the process for making a drawing.

Figure 7.6 The selection in Figure 7.5 within the whole drawing.

7.2.1 Schön

Schön has taken as his point of departure various design professionals, including architects. The original work of Schön has subsequently been used by many others as the platform for the analysis of various work practices; for instance, Christensen et al. (1997) have analysed the work of protocol designers and Lervig (2002) has made an investigation into an artistic production process.

Schön's aim has been to explore how reflection and action are intimately connected in the world of practitioners. According to Schön (1983, 1988, 1992), design is a conversation with materials, where each move contributes to set the problems to be solved. In the design process, the designer works in different media or materials experimenting with different aspects of the design. The design process is a "kind of experimentation that consists in reflective 'conversation' with materials of the design situation" (Schön, 1992, p. 135).

The interaction with materials is a conversation between the designer and the materials in a metaphorical sense. For instance when "working in some visual medium ... the designer sees what is 'there' in some representation ... draws in relation to it, sees what has been drawn, thereby informing further designing" (Schön 1992, p. 135).

To keep the metaphor, the materials talk back to the designer, thus guiding further moves and the process develops into one where the designer sees, acts while taking account of any previously unanticipated result of his moves, and then sees once again (Schön, 1983, p. 158).

The essence of design is not to solve a set of well-defined problems but rather to set the problems to be solved.

> Problem setting [is] the process by which we define the decision to be made, the ends to be achieved, the means which may be chosen (Schön, 1983, p. 40).

Each move in the design process contributes to setting new problems to be solved, which, in turn, guide further moves.

> In the designer's conversation with the material of his design, he can never make a move which has only the effects intended for it. His materials are continuously talking back to him, causing him to apprehend unanticipated problems and potentials (Schön, 1983, p. 101).

The move causes the designer to appreciate things in the situation that go beyond his initial perception of the problem. The designer shapes the situations and "plays his game to a moving target, changing the phenomena as he experiments" (Schön, 1983, p. 153).

Rather than looking for standard solutions, the designer sees the situation as something already present in his repertoire of paradigm cases or prototypes. In the process of *seeing as,* the designer sees the situation as a unique one, paying as much attention to the dissimilarities as to similarities (Schön, 1983, p. 138). Though the designer sees the situation as something already present in his repertoire of paradigm cases, he manages to make something new by making experimental moves, which may result in something which goes beyond his initial expectations. Such unintended consequences give new meaning to the situation (Schön, 1983, p. 101).

The designer works selectively in different media or materials, experimenting with different aspects of his design at different stages in the design process (Schön, 1983, p. 159). The design representations are virtual worlds which may facilitate experimentation at low risk and cost by eliminating or inhibiting constraints of the built world (Schön, 1983, pp. 157–58). In this way, several alternatives can be easily created and explored. The designer is able to move in the virtual world and experience what it would be like in the real world (Schön, 1983, p. 157). Events that take a long time in the built world can be made to happen immediately in the virtual world and variables that are interlocking in the built world can be separated from one another in the virtual world (Schön, 1983, p. 157). Schön uses the term "virtual" in the sense of some kind of physical representation, like for instance a drawing, which is *almost as real as* the object being designed, whereas the term virtual in the context of computers also is used to denote computer applications, which are *almost as real as* our physical reality.

7.2.2 A Dynamic Three-layer Model

In the mid-1980s B. Laursen (1990) developed a model of the process for making a drawing, which systematically addresses the dynamic and complex interplay between three dynamic layers: (I) the concrete world we live in; (II) representations of the concrete world in our mind; and (III) depictions on a picture plane.

The world we live in (I) is constantly changing. Luckily, in our mind (II) we are cognitively able to some extent to follow and conceptualise dynamic phenomena (Neisser, 1976, p. 112) so we can interact with them. That is what we are also doing when we try to depict phenomena on a picture plane (III).

B. Laursen (1993) has illustrated the interplay between the three layers by the example of what happens when one wants to draw a horse. Initially one starts out from a mental image (II) of a horse. But how do the hind legs (I) of a horse actually look? Your mental imagery (II) may turn out here to be vague and without relevant details. A good idea will be to go and look after these details on a real horse (I) (Eisner, 1991). Perhaps you choose to make a sketch (III) on location to make sure you store the details in a relevant form. These are typical aspects of a development of a drawing process. The actual cognitive complexity, taking place during an artistic process, will never be captured in all its details; it may, as Sven Sandström (1983) has suggested, be described as that which happens when a stone is thrown into an anthill: it is simply impossible to grasp the process in its complex totality. On the other hand, the model actually has the advantage of being able to indicate the change in the address of the creator's attention over time, that is, when it jumps between all three scenes. In that way, the model is able to capture the complex flow of the designer's attention.

If we take a closer look at an illustration of the process of drawing, we may get the following picture of what happens (see Figure 7.7).

1. How does a horse look? (II)

2. The designer relies on mental imagery (II).

3. The drawing process is started (III).

4. Some part of the drawing is left out (indicated by -//-) so the model in this example does not illustrate what is happening until:

5. The drawing is getting close to depicting the back part of the horse (III) and a question (II) turns up:

6. How do the hind legs look? (II)

7. The designer confronts a concrete horse (I).

8. The designer observes the back legs of this concrete horse (II).

9. The designer interprets how the hind legs of the horse (II) look.

10. The designer draws the hind legs (III).

11. The designer inspects the appearance of the drawing of the hind legs (II).

12. Here the designer may criticise the drawing (II),

13. and again observe the concrete horse (I),

14. which of course is re-interpreted (II),

15. and this might be part of a more final interpretation of necessary corrections of the appearance of the drawing (II).

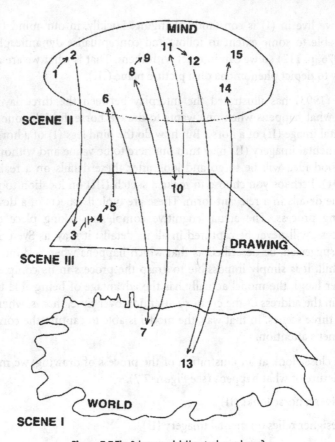

Figure 7.7 The 3-layer model: How to draw a horse?

Steps 1–15 sketch what happens and leave out a lot of details, which is clear from a look at point (7) compared with John Kennedy's (1993) analysis of perception:

> Perception occurs only when a chain of events is complete. The chain starts with an object in an environment and runs through to the actions of an observer in the environment. For vision, the object provides light – typically, light reflected from a few luminous sources in the environment. For touch, the object provides resistance –typically, resistance at a surface to compression. The actions of the observer, in the case of vision, include adjustments of the eye and changes in vantage point to gain more information about the object. The actions of the observer, in the case of touch, include adjustments of the hand, the chief tactile organ (Kennedy, 1993, p. 8).

In the following quotation, he addresses all the links of the chain:

> Between the object and the observer's actions come many links. The complete chain is as follows: object; medium; receptor system; the nerves; brain reception, cognition, and motor areas (none easily distinguished from the others); and the adjustment and exploratory actions that change the vantage point (Kennedy, 1993, p. 8).

Using a model – like the three-layer model – you always face the weaknesses and advantages of reducing complexity. It would be possible to include more details corresponding to what Kennedy mentions, which would make the model more valid, at the expense of clarity; it would be so complex to look at, that it might cause more confusion than clarity. The advantage of the level of detail we have chosen is that it visualises quite a complex process in a compact overview.

7.3 The Early Sketches of *Skuldelev 2* and *3*

Archaeologists working with these maritime subjects have highly specialised visual knowledge of the boats, so any constructed details that are illustrated must be absolutely reliable, otherwise it will be pointed out immediately. This means that the artist works with a lot of specific demands, and has to be extremely exact about the spatial visualisation and details of the specific Viking ships. One of the initial tasks of

Figure 7.8 The preserved wreck *Skuldelev 2* – a major warship – at the Vikingship Museum in Roskilde.

B. Laursen was to read the book by B. and E. Andersen (1989), which describes in detail the work involved in reconstructing the appearance and complex functionality of the five *Skuldelev* ships. Beside this initial reading, there are also studies on the findings of ships at the Vikingship Museum (see Figure 7.8); these are reconstructed on iron skeletons and pieces of preserved wood are placed so that you can see where the single pieces are placed on the boat.

The iron skeletons are of course built on a 1:1 scale and they show clearly the most important lines in 3D of the shape of the ship. The point of view in Figure 7.8 is a position on the side of the boat. As a visitor you cannot go onboard these ships, because the restored original wooden findings are situated on these metal constructions.

Following the three-layer model, B. Laursen's initial perception of one of the wrecks placed on an iron skeleton could look like Figure 7.9.

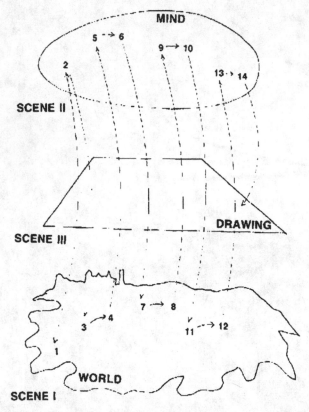

Figure 7.9 Sketch of the cognitive process of experiencing the form of a ship. (1) B. Laursen is present in the area around a Skuldelev wreck. (2) He perceives the wreck, looking at the 3D iron skeleton reconstructions which carry the preserved original findings. (3)–(4) B. Laursen contemplates the discovered materials, (5) and interprets the observations of (3)–(4). (6) The new focus of attention is the 3D lines of the skeleton. (7)–(8) He contemplates the lines of the skeleton, (9) and interprets the observations (7)–(8) of the skeleton. (10) He reflects on the quality of the improvement of the 3D understanding of the shape of the ship-skeleton, at the same time reflecting the fact that he moves his body round the wreck. (11)–(12) He walks, experiencing 3-dimensionality. (13) He interprets his spatial experiences when walking, gazing at the iron skeleton, (14) and associating the process of depicting and its potential to reflect these fresh visual experiences.

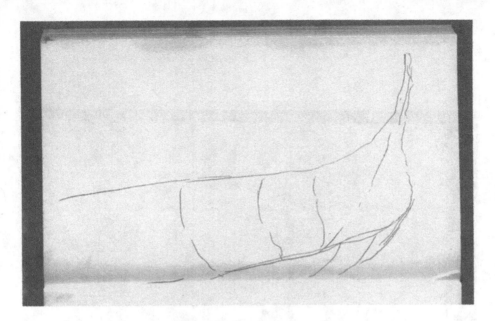

Figure 7.10 Sketch drawn in Indian ink on paper.

Using the exhibition in the museum B. Laursen was led to the production of four small sketches showing the big warship *Skuldelev 2* (Figures 7.10–7.13), drawn in Indian ink on paper. Clearly, the iron skeletons have been important guidelines.

In the second notebook drawing, Figure 7.11, B. Laursen's interest is to study the space in the bow of the ship, still seen from outside the ship, but at a closer distance. Notice the change of format; in the outside position drawings, Figure 7.11, the format is a high rectangle, in the onboard drawings, Figures 7.12 and 7.13, the format is a wide rectangle. That is, the book is turned 90 degrees; this detail is important particularly from a spatial point of view, because it shows indirectly how the space required plays a role. The problem is more or less solved by turning the book, a fact which also shows the flexibility of the medium, a small sketchbook. In the third notebook drawing, Figure 7.12, the boat is seen from an onboard position.

It has been drawn from the farthest end of the boat, but it nevertheless gives an impression of being drawn from within the boat. The point of view – the level of observation – is lower in this drawing than in the two previous ones. In the fourth notebook drawing, Figure 7.13, the space in the middle of the ship becomes a dominant part of the experience.

From the overall perspective of the process, the four drawings explore the following characteristics: (a) from outside to inside the ship; (b) from high point of view to low point of view; and (c) approaching the phenomenon of how to show the experience of living on these kinds of ships.

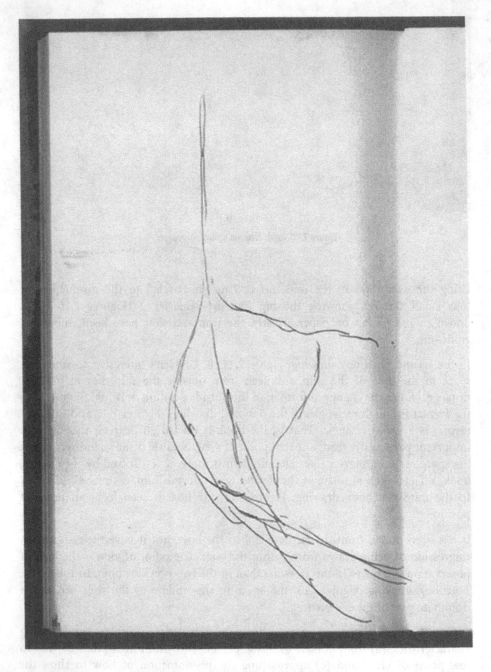

Figure 7.11 Sketch of the ship as seen from outside the ship.

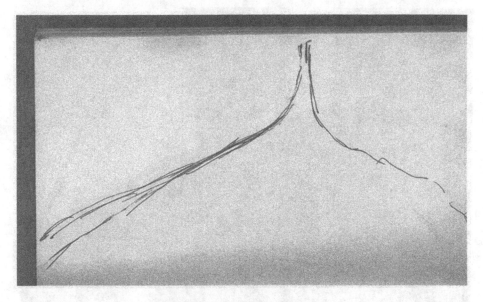

Figure 7.12 Sketch from an onboard position.

At the museum you can find a small model of one of the ships, a knarr, which is built on a 1:10 scale, see Figure 7.14. The model may be viewed from most perspectives – though not from an onboard position, because it is behind glass in a showcase at the museum – but you can walk around it.

In addition, another miniature of the Norwegian Oseberg-type, was built by B. Laursen for experimental purposes, so that it could be used for different kinds of experiments without any worry if it were to be damaged. The sails are reconstructed

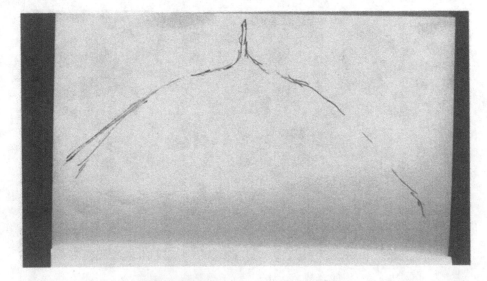

Figure 7.13 Sketch of the space in the middle of the ship.

Figure 7.14 Miniature 1:10 of a knarr, an ocean-going merchant ship in a showcase at the museum.

following measurements in the book by B. and E. Andersen (1989), and the model was put into various environments to get an impression of mirroring, shadowing, silhouettes and authenticity (see Figures 7.15–7.18). A small-sized model is easy to move around if you put it in a swimming pool. You may get the impression of a ship in mirroring water, and the impression is even better if you jump in the pool yourself (Figure 7.15).

Figure 7.15 Miniature in the swimming pool.

Figure 7.16 Shadows.

Creating interesting shadows is facilitated by having a relatively small object and lamps which are easy to move and position (Figure 7.16).

Also if you hold the ship model up in the yellow sunset you may visualise a flying ship in full size (see Figure 7.17).

Figure 7.17 Silhouette.

Hold a hand over the house in the lower left corner (in Figure 7.18) and replace it imaginatively with a Viking-age house. Notice the authenticity of the ships acting as if they were not reduced but full-scale models.

Figure 7.18 Out in open-air, looking as if it was full scale.

Figure 7.19 Pencil drawings of details.

Figure 7.20 Photo of an anchored minor warship called *Helge Ask* with *Roar Ege* in the background.

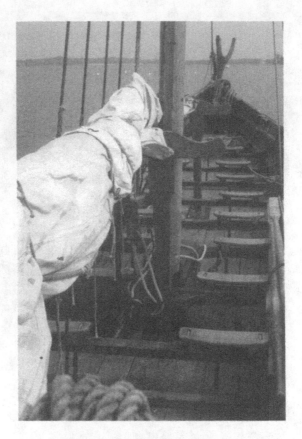

Figure 7.21 Photo of the interior of *Helge Ask*.

According to mythology, these ships were said to sail the dead Viking to Valhalla, where they could live an honourable existence with others who died fighting. But how would that look? How can these phenomena be illustrated in a convincing way? The answer is to use small-scale models. It is astonishing how authentic they can look and how realistic they can make these mythological phenomena appear, see Figures 7.17 and 7.18.

An additional early activity undertaken was the detailed studies of a reconstruction of *Roar Ege*, a smallish boat used for transportation of commerce material round in Denmark and Scandinavia, and secondarily *Helge Ask*, a minor warship; both lay anchored outside the Vikingship Museum in Roskilde. One of the drawings of details made onboard these anchored boats may be seen in Figure 7.19.

The drawing is an experiment with the quality of texture and visual style of the final product.

In addition, photographs of the two boats were taken, see Figures 7.20 and 7.21. Such pictures may of course be shot from many different angles, but once the pictures are brought back to the studio, they are not easy to change.

The pictures are very naturalistic representations of the ships and, in this case, are used to focus on details of the ships, including details of the interior such as the number of seats in the ship.

7.4 Developing the Basic Form in Conjunction with the Viewfinder

The materials and knowledge collected during the initial preparations provided the platform for the subsequent experiments. One of the visual experiments focuses on how to draw the form of the boat so that it gives you the feeling of being onboard when you see a small part of the drawing and, at the same time, the feeling that you can experience the whole ship without using a 3D construction (see Figure 7.22).

Figure 7.22 is the first sketch of the form of the boat in the final drawing. The drawing is 50 cm wide and it should be seen from an extremely short distance, such as 4–5 cm when viewed with one eye holding the other eye closed, or, alternatively, through a small viewfinder as in Figure 7.23.

The very rough sketch served two purposes. First, when B. Laursen viewed it from a very short distance, holding his left eye closed and with his right eye approximately 4–5 cm from the surface of the drawing, it gave B. Laursen an initial impression – when he moved the drawing around examining each single part of it – of how the later final detailed artwork would appear. Secondly, during this process of moving the drawing, the very rough sketch at the same time left it up to his imagination to fill in the gap of the missing details. This was a low cost approach, because, as illustrated in Figures 7.24–7.27, the form could easily be changed. In Figure 7.24 (points 15–19) and in Figure 7.25 (points 1–4) you see that the changes are taking place in the bottom of the picture. Four experiments were conducted to get a satisfying result. Figure 7.24 is a schematic representation of the process.

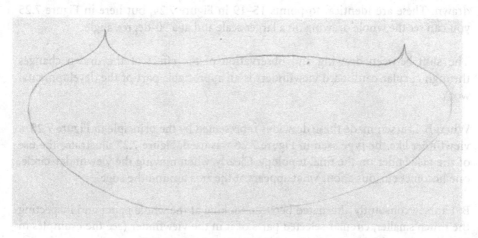

Figure 7.22 The initial sketch of the form of the boat.

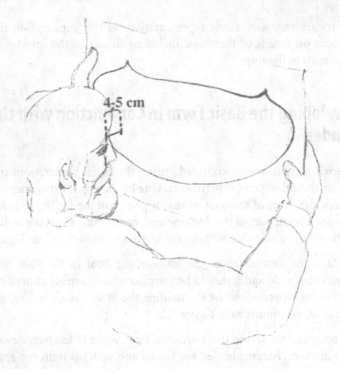

4-5 cm

Figure 7.23 Viewing the sketch from a short distance.

Figure 7.24 illustrates attempts to demonstrate realistically how B. Laursen's introspective imaginings of how it looks to be onboard a concrete visualisation merge and are transformed into a concrete drawing, which, seen through a sharply defined circular viewfinder becomes similar to the final formal appearance of the drawing in the final large touch-screen installation.

In Figure 7.25, the numbers indicate the order in which the lines 1, 2, 3 and 4 are drawn. These are identical to points 15–19 in Figure 7.24, but here in Figure 7.25 you can see the whole drawing on a larger scale and at a 90-degree angle.

The shift between drawing and observation of the effect of the drawn changes through circular cardboard viewfinders is an appreciable part of the developmental work.

When B. Laursen made these drawings represented by the principle in Figure 7.25, a viewfinder like the type seen in Figure 7.26 was used. Figure 7.27 illustrates the use of the viewfinder on the final topology. Clearly, when moving the viewfinder-circle, one becomes curious about what appears at the area around the edge.

B. Laursen constantly alternated between looking at the whole paper and inspecting the much smaller, circular selected parts of it in the viewfinder (see the examples in Figures 7.27 and 7.28).

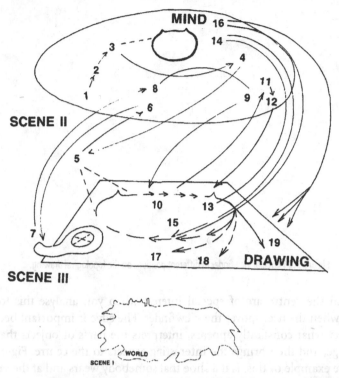

Figure 7.24 The 3-layer model of drawing the first sketch of the final form. Scene I is not directly active here, therefore it is reduced in size. (1) Signalises in principle all the spatial, visual experiences gathered until the beginning of this drawing process; (2) indicates brainstorming, imagining, attempting to generate a possible functional external shape of the ship; (3) illustrates visual speculations on this schematic form and the "drawing" is an attempt to make a "sketch of this imagination", a schemata as Ulric Neisser (1976, pp. 9 ff) would probably describe, of the outer shape of the ship; (4) represents this schematic raw form, which is the imagined visual form that the drawing process elaborates in (5)–(19). (5) is where the very first line is drawn; (6) means interpretation of the signals from the first line drawn; (7) shows the use of a circular viewfinder examining the signals of the line as it appears in parts; (8) indicates interpretations of the spatial results of moving the viewfinder around; (9) represents an idea with consequences for the continuation of the rest of the drawing; if you follow the edge, you will meet the other end of the ship after a while; the distance becomes focal spatially; (10) shows how B. Laursen extends the length of the line considerably if you compare the schemata and the drawing which appears in scene III here; (11) is the interpretation of the extended drawn line; (12) represents the idea of mirroring the ship form, because it is identical and symmetrical; (13) mirrors the form of the ship; (14) indicates imaginings and reflections about the shape of the lower line in the drawing; (15) shows drawing the first attempt to create the form of the lower line; (16) means critique of the form of the lower line; (17)–(19) are analogous to (16) and (18), which are also failed attempts to create the lower line; to reduce the numbering on the model, these cognitive processes have been cut down here because they seem to be so similar; actually the final solution turns up in step (19), radically solving the underlying spatial problem, so that by making a lower line in this drawing you will feel at lower positions in the viewfinder that you are outside the ship, which contradicts your former spatial anticipation of being onboard.

The studies on the perceptual process taking place through a movable circular viewfinder were concerned with the general authenticity of the form of parts of the boat as they appear in the viewfinder. The purpose of these activities was to test whether any possible effect due to the positioning of the viewfinder on the picture plane and its movement and location is achieved to create the illusion of being onboard the ship.

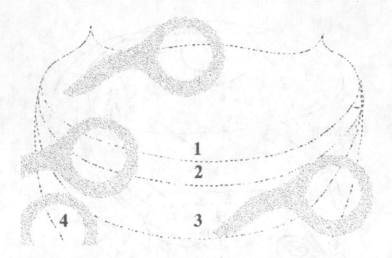

Figure 7.25 Circular viewfinder in different positions on the topological drawing.

The edge and the centre are of special interest when you analyse this topology's functioning when the user moves the viewfinder. The edge is important because the eye can detect what constantly appears, interprets the parts of objects that appear along the edge, and then brings the interesting aspects to the centre. Figure 7.27 is an illustrative example of this. Is it a shoe that somebody wears and at the same time is bound up with ropes? Will I meet a prisoner if I continue to move in the direction of the shoe? The centre is where you can examine the object more closely, as in Figure 7.28, where the furs are the focus of attention and placed centrally.

R. Arnheim (1988) has demonstrated the power of the centre whereas this case clearly demonstrates the power of the edge. Why the edge becomes so interesting could be described considering J.J. Gibson's (1950 and 1986) descriptions of visual field where he demonstrates the elliptical form of the impression while viewing, but where we do not feel a sharp edge in what we perceive, but actually do not feel any edges at all. This is in deep contrast to what is happening when we are confronted with B. Laursen's large visualisation, which always appears as smaller parts in a sharp circle. Here we *do* see the sharp edge, which triggers the users' curiosity about what is visible at the edge – potentially at any place of the 360 degrees of the circle.

Figure 7.26 Circular viewfinder with a cross to indicate the centre.

Figure 7.28 Exploring the far end of the boat.

The circle-construction has become a tool, which establishes a cognitive and perceptual dialogue with our surroundings. The field of vision is seductive from a consciousness point of view, because we do not feel that we just see a smaller part of our surroundings.

In addition to the use of the circular viewfinder experiments were carried out with different shapes of viewfinders, both rectangular and elliptical, and with different sizes. These experiments were of course much easier than would have been the case with a software prototype.

The use of a viewfinder placed directly on the surface of the drawing during the construction of the drawings, established a kind of multi-modal cognitive dialogue, bringing together perception and visual imagination, while evaluating and exploring experimental changes to the picture.

The end result will be functioning on a big screen, so that for the audience it appears to be a 1:1 world-sized experience. Therefore additional testing was performed using a mock-up construction of what is intended later to be a big touch-screen. The mock-up construction made it possible to mime the final interactive process, where people are to use their body to navigate on the topology (see Figure 7.29). People move the topology by dragging it with their hand, so you will also have to use your arm and to some degree the rest of your body to explore the universe of this ship.

Years before working with the development of the topology, B. Laursen was inspired by Howard Gardner's theory of multiple intelligences (Gardner, 1983):

> we are a species that has evolved to think in language, to conceptualize in spatial terms, to analyze in musical ways, to compute with logical and mathematical tools, to solve problems using our whole body and parts of our body, to understand other individuals, and to understand ourselves (Gardner, 1991, p. 81).

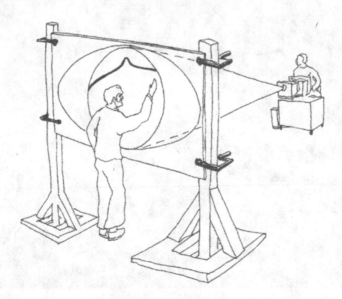

Figure 7.29 Mock-up test screen.

Gardner's theory was an important and an integral conscious part of the working process of B. Laursen, and it was the intention that the topologies would require the user to interact with the topology using the whole mind and body:

- *Spatial* intelligence – how does the space of this ship look? What do you typically pay visual attention to when sailing? Horizon? Objects round you 360 degrees? Signs of wind on the water surface?

- *Bodily-kinesthetic* intelligence – how do you typically use your body when sailing a ship like this? You are in an object that moves in a very complex way; it may follow a direction and at the same time be influenced dominantly by waves and winds. You are attentive in order to be able to keep balance.

- *Musical* intelligence – what kinds of rythms are dominant? Waves? Wind? Working rhythms? Rhythms of movement? Break of rhythms?

- *Logical*-mathematical intelligence – how do you navigate a ship like this? How can this space and these nautical phenomena be depicted or mapped?

- *Linguistic* intelligence – nautical terminology is a craftsman's language.

- *Interpersonal* intelligence – here we have teamwork, where typically 3–4 persons will be sailing smaller merchant ships like these, a situation that might be analysed as an example of distributed cognition.

- *Intra-personal* intelligence – experiencing? Making and adjusting strategies for the tour?

However, technical limitations implied that a multi-intelligence system was not fully implemented. First of all, it was not possible to make the topology mimic the move-

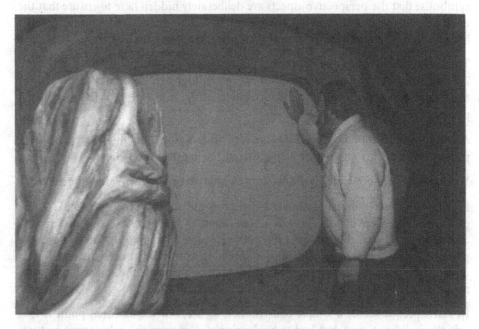

Figure 7.30 B. Laursen using the final touch-screen.

ment of the waves. The idea was to give the visitor the feeling of being onboard a ship, so that during a storm the wheeling of the ship would be dominant, but in the harbour, the surface would be calm.

Another unfulfilled goal was to make the topology work as a dragging system; instead it became a pointing system. This changed the bodily involvement radically, because using a dragging system, the user becomes curious about what will appear at the edge simultaneously with his own movements, whereas in a pointing system the movement of the topology is not simultaneous, and since it does not start to move until you have pointed at something, in this type of system you lose some of the curiosity and intensity; the user has to wait after pointing to see what will happen, instead of experiencing immediately.

7.5 Identifying the General Principles for the Construction

In spite of the unusual angles we see in the drawing as a whole, it looks as if selected parts are based on familiar rules of perception. Figure 7.31 shows two parts of the ship separated and moved apart so that they do not affect each other to any extent.

In the final picture, see Figure 7.32, we find a double perspective, but it was not just made initially in the manner described in this chapter; it is a result, an effect, of other initial considerations to be described in the following.

The two big arrows in Figure 7.33 indicate direction in the two basic perspectives. In the middle we find a smaller bundle of arrows pointing in all directions, which symbolise that the perspective aspects are deliberately hidden here to ensure that the user will not be doubtful about the perspective. The double arrow indicates that here we find an area where the line of the horizon is dominant.

The two sets of arrows (one with white pointed ends, the other with black) in Figure 7.34 illustrate that the two perspectives are woven together. Both pictures are part of the overall process of testing the seductiveness of the integration of the two overall perspectives of the picture.

An additional feature developed was the idea of changing individual elements of the picture. Figures 7.35 and Figure 7.36 illustrate the use of such elements.

You can see these movable layer drawings and the original drawing in Figure 7.36.

Finally, you can see drawings and the first layer put together in Figure 7.37. While producing the drawing B. Laursen tested whether the people using it paid any attention to the twisting of the perspectives, whenever they only saw the smaller parts of the drawing, using the framing intended to make them see the small parts in the circle. Figure 7.37 shows the developed basic principle for constructing ships topologically in 2D with qualities normally found in 3D.

In retrospect, it seems a simple construction to use, but the essential point is that initially it did not exist, but had to be developed. However, the subsequent pictures

(a)

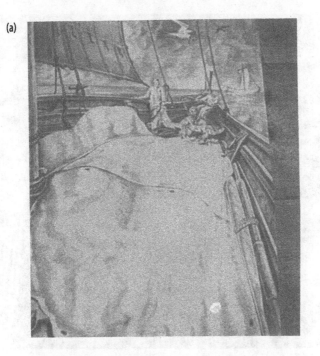

(b)

Figure 7.31 The ship separated into two halves.

Figure 7.32 The final topology.

Figure 7.33 The dominant lines of the perspective drawn on top of the picture in Figure 7.32.

Figure 7.34 The integration of the two perspectives.

were easy to build up following the basic prescription: you stand with your feet in the circular area, so you can see the area around your feet, then you raise your field of vision and meet the two basic perspectives that are weaved together so that they overlap discretely (see Figures 7.32 and 7.33).

Figure 7.35 Parts of the drawing are made in an extra layer, which can be moved so you see the drawing beneath.

Figure 7.37 The final construction principle.

7.6 Summary of Materials Used

Table 7.1 summarises the main qualities of the materials used throughout the process. Clearly, the process that led to the final digital drawings part of Wodan's Eye grew out of a complex process involving a diversity of material ranging from the actual findings, scale model, cardboard, photos over paper and pencil sketches to pencil drawings. The quality of the material in quite different ways facilitated test ranging from quick line drawing to still photos. Each of those intermediate steps focused on their own aspect of the ship.

Table 7.1 Materials.

Fig.	Material	Focus	Facilitate testing	Quality	Dimension	Ease of modification
8	Wood pieces and metal skeleton	Shape of ship	May be viewed from some perspectives	Close to 3D drawing	3D object	Practically impossible
10–13	Paper and ink	Shape, point of view	Quick. Enables many versions	2D. Sketchy	2D	Easy and fast to modify
14	Wood	Shape of ship	May be viewed from most perspectives	Miniature	3D object	Practically impossible
15–18	Wood	Shape, surrounding	May be put into various scenarios	Easy to move around	3D object	Position easy to change
19	Paper and pencil	Texture and visual style.	Hard to change	2D detail of the final product	2D	Possible
20–21	Photos	Certain exact aspects of the ships	Hard to change	Realistic	2D	Hard
22	Paper and pencil	Shape of topology	Easy to test the topology	Rough sketch	2D	Easy
25	Paper and cardboard	Authenticity of basic form parts of the boat	Easy to experiment with viewfinders	Simple	2D	Easy to move viewfinders
26	Cardboard	View	Easy to test the topology	Simple	2D	Easy
27–28	Pencil on paper and cardboard viewfinder	Focus on content and narrativity	Easy to make detailed experiments	Detailed picture	2D	Easy to move around the selected viewfinders
29	Wood and cloth	Bodily navigation	Easy to experiment with	Physical	3D	Fairly easy
31	Pencil on paper (grey scale)	Perspective	The final part of the grand experiment	The final picture	2D	Hard
33–34	Computer coloured and digital	Integration of perspective	Visual testing	Interprets visual complexity.	2D	Hard
35–36	Pencil on paper	Part elements	To test combinations of elements	Building blocks	2D	Easy to change combinations
37	Computer coloured and digital	Construction principles	Not intended for testing	Final drawing	2D	Hard

Acknowledgments

The installation at Ribe Museum was produced as a co-operative effort between the Antiquarian Collection in Ribe and researchers from the Department of Information and Media Studies, Aarhus University, Denmark, in the period 1990–93 with a budget of approximately €400,000. The Vikingship Museum in Roskilde kindly provided access to their collection of ships. Associate Professor Søren Kolstrup assisted Bjørn Laursen during the sculpturing of the wooden figures.

References

Andersen, B and Andersen, E (1989). *The Square Sail: The Wing of the Dragon*. Roskilde, Denmark: Vikingship Museum, Roskilde.

Arnheim, R (1988). *The Power of the Centre: A Study of Composition in the Visual Arts*. Berkeley: University of California Press.

Eisner, E (1991). *The Enlightened Eye: Qualitative Inquiry and the Enhancement of Educational Practice*. New York: MacMillan.

Christensen, S, Jørgensen, JB and Madsen, KH (1997). Design as Interaction with Computer-based Materials. In G van der Veer, A Henderson and S Coles (eds.) *Proceeding of DIS 97*. New York: ACM, 65–71.

Gardner, H (1983). *Frames of Mind: The Theory of Multiple Intelligences*. New York: Harper Collins.

Gardner, H (1991). *The Unschooled Mind: How Children Think and How Schools Should Teach*. London: Fontana Press.

Gibson, JJ (1950). *The Perception of the Visual World*. Cambridge, MA: The Riverside Press.

Gibson, JJ (1986). *The Ecological Approach to Visual Perception*. Cornell University/ Lawrence Erlbaum Associates.

Kennedy, JM (1993). *Drawing and the Blind: Pictures to Touch*. New Haven and London: Yale University Press.

Laursen, B (1988) *Blyantetegning – en indføring I kreativt billedarbejde* [Pencildrawing – an introduction to creative visualisation]. Copenhagen: Gyldendal.

Laursen, B (1990). *Tegning og Kognition* [Drawing and Cognition]. Aarhus, Denmark: Department of Information and Media Science, Aarhus University. VENUS-report no. 06. 39 p. 1990. ISBN 87-89271-24-6.

Laursen, B (1993). *Paleolitic Cave Paintings, Mental Imagery and Depiction – A Critique of John Halverson's article "Paleolitic Art and Cognition"*. Aarhus, Denmark: Department of Information and Media Science, Aarhus University. VENUS-report no. 19. 1993 ISBN 0907-3019.

Laursen, B and Andersen, PB (1993) Drawing and Programming. In P Bøgh-Andersen, B Holqvist and JF Jensen (eds.) *The Computer as Medium*. New York: Cambridge University Press, 236–62.

Lervig, M (2002). From Music to 3D Scenography and Back Again. In this volume.

Neisser, U (1976). *Cognition and Reality*, New York. W.H. Freeman and Co.

Sandström, S (1983). *Se och uppleva*. Lund, Sweden: Kalejdoskop förlag.

Schön, D (1983). *The Reflective Practitioner*. New York: Basic Books.

Schön, D (1988). Designing: Rules, Types and Worlds. *Design Studies*, 9(3) July.

Schön, D (1992). Kinds of Seeing and their Role in Design. *Design Studies*, 13(2) April.

8

Dramaturgy in Building Multimedia Performances: Devising and Analysing

Torunn Kjølner and Janek Szatkowski

Torunn Kjølner has a BA from the Royal Scottish Academy of Music and Drama in Glasgow, and a Mag.art degree from the Department of Theatre Science, University of Bergen, Norway. Apart from university teaching she has worked extensively with different forms of theatre and is an educational consultant for theatre schools.

Janek Szatkowski has a degree from the Department of Dramaturgy, University of Aarhus. He has worked as a professional dramaturge for years and headed the First National Danish School for Playwrights.

8.1 Introduction

It is often believed that art can challenge technology because artists ask questions that scientists do not ask or anticipate. Likewise, there is a belief that technology – that is, digital technologies – challenge art because the program developer can provide the artist with means of creating completely new forms of art. We have met many myths and thinking habits that indicate the general idea that art and science are each other's counterparts, that there is a scientific way of doing things on the one hand and an artistic one on the other. The point, the problem and in fact, the real challenge, is that there are many scientific and many artistic ways of doing things, or *creating* things, which is what we will deal with in this chapter. If we try leaving the idea that scientific or artistic activity is directed towards discovering universal laws and elucidating things that bring us closer to the truth, we might end up supporting the American neo-pragmatist Richard Rorty. He argues that it is a better idea to stop asking whether we have come closer to truth, and rather ask: "Are there ways of talking and acting that we have not yet explored?" (Rorty, 1989). Then the will to create new vocabularies could bring art and science into an interesting dialogue and make us question general and conventional ideas, such as whether art has an antagonist in science. From our experience, we would tend to agree with Rorty, however, when he suggests rather that both art and science have an enemy in common sense. Common sense often relies upon simplified, down-to-earth thinking that easily kills a creative process by asking questions already formulated. This is why in this chapter we are looking for ways of thinking and acting to produce multimedia products where competencies from several fields meet. We start out from the field of theatre, and we have chosen to express our experiences in vocabularies derived from post-modern production strategies, where the term 'devising' has gained a lot of interest.

There is nothing inherently theatrical in the English word 'devising'. It means to plan, contrive, invent or scheme and is used in various thought traditions including development of multimedia products. Nevertheless, devising has become a commonly used term to explain main principles for the production of contemporary theatre performances. Devising usually points to the importance of collaborative and compositional processes in such productions, although it would be wrong to say that devising is a method or a particular set of rules and regulations for theatre companies or performance production. Devising can be considered to cover a collection of practices that have certain characteristics in common. Apart from collaboration and composition, generation of material is considered essential to a devising process. Practically anything can be the focus or the starting point for a performance production: a theme, a group, a location, a site, a culture, a ritual, a photo, an article, radio or television programmes, an institution, a biography, etc. A typical devising process will start with a decision about how this particular group will generate the material for its performance.

In a process that is based on collaboration, there are many forms of co-operation involved, including a mixture of many different competencies. So generating material means to explore and test the crafts and skills of the individuals to see whether anything that could be interesting for performance use is created. Some devised performances take the human body as the main theatrical element, but any element or piece of material might gain the importance of a performer in the end result. Indeed any kind of material, ready-made or created for the purpose can be considered for use in the theatrical composition of a performance.

As professional dramaturges we are accustomed to work in artistic and scientific processes. One challenge in producing multimedia lies in gathering the right combination of people who can start a process that will make sure that each individual's crafts and skills are explored and, furthermore, linked together. Another challenge is that all the members of such a group have to accept and endure a situation where nobody has the full control of either the process or the product, where, as a matter of fact, nobody can know what at all will come of it. So devising is a highly investigative and experimental practice. A devised performance is a composition of material, which is created by a production group.

A main point in devising processes is to generate material from the actual competencies and skills of those who participate in the production of the performance. We see lots of more or less successful products, which result from all sorts of combinations of competencies and people, and these have led us to consider creativity as something you practice. In our opinion devising a performance is an interesting enterprise because it allows us to think of creativity as something that can be *made to happen* and that *being creative* can best be thought of in terms of decision making and coherent thinking, rather than as inventiveness or alternative thinking. Creativity in our understanding will then be treated more as an attitude towards solving a task, and towards the people you are working with, than the actual ability to be original. Devising obviously asks for what we understand as general creativity, like the ability to take an initiative, to invent, to think alternatively, to associate interestingly, to create metaphors and images. More than anything, however, it asks for an ability to think coherently and the discipline to act accordingly, to be able to work out the consequences of decisions made in the flow of things, to endure unfinished processes, to oscillate between having control and letting go of it, to accomodate lots of things in your head at the same time, to remain open to suggestions etc: in short, to co-operate professionally and develop decisional powers that match the notion of a professional product. Whereas artists tend to think in terms of unique products, designers and researchers more often aim at creating prototypes and other kinds of master references for the production of sellable products. Processes of scientific research, design and art production mix and merge in many ways these days, however. Multimedia is but one of many fields where it soon becomes uninteresting to insist on being artistic or scientific. The question is rather directed towards finding different means for different purposes. Our perspective is mainly dramaturgical, which means that we are concerned with how actions can be created and composed for performances, installations or exhibitions. Theatre, both traditional and contemporary, either for an audience or with participants, is our professional reference.

8.2 Manpower: An Example of a Devised Performance that Turned Into a Theatre Exhibition

The product we will focus on ended up being a 28-minute long performance, which we eventually chose to name a theatre-exhibition. An audience of approximately 20 people could walk and stand inside ten mobile projection screens (2 m × 3 m). Eight people operated the mobile screens and projectors. During the performance the space was changed four times. The screens were used for projections of slides, live video, 3D animation and shadow work (carried out by the live performers and the stage crew). From the start, the audience saw an animation of a bizarre, almost grotesque, male body, while a male voice was heard talking. The projection screen was removed from the entrance of the space and gave way for the audience to enter into a space where the two walls met in a central perspective. The audience could watch a kneeling man watching two girls in red dresses, dancing. They performed a tango-inspired choreography accompanied by Italian circus music. The kneeling man had a "double" who could follow his gaze through a video camera, that is, zoom in on their high-heel black shoes (see Figure 8.1). The gaze of the man was then

Figure 8.1 Manpower: dancers and projection screens.

projected onto the 12 m long wall of Altuglass screens. The other wall was showing black and white slides of old drawings and paintings of courting situations.

The wall then changed into a spiral. The voice-over was restarted and turned into a Piazzola tango, as the male performer danced a short solo. His "shadow" continued video-filming him and thus the contours of his movements were projected onto four of the screens. More black and white slides, this time kissing scenes from American movies, were projected onto the remaining screens. The audience surrounded the male performer inside the circular space. Teasingly, the two women entered his dance, only to leave him on his own shortly afterwards. Again the screens moved and a new text, a dialogue between a man and a woman, was presented as voice-over. The third space was formed as a corridor: five screens on each side divided the space into a male and a female side. Animations of a match-stick man, made from motion-captured movements of the male dancer, in a red spiral and other animations, covered the male side. On the female side, four women performed repetitive movements, undressed in various ways as shadow "puppets" and eventually just vanished as distorted bodies. The fourth space had no performers at all. The screens moved into a square, like the space of an exhibition room in an art gallery. Black and white pictures of staring men and women were projected in small format on to the four walls that closed in the audience. A double-sized slumberdown was placed in the very middle, and from the ceiling a video of a sleeping couple was projected. A male and a female icon were also projected on to the slumberdown. It was now possible for the audience to put their hand on top of the icons to decide whether there should be (1) a female only, (2) a male only or (3) a couple sleeping there. On one of the walls, a 3D-animated, stylised character danced tango using motion-captured movements from one of the female dancers. This interactive installation was open-ended, but the performance ended when the music stopped.

8.2.1 Framing the Work

Creating or setting up frames for a production process inevitably means excluding some possibilities. So some decisions as to the final result are in fact made very early in the process. Anything might still happen, but everything will not. We see enclosures as artistic necessities and frames that make it possible to act creatively.

Flirtation

One of our dramaturgical research aims had been to explore interaction (between humans) and interactivity (between humans and machines). The notion of flirtation was a notion we had worked with in relation to play and improvisation and inspired by Adam Philips' book *On Flirtation* (Philips, 1994). We thought it interesting to look closer at flirtation as a possible dramaturgical model. So a narrative with no definite ending was a possibility. The research question was: "Could we make machines participate in a flirtation?" Why this interest? Primarily because flirtation is a process that can only be kept alive if two partners participate on equal terms in the activity, and if they are able to suspend the idea of a particular ending. If one (or both) wants to end the flirt with a definite result, the activity changes and turns into something else, for example, seduction. We found flirtation interesting because flirtation seems to be *paradigmatic interaction*. A flirt needs another flirt, which means that flirtation, as a necessity is a *subject-to-subject relationship*. Like children's play, flirtation is *without a specific purpose*. This *purposelessness* allows you to improvise. Flirtation only really works when there is *no anticipation* on the part of the participants and when the *rules are constantly negotiated*. So we consider flirtation to be a pleasure, not a need. To be able to flirt you have to want to get involved in the game and to enjoy constant reconsideration and adjustment. Flirtation is about taking risks. Flirtation means to give a chance and take a chance and to suspend disbelief. Losing in a flirtatious situation is not the same as really losing. Flirtation works on some kind of border between fiction and reality. Flirtation creates an uncertain repertoire of possible relationships and possible modes of relationships. Flirtation playfully questions what is possible and what is not.

We looked at flirtation as a dramaturgical challenge. We saw flirtation as a kind of fluid dramaturgy, which challenges our sense of beginning, middle and, in particular, the need for an ending. To study flirtation means to study unstable relationships, where everybody and everything can be treated as uncertain: values, ethics, words, behaviours, chance and circumstances. So a dramaturgy of flirtation slows down real-time interaction and ways of extending time limits. In doing so, it practises controlling time and space from the inside, as part of the interactivity. We found that flirtation was a good metaphor for the kind of interactivity that a lot of the new technologies seem to be aiming at.

Spatial Experiments: Live and Virtual

We wanted to explore the idea that experiencing the stage as a three-dimensional space could be part of the experience of the audience. In other words, we wanted to see if we could *include* the audience in the performance space in some way. We wanted the audience to be able to move around and possibly to take some kind of a responsibility for what they experienced. We saw this as a very delicate and cautious first attempt to work on a borderline between theatre *for* an audience and theatre *with* an audience. It was also an expressed aim of our research project to explore both real and virtual 3D spaces. Another part of our research project was to investigate relationships between live and the virtual, such as the real theatre space and projected and experienced 3D spaces, real 3D performers and virtual performers or moving objects. We were dreaming of making live performers interact with 3D animations or projections of their own images videoed and digitally edited in real-time.

Fictional Contracts

Knowing where and when and under what kind of circumstances the performance is going to take place, obviously set some restrictions and we knew that we had to spend a lot of energy looking for ways of negotiating the fictional contract with movable spectators. Plotting a story draws on dramaturgical tools and competencies that are somewhat different from the dramaturgies demanded by a devising process. A dramatic play requires calculations that make it possible to place a dramatic situation somewhere in an untold story and the ability to plot this story backwards, from an ending to a beginning, and forwards, towards an end that causally relates to the beginning. A dramatic story is told through the characters that it takes to set up such a plot and the situations that bring out the conflicts of dramatic action. In principle, devising does not set up a hierarchy of theatrical elements, but investigates how all elements of the theatre, so to speak, can tell their own story. Devising is an attitude that favours the production of experimental tales or those special narratives, which draw on several kinds of artistic logic. Devising does not make it easy to make coherent performances, but it provides opportunities of testing paths towards interesting findings.

The first enclosures implied that we knew *something* about the end product and how this product might negotiate its methods with the user or spectator in much the same way as deciding whether one wants to design for fun or for functionality.

8.2.2 Generating Material

One of the most important elements in devising processes is the ability to produce material without having an ultimate thematic or aesthetic aim, namely not knowing how, why and where the material produced will find a place in the final product. This means that you have to be able to produce something from loose ends, from bits and pieces of a concept. This is often done in terms of *generating responses* to things, both concrete and abstract, and to spend time on things that might look impossible, see things used in ways they were not made for, etc. It also requires an ability to abstain from aesthetic judgments and avoid discussions of immediate purposefulness or stage potentials for a rather long period of time. It requires strong decisional powers to avoid aiming at immediate results.

In this particular case, it was rather obvious that we had to start investigating what kind of technologies would be interesting (and possible) to integrate into the multimedia product. A dance and technology expert, Scott de Lahunta, accepted an invitation to be our researcher and advisor to set up a program for digital art experiments. His knowledge and ability to make international contacts became crucial for us, as we had to figure out what happened in this field in a fairly short time. Scott de Lahunta helped us develop a complete concept for a digital "experimentarium" based on a combination of lectures, demonstration of technologies and workshops.

The next step was gathering a group of interested performers, visual artists, researchers and students to participate in this experiment. The original idea was to form four different groups and make four performances or installations that could be presented together. For economical and practical reasons we ended up with only two productions, one of which was to be a team of professionals: dancers and digital animators. This dance-oriented performance was to be led by a professional choreographer, Susan Rethorst. The other group ended up working with students and Torunn Kjølner directed it. Janek Szatkowski and Niels Lehmann were dramaturges.

In an intensive period of approximately six weeks, we researched four areas:

1. Motion capture (Ascension)
2. 3D-animation (Maya)
3. Projections (projectors and material to project on), and
4. 3D space.

A fifth seminar was held after the presentations of the performances and it focused on reflecting on experiences from all the phases.

The five seminars were open to a public of artist and students of the arts and multimedia and were well attended. National and international guest speakers presented papers that introduced the audience to the state of the art within the given areas. So we had technical reports, work demonstrations, philosophical and dramaturgical reflections. A group of approximately 15 people, artists and multimedia students, was allowed to spend a lot of time in the workshops that ran for a week or so after the public seminars in order to come to grips with the technicalities of motion capture, animation techniques and projection material. During these workshops everybody just tried to produce something. A lot of powerful computers were installed in our black box theatre at the Department of Dramaturgy for almost two months. Other technological equipment, like projectors, sound systems, etc., was also in use, so the space functioned as a freely accessible laboratory open at all hours of the day. This intense working period ended with an informal exhibition of digital products from the workshop. Below are two examples of some of the very fascinating material that was produced in those workshops. Both were used in the final performance.

Elastica (Vibeke Bertelsen and Lone Koefoed Hansen) had combined motion-capture data and 3D animation. The students who made it wanted to experiment with the creation of an image expressing the desire to move, without really being able to do so. The images were made as responses to a poem written by the Danish poet, Henrik Norbrandt. Separately, they motion-captured movements of arms and legs of a person sitting on a chair trying to get away from it, while being tied down on both feet. This movement was attached to a rather abstract animation of an organic, brownish archway (see Figure 8.2).

This experiment reflects an attempt to generate material that tried to avoid using motion-captured movement and 3D animation to make things look realistic. The resulting images seemed eerie, something we had not seen before. The same applied for another experiment carried by Sonja Tepavcevic, who modelled a male body. In the animation process she attached motion-captured points from moving arms and legs to the face of the man, so that separate parts of the face started dancing (see Figure 8.3).

Several of the students had produced things that had qualities which were thought to be of possible interest for further use. Nevertheless, at the time we were very troubled by a feeling that something was lacking. We had been looking for themes and narratives ever since the idea of flirtation was mentioned. So we had noticed that there was a lot of interest involved with gendered gaze and later with a feeling expressed by some of the male students, namely that the proud, strong male gaze seemed to be fading in certain Danish cultures at the turn of the millennium. This, to them, made it rather difficult to be a man. In fact, some of the young men did not really dare flirt, nor did they feel secure about how to do it. It seems striking to us too, that the young women responded to these stories by laughing. So what was it we were looking for? We thought we had a theme: an asymmetrical distribution of power: strong women versus weak men, or rather, a male *feeling* that women had an easier access to their life powers, and that this left men with a sense of losing the

Figure 8.2 Elastica: expressing the desire to move but not being able to do so. A 3D animated figure using motion capture data.

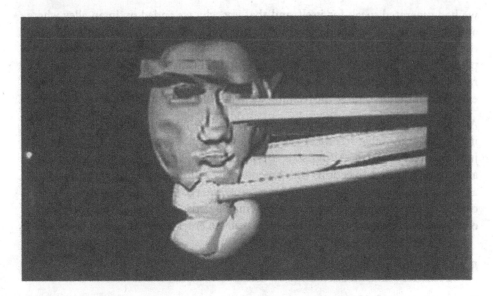

Figure 8.3 3D-animated male face, exploding with motion-captured body movements.

ability to act. So we had a theme: Manpower. What we needed was the right material. Or *was* that what we really needed?

Continuing from here, we worked on several levels simultaneously. Three performers were asked to make some improvisations on the theme flirtation, and especially the male versus female gaze. The task was to improvise a response to the idea of strong women versus weak men. These improvisations were taped and analysed by us. Several interesting scenarios and movements had emerged. Some of which were actually used in the final performance.

To generate more material we all read Norbrandts poems, and even some biographical studies to see whether there was a "weak man" to be found. Could he be a central reference for a kind of character for our performance? There certainly were lots of things to respond to, and we did. We tried out sequences, looked for narratives that could be expressed through dance and movement, etc. One of Norbrandt's small poems in particular attracted us. It was about a woman in a dress, a tent in a desert, and wind. Our idea was to set up some kind of tent across the big space of the black box and to use its material to project onto. Students from the School of Architecture, who had followed some of the workshops, designed an impressive scenography that worked with huge constructions of projection-screen material stretched out from the ceiling and across the whole space. We tried to motion-capture the movements of a dress swaying seductively, the movement of a zipper being unzipped in a seductive way, and lots of other things.

All these attempts were fine, but they missed "it" – that special feeling of quality. Some time passed before we really understood why. Looking back at it now, we will say that we learned a lesson about the dramaturgy of devising. What was wrong was that we had tried to illustrate a poem and a theme. We did not really let the material we had generated speak for itself, and that was why we ended up in an alley where all exits seemed to be blind. Because we had chosen to build a narrative from the outside of the material we had generated, we found ourselves missing bits and pieces everywhere, so that the loss of technical skills became very prominent. The rather fantastic things that were produced lost interest, and so it had become extremely difficult to force the technology to do what we had in mind.

Architect and stage designer Lucca Ruzza then came up with the idea of constructing ten huge movable screens made from a new projection material, which he had just discovered existed. Altuglass is a type of black Plexiglass, which is polarised, allowing very clear projections with exceptionally little loss of light. So the notion of a performance space with movable screens emerged. All the material was reevaluated for use, and we were now moving towards something, which seemed to end up as a performance. At least we were ready to enter a new phase.

8.2.3 Selecting and Composing

From now on we did not enter into many thematic debates. We looked for ways and guidelines to structure the material we had, in order to try to compose it. The structure – in other words, the dramaturgy we were looking for – had to be flexible enough to stand up as a reference for our selection process. This is the phase in a devising process where the decisions about the dramaturgical structures and the final aesthetics of the end product are created so it is crucial that the actual material and other actual facts of life are taken into consideration. It is now a question of finding the best possible dramaturgy, narrative or compositional entity that can "include" the material. If the compositional structure is good enough, almost no new material should need to be produced. Sometimes it is a question of creating a deadline, yet another artistic restriction, or self-imposed frame, *created* in order to limit possibilities and thereby promote productive creation.

When we devise, we do not usually choose classical dramaturgical narratives, but we have them in mind, because there are always elements of dramatic action in any performance, and personally we like to know what rules and models we break and play with. Again we have found it fruitful to think in terms of creating enclosures or dogmas. Any performance will still have a beginning, middle and an end, and we still might need a sense of variation in energy or excitement, a pulsating feeling of change, made clear and readable for the audience. It might not be a what-happens-next kind of fictional contract we are after, but we are looking for something to let the audience into our universe to make them able to start a process of interpretation. We considered questions like "What kind of tensions next?", or "What energises what?", "What kind of formal linking systems do we set up?" as basic dramaturgical and compositional questions. The following is the example of how we created a compositional framework for Manpower.

The notion of some kind of theme and a space was formulated during the workshops. Looking back it was fortunate for us that the material we had neither combined nor suited the idea of the space and the tentative plot. We had wanted to see what happened to a weak male and a strong female living somewhere in some desert-like landscape enclosed by tent-like screens. We had to realise that we were about to do exactly what we did *not* want to do: use the technology to illustrate and conceptualise a story that had been created as a result of metaphysical dreaming, not a pragmatic understanding of what material we had at our disposal.

This new order of production procedures goes for *use value* rather than *truth value*. What we already had at our disposal would act as guidelines for what we could produce. We did not really have a lot of material; so producing more material more or less at random now went hand in hand with searching for the right compositional restrictions. Eventually, we looked for some kind of formality to adhere to whatever could give us an idea of a sequence. The study of flirtation had reminded us of the love sonnets of Shakespeare. So we came up with the idea of using the structure of a sonnet, which has twelve lines composed in three parts, to act as a guideline for our dramaturgy. The addition of a concluding, but open couplet, which Shakespeare had added to the Italian sonnet, seemed in very good tune with our purpose. So we created a dramaturgical model from the very strict structure of a Shakespearean sonnet and started to organise the material from there. By dividing the fourteen lines into four (3 × 4 and 1 × 2) and formally equating each line with two minutes of performance time, we had a compositional structure in four parts and a running time of 28 minutes.

Each of the four sections was then given a heading in relation to space with metaphorical connotations: "The Central Perspective", "The Spiral", "The Divided Space" and "The Open Space". By moving the ten screens, we could create spaces that would both feel and look very different. These spaces were tried out and we decided to use them as walls of an architecture that also included the spectators. In this way the audience would have to move within the walls and thereby experience stage design as architecture, in the sense that these walls would work on the audience in much the same way as they worked on the performers. The audience would be able to walk around inside these walls and we would be able to change the spatial experience by projecting different images on the screens (slides, video, and animation).

When the time and general structure had been decided we needed to compose a soundtrack for the multimedia performance. Our director had always wanted to work with accordion music. After a lot of research, we ended up with three rather different pieces of music with only one thing in common, the accordion. The sound technician digitally mixed a composition for the fourth part of the performance.

We had not worked with any idea of spoken dialogue, but on coming closer to the creation of a scenario, we commissioned a young Danish playwright, Jens Blendstrup, to generate some text starting from the general idea of weak male versus strong female power, and preferably from the perspective of the weak male gaze. He seemed to enjoy this gaze and after having watched the animations and some of the recorded improvisations he came up with a lot of material that we were allowed to edit and use according to our needs. We recorded the soliloquies and dialogues with actors, and used the taped version as a voice-over during the performance when screens were moved.

When the ten screens were mounted on their frames and wheels, new discoveries about the material were made. The special qualities of Altuglass, combined with the various options in the construction of the frames, made perfectly sharp shadows even at a distance of a metre, but they also allowed some fascinating effects with dissolved bodies when the performers climbed the metal structures. This was used as the main input in the divided space. This was an example of work that shows how to explore the material actively (see Figure 8.4).

Another thing about the Altuglass is that the front surface is very shiny. This creates lots of reflections. At first we considered the reflections to be a disaster and a huge problem to be resolved. Having worked in the space for some time, though, we gradually began to see that some options offered an extra bonus – the magic of these reflections. Complex images were interesting results of this. The audience could see themselves reflected on top of the images we projected on the screens. It turned out to be an interesting addition to our concept of the gendered gaze.

As we tried to investigate the (male) gaze, it was decided that we needed a person with a video camera who would produce live pictures to be projected on to the screens. We were interested in the possibilities of making real-time digital adjustments to the live video signal. So we asked a programmer to come up with something for us. Thomas Moeslund took up the challenge, and he made a program that caught the outlines of

Figure 8.4 Shadows creating optical effects due to construction of projections screens.

a figure and displayed them. After having worked with us for some time, Thomas appeared one day with a new version of the program. He mentioned that he had a version that included an error, but he had observed that this error had the interesting visual effect that it allowed the edges to hang onto the picture for a short time before being erased. He had kept that version of the program as well, thinking that we would probably like it. We did, and we used it (see Figure 8.5).

Apart from the sonnet-structure, we obviously wanted to work with some other kind of recurrence. So the same theme or image was to appear and reappear to create redundancy. To create one such element, we motion captured a segment of the male performer's movements from the spiral part of the performance. Peter Skaarup, a student in multimedia, used the data to produce a short dance of a matchstick-like man, miming the spiral in a 3D surrounding. This was used as projection in "Divided Space".

Selecting the slides we would use was simply motivated by the wish for a historical perspective. We wanted the pictures to give a notion of courtship through the ages, so we used scenes of seduction from art and film history. These pictures were displayed in chronological order as a simple slide-show.

As material for the last interactive installation, we needed to record some video of a male and a female sleeping. The idea emerged that the audience should be given the option of deciding how the performance should end, whether one, both or none of the figures appear on the slumberdown.

We could now make a storyboard, using the 28-minute long soundtrack as continuity line.

Figure 8.5 Video input edited digitally real-time projected on screens.

8.2.4 Rehearsing

As we have pointed out earlier, we were not concerned here about plotting a story into this performance. This does not mean that there is no order. On the contrary, one could say there is almost nothing besides order in a performance like this. The rehearsals of a performance must concentrate on running orders and all kinds of details to avoid the wrong kind of confusion in the audience. During rehearsals one looks for *ways* of presenting the material so that it comes across as a deliberately created entity. We were trying to avoid the cold and cool quality of digital technology, so we looked for qualities like warmth and calmness. It was important that the spectators could feel comfortable inside this installed performance. All the technical gear was hidden behind the screens in semi-darkness. The energies should decrease, after a rather energetic and emotional start, through an almost lamenting piece when the females surround the male. A meditative mood invoked by people moving as shadows followed and finally towards an open end, where the audience become more aware of each other than of the finish of the performance.

All such choices are, of course, matters of aesthetic judgment, and in this case left up to the director of the performance. An art product involving human bodies always risks losing full control of the material. Anything can happen, especially when eight people have to move ten huge screens four times during half an hour and at the same time they have to push wagons with projectors, set cameras, change slides, etc. We think we actually reached a satisfactory level of flow in Manpower.

What we did not achieve, however, was an interesting interaction between the live actors and the virtual, digitalised projections. In the process of devising Manpower, we learned several lessons about this. When we worked with the performers, we reached the point where we had created a complete score for the entire dance sequence. To compose this into an interesting interaction between live performers, projected animations and video, did not seem possible in the given time. To be able to work with such interactions, it would be necessary for the performers to work with the technicians in order to generate material together. We did not have the chance to re-compose the sequences and ended up with a rather simple montage of sequences one on top of the other, which, due to the fact that the screens surrounded the audience, turned out to concentrate the main attention on the performers, rather on the projected images of their contours. A lot of spectators did not even look at the moving images behind and therefore lost out on what we had wanted, namely that the images could be seen as commentaries and supplements to the real movements. One could conclude that we possibly aimed at results too early in the process. One could also say that we did not have the right material for such a montage, and therefore might have avoided including it in our composition.

Most valuable for us, however, has been to learn about the importance of *how* to conduct the initial enclosures. If you want to do research via art, that is, in an art form, it seems crucial to share the aims of the research and all the given circumstances before starting to generate the material. Only then is it possible for everybody involved to explore not only individual skills and crafts, but also the possibilities of synergies.

8.2.5 Reflection

Our final seminar was very rewarding for us, since the invited scholars and theatre people came up with very interesting responses to our work. Let us briefly recapitulate here what Professor Morten Kyndrup said (Kyndrup, 1999). He pointed to the fact that the work itself did not establish any hierarchy between the levels of expression. He saw the work as having zeugmatic character (from the Greek forced conjunctions).

> The different levels of expression are present simultaneously, and even the traditional subject/object relation between artwork and beholder is sort of wiped out. That is because the beholder feels herself as part of the work by being inside it, and also because the other beholders seem to be part of the work too, even to the physical senses, since from time to time they create shadows and bump into you, and hence become part of your sensuous impressions.

Kyndrup stresses that there is a quite extensive thematic coherence in the performance, particularly in the man versus woman problem. The text seems to be represented by the dancers, and the theme is also apparent in the still photographs that are projected on the walls. The dances are doubled and mirrored by the motion-captured sequences, which in turn more or less directly touch upon the identity problematic of the text. All this, concludes Kyndrup, makes the performance at one and the same time both open and closed as an artwork.

> This work, Manpower, is open in the sense that it completely desists from pointing out any order of priority between its levels of signification. It just makes its significations available in a paratactical exhibition-like universe in which everything, even yourself as a beholder, seems to belong to one and the same level. But the work is also closed in the sense that thematically it has quite a lot of redundancy in the man/woman problem, and in the formal self-referentiality too. ...the work is closed in the sense that the beholder is sort of locked up by it, indeed is actually being pushed around by the work from time to time. The work does not just consist of a number of juxtaposed offers, which you can take or leave. No, quite literally this work is closing around you, and this I believe, is one of the quite decisive properties of its aesthetics. There is something intrusive about a work like that being around you and moving you around, an intrusiveness which engenders from time to time an almost obscene effect, an almost uncanny, unheimlich feeling of the fact that at the same time this artificial space is damned real as well ... This distinct touch of obscenity or uncanniness in this surrounding prisonlike zeugmatic or paratactical theatre is, I believe, a decisive force of its aesthetic construction, and basically this is substantial to its status and quality as an artwork.

We must mention that Kyndrup points out the weak spots as well. He would have preferred a text with a higher level of literary quality and he asks whether perhaps we might have overdone the redundancy in Manpower.

> The pure redundancy creates its own chain of signification, but this also makes it easier to reject it as just symbolicity. The rejection is far more difficult when the elements become intrusively real.

By this, Kyndrup refers to the weirdness of some of the 3D-animated elements (see Figures 8.2 and 8.3).

8.3 Reflections on the Art of Devising

We have tried to show that devising is best thought of as a process that takes place in distinctly different phases. This is not just common sense. It suggests a rather specific belief in what it means to be creative in collaboration with others and what it means to be able to end up with a product one can present to a public. First of all, one learns from devising that it is important to learn to jump between relinquishing control and taking control. One learns to accept that in order to generate interesting material, many, many sketches and trials must be done and completed before evaluating the resulting proposals as potential performance material. Devising means to endure not making decisions about end results during the early phases of exploration and generation of material and creating frames. Devising also means daring to stop producing, to create strict limitations and to work coherently in order to link the material whenever the compositional phase starts. In other words we imply some kind of method by arguing that devised processes should be divided into phases, each with a specific focus and means, in order to be able to apply different kinds of creativity for the different purposes. The distinct phases may be as many as we suggest below. Our point is not, however, that these elements of devising are necessarily to follow each other in this order, but that by distinguishing between them, the whole production for a performance may be more creatively and more professionally handled.

- Starting
- Teambuilding
- Collaboration
- Generating material
- Looking for compositional principles (a dramaturgy)
- Composing
- Rehearsing
- Presenting
- Reflecting.

It will be obvious for anybody who devises a performance (or any other multimedia product) that each phase influences another in various ways, backwards and forwards. The distinction then should be considered as a working tool, particularly when one works with time-consuming and complex programming and technology as one does in multimedia production.

The only opportunity of really including technology as part of the generation of material is to calculate with a lot of time to explore technological inputs. It is our conviction that a good devising process should allow different forms of creative work, different methods, purposes and procedures. What gives the best result is often where the rules are made perfectly clear to everybody involved.

It makes a small difference whether you think in terms of creating, generating or producing material. We have stuck to the concept of generating material because we usually work from a starting point, the aim to investigate virtual and real movement and space. So generation of material means, not to illustrate themes, but to create different kinds of responses to a chosen starting point. Our experience is that, during devising processes, certain notions of form and narrative structures generate from the work done. We see it as an important element of being creative in a devising process to be able to endure complex, sometimes chaotic and often seemingly purposeless inputs and simultaneously to keep an eye open for possible orders of and in the material produced. So we suggest that one can jump from one practice, which is to create frames that can generate diverse material to another, which is to create a productive order, which will include and capture main bulks of the material produced during the first phase. This phase can be described in rather scientific terms: what matters are to calculate consequences, to work out coherent structures and to decide what is usable and what is not. Analytical skills then marry repertoires of dramaturgical models and possibilities by a creative act of composing a performance without missing links and freed from common sense. This is not an easy task, but a challenging one.

The last phase, rehearsing, can start when the frames have been created and the material is ready for being replayed and adjusted to the decisions made in the second phase. The rehearsal time can be long or short, depending on the state or finish in which the first phase has left the material.

Reflection, documentation, and analysis of each phase of the process are often vital parts of devised theatre productions for strengthening the awareness of what happens and how the team functions.

8.3.1 Starting

The idea behind paying special attention to the point of departure is that one wants to avoid starting with something that is already well known and explicitly formulated, in order to prevent the process from ending up as an illustration of an idea. Some devising procedures will spend time on exercises and practice that can bring forward matters, which can catch the interest of the participants. Personal investment is a key notion since part of the concept of devising implies that the end product is a result of what a collective can produce as synergies.

Art processes are often unpredictable in that there are many accepted ways of finding what kind of ideas, matters, issues or phenomena catch interest. So physical responses to concrete things, voice experiments, writing, painting and other kinds of expressive exercises, might be a way of opening some fields of investigation, or of closing others. Bringing in, or reflecting about, pieces of art already open to the public (poetry, music, film images, etc.) might direct the interest in new directions. Tasks that are specifically directed towards the exploration of, for example, digital technologies, as we did with the Manpower experiment, might serve equally as a beneficial starting point for devising a performance. A research aim or ideas about trying to stretch the uses of known technologies might, for example, assemble a good team for a devising process.

In devised theatre anything can be used as a starting point, a newspaper article, a film, a book, a site, a character, a technological device, a common experience, a mysterious phenomenon, a quotation, a specific feeling, an effect, a journey, a projection material, a research field. Even a dramatic play can be used as initiating the process of generating material!

Rules and restrictions that the participants can accept or give credit to usually frame a good start. The (explicit or implicit) negotiation of such rules should probably be considered as a crucial tool in devising. The fact that everything is possible does not mean that anything goes. To achieve an environment "where creativity can happen" is not a totally mysterious endeavour, although it might be totally impossible to prescribe something, which guarantees that creativity happens and ends up as a good result. Starting can be an interesting test of who and/or what provides standards for formal and aesthetic ideals that in turn affect the end product. Our issue is to make sure that starting means that we talk about an experimental phase in all the meanings of the word. Experimenting is like flirtation, a practice that exits beyond a thought of an end result.

8.3.2 Teambuilding

Teamwork is at its best when the people involved find a productive balance between being understanding and being questioning, between doing and not doing, between talking and not talking, etc. This is obvious, and only really noticeable when it does not work. Only dreamers would try to set up criteria that have to be fulfilled in order to make a team work. Experience has shown us, however, that some elementary rules of conduct, like a basic respect for other people and their competencies, and a fair portion of self-awareness, need to be taken for granted to make teamwork happen. Having worked in many artistic processes, we know very well that just one person who continually insists on doing things in a different way can destroy a team. Dealing with problems in ill-functioning teams often differs from solving the problems. In a basically democratic society it might be difficult, for instance, to accept the fact that a particular team, due to different attitudes towards the work, might not be able to select good means to deal with the case. So such a team should probably be allowed to stop working. To work professionally and creatively in a team should be based on *choice*. Our point is that the idea of devising in fact asks for something in the direction of a pragmatic attitude towards what a creative process is and what it means to create something collectively. One of the questions asked is whether one expects to produce something as somebody else's material (e.g. for a director who is staging a play) or whether one is willing to join in with the idea that "my aim" is to be subordinated to a notion of "our intention".

Finding such notions of common attitudes towards work may easily become a vital part of teambuilding. A team can find each other, or be collected by someone who can provide the economical and spatial frames for something to happen. In any case there is continuous work to do in negotiating the understanding of how creativity can happen.

8.3.3 Collaboration

A team can start with a variety of competencies and then see what happens, or gather competencies from an idea of what is needed to make a specific investigation happen. Necessary in collaborative work is a *will to understand* what is happening. Niklas Luhmann (1968) has shown us that trust is a basic social and personal ability. As such, trust is an ability to realise that the future cannot possibly be controlled and that we therefore have to trust a selection of different systems in order to be able to act at all. For Luhmann it is crucial to understand and accept that the future always has more possibilities than can be realised at any given time. Luhmann points out that some people do not acknowledge, let alone accept that. So they will hurry to try to restrict the possibilities of future actions, and even see this as a scientific attitude. Devising could easily be understood as an activity built on trust. Only people, who can endure that the future always has more possibilities than any one work can achieve, should join a team of devisers.

Something new is often created through a kind of confrontation with what is well known. Devising can be seen as an explicit exploitation of metaphorical universes. A metaphor, then, not only acts as a creative tool, but also as a means of communication when one is trying to understand and exploit unknown competencies and their traditions. In order to understand new approaches, one creates images of what is already understood. In such image-oriented communication processes many problems and many ideas arise. Devisers accept and make the best of such meetings.

Looking at theatre art leads to the issue of collective art production. Again many practices have been tried out, many methods investigated. Experience quite obviously shows that it is very problematic to link art and democratic decision-making. Democracy is usually understood in a way that gives members of a collective equal rights to have an opinion and that each member represents something as equally important as other members do and, if consensus cannot be reached, the majority gets the decisive power. This notion of democracy might make it difficult to create interesting material. So we have found it essential that each team and each production spend the energy it takes to establish workable rules and codes of conduct, and that these negotiations are reflected in relation to the given circumstances. Special attention is usually paid to how the process is organised in terms of coaching, researching, directing, stage management, etc. Devised performance does not exclude the idea that there are different roles and functions in a theatre production, but there can also be an artistically, educationally or research-oriented point in incorporating the functions of each individual competence into the compositional process. So, there might be a director. Or it is possible to let the function of a director rotate among the members, or there might be a point to do without a director altogether. The same will go for other functions, like a writer's, stage designer's, performer's role, etc. To work professionally in a type of collective means to have a flair for collective processes and experience that the collective does better than each individual member separately.

8.3.4 Generation of Material

The idea of generating material more or less at random is that a performance is a product, which should be *made or created*. So the production does not start with an order of events waiting to be staged. In principle, all the material produced will be considered as suggestions, which later will be evaluated as usable or unusable, and in relation to other suggestions. The material produced can be short texts or small images or other elements that is shared within the team, or it can be sequenced movements, even performances that are practised so that they are more or less ready to be staged. An investigation of a site can generate a lot of material and become the sine qua non of a particular performance. All tricks of the trade should be allowed in this process.

There are many ways of enhancing the material for stage use. Some find it important to set up frames for the production of material, which ensure that the participants surprise themselves, that they do something they have not done before, build something not seen before, see something that takes them away from their old habits of doing, thinking and seeing.

Practice differs when it comes to deciding how finished or artistically fulfilled each piece of material must be in order to be considered worth entering the selection process. When complex technology is involved, it is important to accept that it is not easy just to change it. This in fact might prove very productive in a devising process, since special care about technical things often leads to unexpected uses of the technology involved. Thus notions that are important for the compositional backbone of a performance might stem from paying attention, for example, to technological inputs. Sometimes it is most beneficial to sketch material, and then leave the rest to the rehearsal period. This will ask for a longer rehearsal period, where composition and rehearsals easily merge into one activity. This often makes it more difficult to let the material speak for itself.

8.3.5 Composing

Composing is a term one has chosen to use in devised performances to signify that we are not just talking about dramatic plotting, narrative structures, and even text-based work at all. We use the term "composition" in close relation to "dramaturgy" because we tend to practise dramaturgy both analytically and creatively. Thus we tend to think of dramaturgy as a reference for analysing plays, films and theatrical performances as well as a repertoire for creating fictional events. We have introduced the dramaturgy of devising as a compositional tool. Dramaturgy can be understood as a kind of craft, which makes it possible to formulate how the images and actions work when they are linked up with each other. "Dramaturgia" is a Greek word derived from drama, which means action, and urgia (ergon), which means either a work (of art/actions) or to work. Applying a dramaturgical perspective on a process means to us to analyse what actually happens on stage and to suggest systems and other guidelines for how actions can be made to affect the audience. The knowledge of how actions work as part of a performance is a vital working tool in devising processes.

One will find a variety of usages of the word dramaturgy in devising practices. Some will insist that dramaturgy can only be related to understanding how a drama is composed and staged. Basically drama is then understood as an art form, a literary genre of its own, like poetry and epics. Originally a drama was composed as a series of actions and interactions between people. A complex relationship between time, space and characters is composed to form a plot or a story. A drama is *dramatic* because it is told through the actions and interactions of living performers who play somebody else. A drama is rehearsed so that it seems to happen here and now, right in front of our eyes. The paradigmatic dramatic genre is basically causal in structure and effect.

Two thousand years of theatre practice has challenged Aristotle's (1968) first insistence on such a dramaturgy as a more or less universal artistic law of methods and effects. The German playwright Bertolt Brecht (1967) and others have insisted that the theatre could happen as the effect of different mixtures of dramatic and epic narratives, etc. The French actor and philosopher Antonin Artaud (1954–96) insisted that we should drop the dramatic text as the main reference for theatre and that the potential effect of theatre could be something much more powerful, made up of colours, sounds, words, movements, etc. which would work on the performers and the audience with the dramatic power of life itself.

The dramaturgy of devising acknowledges that certain theatrical narratives are inherent in our Western cultural tradition. The ability to see what kind of plots such rules lead to, and which effects it has available to break them, has become a field of dramaturgical research. Montage is, for instance, a dramaturgical model with countless variations.

Composing has, of course, other connotations than dramaturgy and that is why we want to keep the term composing. Composition is less focused on action than dramaturgy. Composing is a term used in non-dramatic art forms like painting, architecture, poetry and music. Composing is closely linked to a basic under-standing of devising, but in devising compositional practices differ. Some think of composition as an organic process, as something that happens while you work. More or less intuitively one *discovers* the composition of a performance. Others, like us, tend to insist that composing is a matter of creating structures, or of *making* or *giving form to* the material. So composing can mean to create a structure or to devise a principle and a linking system to care as much as possible for the material produced.

Theatre research has made a point of trying to find good categories and systems of dramaturgical strategies, such as epic theatre, simultaneous theatre, meta-theatre, etc., in opposition to the classic Aristotelian dramatic model. Creative references like organic, spatial, formal and symbolic, have also been used as more or less abstract hypotheses to look for alternative strategies to produce performances. Our experience tells us that one might as well make a point of *creating* such a "model" as a unique structural reference for a particular production. We consider that dramaturgies can be devised as productive imposed artistic restrictions.

8.3.6 Rehearsing

Rehearsing is not a key word in devising processes. A lot of devising practices high-light the process and think of performances as a constant work in progress. We will argue, however, that the idea of devising does not necessarily support the hegemony of process work. So to rehearse might as well be looked upon as a closing phase, another self-imposed artistic restriction, where the material is being tested in order to stand out as a unique artistic product. Rehearsing devised material might take place in much the same way as it does in theatre institutions, with the director as the main decision-maker. A crew of other arts and crafts people makes sure that the deci-sions are carried out in the best artistic way and a dramaturge might try to make sure that the structures and conceptions created in the compositional phase do not fall apart.

Since there are many ways of exhibiting a devised performance, many kinds of aesthetic ideals involved and a great variety of professionalism to draw from, one will find a variety of ways of relating the material to a stage or a site. Some will insist that devised theatre asks for something completely different from the rehearsal of a play, because devising relies on the principle that theatrical components can gain a status equal to that of the performer. Seen in this perspective no medium should illustrate or work for something else. An example would be to look at the lights as a narrative element, not as something that is supposed to represent, for example, the time of day when it occurs or a mood of an actor. Equally, scenography is not thought of in terms of a backdrop for the action for the audience to understand that the action takes places in somebody's living room. The performer is not expected to "suit the word to the action and the action to the word", as Hamlet advises his players to do. In principle, all the elements exhibited by the stage could be considered as elements in their own right, with stage potential and as part of a compositional whole.

8.3.7 Reflection, Documentation and Analysis

It goes without saying that reflecting devised process can be done in many ways. It can also be left out altogether. Most theatre academies have developed rather effective ways of reflecting on the practical work, so that the students learn how to devise and how to learn from it. Since devising is about *making* theatre, it becomes crucial to examine which creative strategies were implemented to achieve what was achieved. One might insist on documenting what happened all the way through the process, because all experience tells devisers that it is very easy to lose track of what is happening. Logbooks, videos, photos, written assignments, etc. can be used for this kind of "cold" documentation. Another reason to document each step of a process is, of course, to have something written to go back to, when the material is to be re-evaluated for compositional purposes. Last, but not least, a team of devisers who have a successful process will most likely end up with a lot of good material and ideas for later use. Thus documentation can help to order creative processes and make distinctive choices. A well-known fact is that groups of people often experience, and of course remember, things quite differently. Therefore, taking the time to decide what to document might function as that "stitch in time that saves nine".

8.3.8 Devising Dramaturgies

Designing multimedia products still challenges designers, as well as more traditional artists at a very basic level. There are several reasons for this of course, but the fact that people who work with multimedia are presented almost daily with new tools, new programs and even new forms of media, makes it almost impossible for one artist or designer to reach full mastery of methods and materials. This is an artistic challenge because most art forms and design work have relied heavily on specific crafts and traditions where new forms often have been found or created by breaking the rules of old traditions or where traditional crafts have been used in new ways or applied in unusual contexts. We have seen various forms of conceptual art, where crafts and traditions are considered less important and where ready-made material is considered as interesting as mastery of specific arts or crafts.

Art production could very well be considered as a fight between creative thinking and professional crafts. Multimedia art is a prototype of such a "battlefield" where artistic and lots of other competencies have to meet in order to challenge and explore each other. Limitations of each art tradition and definitions of genres necessarily require questioning, to the point of transgression, in multimedia production. So traditional differences between art and design are challenged too.

This chapter has attempted to reflect on some relations between thinking and practice in the production of multimedia art products based on devising. The meeting of professional competencies from very different traditions of thinking has made it an issue to examine *how* we think and act to devise performances. Quite obviously, there are many attitudes towards production processes in itself and these differences accumulate when you look at working habits, research and creativity. In short we practise our thinking in concrete artistic processes very differently.

Our angle of approach has been dramaturgical. We have worked for years with theatre and theatre research, drama in education, playwriting and the staging of performances. Our entry into multimedia production has meant that we have had the opportunity to interchange our competencies and work with computer scientists, software programmers and concept developers who have been mainly brought up in traditions broadly known as natural sciences, and artists, whose background lies with theatre, dance and the visual arts. In 1999 we formed a small theatre company called Digital Theatre. Our experiences with Digital Theatre have made us very aware of some of our own mental habits, which has been a rewarding input for our research work. To further the experiments with multimedia productions, we have been summoned a new art and research group, which we have named the Hyperoptic Art Collective (http://www.hyperopticon.com). In our

Hyperoptic art project we continue our investigation on interactivity between real and virtual, between system, live performers and spect-actors, through the metaphor "The Angel's View". Devising has proven to keep challenging our art and research work in multimedia.

References

Aristotle (1968). *Poetics*. Oxford: Clarendon Press.
Artaud, A (1956–94). *Oeuvres Complètes*, T 5: *Autour du Théâtre et son double et des Cenci*. Paris: Galimard.
Bauerlein, M (1997). *The Pragmatic Mind*. London: Duke University Press.
Brecht, B (1967). *Gesammelte Werke*, vol 17. Frankfurt am Main: Suhrkamp Verlag.
Kyndrup, M (1999). "Bodybuilding. A Short Analysis." http://www.daimi.au.dk/~sdela/dte/kyndrup.html.
Luhmann, N (1968). *Vertrauen: Ein Mechanismus der Reduktion der sozialer Komplexität*. Stuttgart: Ferdinand Enke.
Phillips, A (1994). *On Flirtation*. Cambridge, MA: Harvard University Press.
Rorty, R (1989). *Contingency, Irony and Solidarity*. Cambridge: Cambridge University Press.

9

The Family Factory: Developing New Methods for Live 3D Animation

Jørgen Callesen

Jørgen Callesen MA, is a researcher at Interactive Institute, Malmö, Sweden. He is exploring autonomous agents, virtual puppets and puppet theatre from a background in multimedia research.

9.1 Introduction

"The Family Factory" is the experimental part of a PhD project in multimedia research concerning the creative integration of interactive digital media in the performing arts. It is a play combining animation, virtual puppets and modern puppet theatre. The play was developed through an interdisciplinary artistic process and combined academic multimedia research, animation and theatre production. Production as research, or research as production has become a widespread method to investigate the functional and aesthetic potential of new digital tools and media. In many cases the only way to obtain a proper object to study is to produce it, since it simply did not exist before. Throughout history most art forms such as film, theatre, music and dance have established a clear distinction between production and academic research, but the rapidly changing and multifarious nature of computer-based multimedia often forces artists and researchers to cross the borders.

I have chosen to call the particular art form of this chapter "performance animation", extending the term to cover an artistic approach to the application of motion capture for real-time 3D animation in different genres within computer games, films and stage performances. Performance animation means the manipulation of a computer-generated image in real time by a performing artist. The result can span from 3D animated characters to the manipulation of space and abstract forms. The development of tools and skills for performance animation is interdisciplinary in its core, since it requires the participation of performers, animators/3D modellers, programmers and systems developers. My approach to performance animation has a strong focus on the theatrical use of direct feedback given to the performer and to the audience through screens and projections, with inspiration from the theory and practice of the puppet theatre. Productions where researchers and artists are brought together raises a lot of methodological questions about the scientific approach to an artistic process and practical questions about the development of new skills. This chapter is an account of such an experimental production process, focusing on both practical and theoretical aspects, the motivation of the different groups behind it and the results obtained.

9.2 Motivation and Sources of Inspiration

During my research into computer games and how to make interesting and intelligent characters for virtual worlds, I focused on traditional media because it seemed most adaptable to work aesthetically within the potentials and constraints of live 3D computer animation.

The point of departure was to work with "Agents as Actors", but it soon became obvious to me that by seeing "Agents as Puppets" you can characterise more aspects of this new phenomenon. By integrating the theory and praxis of the puppet theatre you can get a broader understanding of the meaning of the relation between the player and the puppet, in this case the "agent" on the screen (Andersen and Callesen, 2001; Lund, 2001; Callesen, 2001).

I had the opportunity to study this art form at the department of puppet theatre at the theatre school "Ernst Busch" in Berlin, Germany, for 10 months in 1998–99. This became the main inspiration for developing the concept of virtual puppets for stage performances. The department offers a 4-year course, with acting classes combined with training for physical theatre and puppetry. It has a strong focus on the qualities of the physicality of objects and puppets and on the theatrical presence they create on stage (Völker, 1994, pp. 112-40). From this background my motivation for the production was, first, a wish to create theoretical thesis about virtual puppets and, secondly, curiosity about live 3D animation as a new material for stage projections.

As a follow-up to the empirical studies I wanted to carry out practical experiments with the material of the "virtual puppet" consisting of light on a screen. The thesis was that the puppeteer can play with virtual puppets through the use of motion-capture equipment as if they were "physically" present on stage and thereby intuitively transfer skills from playing traditional puppets. Motion capture is a technique to register physical movement and transform it to computer data. It is often a highly technical discipline, where the aim is to measure movement as accurately as possible. In this artistic approach the focus was on the relation between the performer's physical expressions and on the aesthetic and expressive potential in the computer animations they could generate. I saw the potential for creating a project for testing

Figure 9.1 Reality meets virtual reality. Inspiration for the play came from very different sources spanning from social realistic films to computer games. Still from Mike Leigh's film "Life is Sweet" (1990) and screen dump from the computer game "Final Fantasy VII" (Eidos, 1998).

this thesis, with participation from puppeteers, film animators and others, representing the different skills of the theatre. Through such a collaboration I could use motion-capture techniques in direct relation to the performer movements and gestures through feedback from computer-generated images and animations.

As a basis, I had a story that fascinated me and some inspiration from different kinds of visual media art. The story behind the play "The Family Factory" was inspired by Grimm's fairy tales and British social realistic films. Through the story I wanted to find a way to let the virtual world meet issues closely related to everyday problems such as a child getting caught up in her family relations.

The style and aesthetics of the virtual puppets was inspired by the European tradition for animated puppet films (Bendazzi, 1994) and from theatrical puppets and masks. The 3D animation style was influenced by real-time 3D animation in computer games and artistic music videos rather than the complex 3D animation seen in American feature films such as *Toy Story*, *Antz* or *Jurassic Park*.

9.3 Virtual Puppets: From Theory to Practice

9.3.1 Theories of the Virtual Puppet

The concept of the virtual puppet was presented by puppeteer Stephen Kaplin in 1994 and was later included in an overall model of puppets throughout history in an article in 1999 (Kaplin, 1994, 1999). Puppet theatre theorist Steve Tillis describes the virtual puppet as a new type of puppet with distinct features because of its special material. In opposition to puppet theatre traditionalists he and Kaplin see no reason that it should not have the ability to function as a medium for theatrical representation in line with physical puppets (Kaplin, 1994; Tillis, 1999). Their arguments are based on insights about the materiality of the virtual puppet and how it is controlled, in comparison to physical puppets and mediated puppets for film. The virtual puppet is intangible – you cannot touch it since it is made of light on a screen, but it is tangibly controlled via sensors physically present in the hands or on the body of the performer. The presence of a puppeteer gives the virtual puppet "open" movement possibilities compared to the automata of the mechanical theatre or the pre-programmed NPC (non-player character) of the computer game. The NPC is "closed", because it very quickly becomes obvious to the user (audience) that the pre-programmed "automata" can only repeat its repertoire of actions over and over again. This phenomenon is of great interest to the researchers in autonomous agents, because the discipline is concerned with finding methods dealing with the fact that the NPC, from the perspective of the puppet theatre, is similar to the automaton. The puppet theatre has a long tradition of discussing the dramaturgical and aesthetic consequences of hiding the steering mechanism of the puppet or using it openly in actual performances (Callesen, 2001).

9.3.2 Playing/Performing a Virtual Puppet

Performance animation – in the sense of a performer animating a virtual character through motion-capture technique – has already made an impact in the animation world as a promising method to invent new styles in 3D animation and to improve production efficiency (Layborne, 1998, pp. 260–61). The integration of motion capture in actual productions is still experimental and every new film that uses the techniques is getting involved with research and development of the methods. Some call motion capture "the devil's rotoscope", being time consuming and difficult to control; others, especially the developers and software designers, believe that it can cut production costs to a minimum. The main challenge is how natural movement of the performer is transformed into digitally animated movement, which is a new interdisciplinary field between performers, film animators and technicians. It raises the question about the education of the performers and animators who have to use the new equipment, and how to perceive the characters they create in relation to the performing arts, which might be very different to that of the animated film.

In his pragmatic book, *Acting for Animators: A Complete Guide to Performance Animation* (2001), Ed Hooks has set the main goal to bridge these two worlds – the stage performers and the film animators – giving film animators insight into acting techniques, and suggesting methods of how to apply them to the special way in which animated characters look, feel and move. Hooks believes that "method acting", which is giving the actor motivation for his actions and letting him live them out on stage, is more suited for performance animation than other formalised acting techniques (Hooks, 2001, p. 4). The main difference between film animators and actors trained for American "method acting" is, according to Hooks, that "actors actually, for real, do it when they are acting", while "animators actually, for real, describe it when they are acting" (Hooks, 2001, p. 6).

In this way Hooks is raising the question about two main elements in storytelling – the dramatic and the epic. The dramatic theatre is conventionally connected with naturalistic and illusionist styles of playing, whereas the epic theatre uses more

Figure 9.2 The material level of the theatre. (a) Dalcroze's Eurythmic method. Sketch by Paulet Thevenaz; (b) accentuation of movement by anticipation. Sketch from Preston Blair's manual on animation for cartoonists (Barba et al., 1992, pp. 176–77).

stylised effects such as stylised movements, puppets, mixed media and introduces the concept of "Verfremdung", which is breaking the illusion.

"Method acting" is a naturalistic acting technique derived from the Russian actor and director Stanislavsky (1863–1938), very much used by film actors. It is a technique primarily evolved for the dramatic theatre, the story, referring back to Aristotle (384–322 BC), told by "the acts of acting persons". Aristotle defined the dramatic art in opposition to the epic, where the story is told – "described" – by a singer or a storyteller.

But Stanislavsky's very important works are also used successfully in combination with epic or "non-naturalistic" theatre forms as the puppet theatre or, for example, in the theatre of the German author and director Brecht (1898–1956). Here the actor is able to switch between "describing it" and "doing it", a combination often referred to as "the Penka-method" after the German actor and teacher Rudolf Penka (1923–88).

Other methods for acting derive from principles based on the material level of the theatre. This form originates in oriental theatre and is actually the basis of many animation techniques, for example "anticipation – action – reaction" patterns. These techniques were introduced in Russia and Europe by Emile Jacques-Dalcroze (1865–1950), Meyerhold (1874–1943) and François Delsarte (1811–71) who developed methods to express emotional states through opposition of rhythm, movement and stylised physical expressions, which had a big influence on modern dance and physical theatre such as pantomime (Barba et al., 1992, pp. 176-77). These techniques are useful for stylising naturalistic movement in order to work with animated characters through motion capture.

9.3.3 Discussion

Applying method acting to performance animation is based on the idea that it will enable actors to perform in virtual environments with a feeling that "they really are acting it out there". But this approach is too optimistic about the abilities of motion capture as a magic tool transforming emotions from a body made out of flesh and blood into a 3D character made out of light projected on a screen. The "pure" method acting approach does not recognise that the nature of the living body and the animated character is fundamentally different and therefore does not have the same way of expressing emotion. It is, traditionally, the job of the animator to master this art form, finding the right stylised movement to induce emotion into the animated character. For this he can edit and insert motion-capture data recorded from the performer, as the film editor is using the possibilities in the footage for a film.

Performance animation for theatrical productions again requires other methods than those in the animation world, since the animation has to be played and edited live for an audience. This is technically challenging both for the character designer/film animator and for the performer, but it also calls for another conception of the actor, which is specific to the modern puppet theatre.

The puppeteer's approach to performance animation is different. As the puppet theatre is using images and puppets as a means of expression "to tell a story", it is principally not "dramatic" but "epic" in its character. Actors, film animators and puppeteers have a very different approach to acting. The actor is trained to work with the character "present" in his own body. The film animator is trained to work with the character "in absentia". The puppeteer is trained to work with the character "present" and "absent" at the same time. Therefore the puppeteer is able to think like the film animator, even though he is a trained actor. The puppeteer then has to invent new acting styles suited to film animation and the film animator/character designer has to design a 3D character that is suited to live action.

For these reasons I wanted to use puppeteers for the experiment. I wanted to use different forms of "mixed reality" to represent the fictional universe and the psychology of the characters on different parallel levels, which appeals to the aesthetics and dramaturgy of the epic puppet theatre. In this way the production of the play, with mixed techniques from animation films, films and modern puppet theatre and with the use of virtual puppets, became a method to expand the concept of virtual reality by turning it into a theatrical space.

9.4 Producing a Play with Virtual Puppets

Initially the production was conceived as a way for three institutions working with animation, theatre and computer science/multimedia to explore the potential of performance animation. Each institution would contribute with their particular methods, resources and skills and evaluate the result from their different perspectives; theoretically, practically and artistically.

The production plan was integrated into an overall research plan starting with research of puppet animation and motion-capture techniques parallel with script writing, then a puppet design phase, followed by the production of the actual performance, and finally an evaluation phase. During the research phase the roles of the participants and their tasks for the remaining phases of the project were also determined. The students from the department of animation directors at the film school in Copenhagen were responsible for the 3D character design and the animated backgrounds in the trick films. The puppeteers from the theatre school "Ernst Busch" in Berlin would participate in developing the play and playing techniques for the virtual puppets and masks. The multimedia department at Aarhus University would be responsible for project management, creative direction and technical support as well as programming of performance animation techniques for the virtual puppets.

Professionals with a background in theatre and multimedia production were hired to bring in experience and secure the quality of the production. A puppet theatre dramaturge and theorist, who followed the research and helped in developing the script would also support the direction and development of the play. A stage designer specialised in projection technique would follow the puppet design phases and finally design the set. The blue-screen recordings would be done in a TV studio, a costume designer would design the costumes and a digital media artist would supervise and help fit all the graphical digital material together.

An overview of the project phases is given in Table 9.1.

Table 9.1 Project phases: An overview.

Period	Activity
Autumn 1999	Research and scriptwriting • puppet animation and motion capture technique • story and characters
January–March 2000	Design of prototypes • character design workshop • 3D modelling/character design • set design • development of performance animation technique
March–April 2000	Development of the play • acting techniques • devising the play • performance animation techniques • programming of animation techniques • programming of mapping techniques • costume design • trick film: blue screen recordings/animated backgrounds • sound design
28–29 April 2000	Performance • the family factory; four performances, Kulturhus Aarhus
Autumn 2000–Spring 2001	Evaluation and exhibition • exhibition; drama and performance animation, World Art, Aalborg, 2–8
October 2000	• video; interviews with participants • seminar; performance animation as a new art form, Aarhus University, 15 June 2001

9.4.1 Scriptwriting and Character Development

The script was written for epic puppet theatre, which in comparison to traditional drama based on the spoken word aims to tell the story through the creation of images on stage. The development of the story, characters and character relations became the backbone of the project, defining what material was needed and which aspects of the virtual puppets to investigate.

Modern puppet theatre often uses the effect that the puppeteer is present on stage playing a character as well as playing the puppet. The relation between the two opens up a lot of interesting dramaturgical possibilities. This had a big influence on the scriptwriting process and the integration of the puppets in the play.

Inspired from a tale by Grimm, *The Tale of Someone Who Went Out to Learn How to Fear*, the story tells of the little girl who on a magic day sees the alter egos of her family members and herself – as a representation of what they really feel and think – behind the façade of the everyday routine. This frightens her and makes her confront the other family members, big sister, father and mother, with what she sees. The confrontation only creates chaos and terror, and she has to bring things

Figure 9.3 Traditional acting techniques. The council flat: morning – afternoon – evening. What actually happens – stylised absurd style of acting.

back to order, by pretending everything is fine, just like the other family members are doing.

These four characters – father, mother and two children – meant there was one part for each of the four participating puppeteers. They would play the characters as traditional human actors on stage and also play different representations of them as virtual puppets, physical masks and filmed characters in small trick films. In this way we would condense the drama into images, often with symbolic meaning, as in short animation films. All these different media were integrated in the story and outlined in the script, which also contained a description of each character.

The virtual puppets would represent the alter egos and show the suppressed emotions. The masks would represent the revelation of the emotions and the confrontation. Trick films with the family members as filmed characters in their own dreams would be showing their urge to forget reality and carry on as if nothing had happened. Figures 9.3–9.7 illustrate how the different levels were established on the stage in the finished production.

Figure 9.4 Virtual puppets. Big sister and her alter ego. She is cynically giving details about a fellow pupil who had a dangerous accident at the School of Ice Dance, where she is an elite student.

Figure 9.5 Masks. The attributes from the virtual puppets become real. Big sister is confronted with her cold ambition and cynicism – her hands are transformed to lethal weapons.

Figure 9.6 Trick film with blue screen animation. Mother's greatest dream. In the animation she is looking at the applauding family from the stage after performing as a celebrated singer in a Jazz club.

Figure 9.7 The steering devices for the virtual puppets were built into little sister's toys. Father is playing with the toys while talking about work, which causes the movement of the virtual puppet. This was a way to integrate the steering devices in the play, but also created an extra level of representation – the story of the toys. This "3. level" should have been much better integrated in the play.

9.4.2 Research of Puppet Animation and Motion Capture Techniques

From the beginning of the project we had to relate our visions of the virtual puppets to the capabilities and constraints of the available real-time 3D animation equipment and the technical expertise of the staff at Aarhus University. It was very important to incorporate the limitations of the hardware and software into the production from the beginning. For example, it would only be realistic to play one virtual puppet at a time. This meant that the script had to be written with this constraint in mind.

The technical team had never worked with real-time 3D animation for an actual performance, but had prior experience in using the equipment for key framed 3D animation based on motion-capture data mainly from dancers. The animations were then played back from tape in the performances "White on White" and "Body Building" (see Kjølner and Szatkowski, Chapter 8 above). This technique is based on the method that the animator is using pre-captured motion as his creative basis for an animation.

What we had to investigate was whether the conception of the actor from the epic puppet theatre would contribute new technical and dramaturgical possibilities concerning the development of performance animation, as I had defined it.

To determine which puppet technique would be useful for the live animated virtual puppets, research in puppetry and motion-capture technique was carried out. This was done in collaboration with teacher and puppeteer Regina Menzel from the theatre school "Ernst Busch" in Berlin. In the first session she demonstrated different types of traditional puppetry techniques for playing marionette and hand puppets. Then, together with the research group, she investigated the possibilities in the magnetic motion-capture equipment (Ascension; Wireless – eight sensors) connected with cables to dummy 3D objects and 3D puppets in the 3D modelling program, Maya. The teacher had never worked with a computer before, but the principles behind motion capture and the mapping of the movement onto the live animated 3D material very quickly and intuitively became clear to her.

Normally, the motion-capture equipment is used by attaching the sensors to vital parts of the body and mapping it on to a virtual skeleton in a 1:1 relation – that is, the arm moves the arm of the skeleton, the head moves the head and so on. Puppet theatre is usually different to this – very often you will only use your hands to control the whole puppet. Intuitively, the teacher started working with the individual sensor and its response in the animated dummy. This seemed to be the obvious way to work for a puppeteer.

One important design decision was already made at this point, which was to deconstruct the motion-capture equipment to reduce complexity so the performer could understand the role of each individual sensor (see Figure 9.8). This decision was also based on practical aspects; if the sensors were attached inside a suit on the body of the performer, there would have been a lot of costume shifting between the actors, since we only had one suit. In this way the sensors could move from person to person on stage.

During this process we identified six challenges which are specific to puppet theatre and which became crucial to the design of the puppets and the integration of them in the play.

1. *The fact that a puppeteer needs to understand and control all the parameters of the puppet.* When the steering device runs through a black box containing complex dynamic inverse kinematics and mapping models that are only accessible by the technician, the puppeteer is highly dependent on the communication to someone else and the skills he represents.

Figure 9.8 Deconstructing the motion-capture equipment. Regina Menzel would work with a combination of single sensors individually manipulated, rather than the traditional full set of sensors attached to the body. In the middle you see the representation of each sensor on the computer screen.

2. *The sensitivity and naturalism of the motion-capture equipment and the inverse kinematics animation algorithms in the live 3D animation engine needed to be stylised, formalised and reduced to create convincing motion of the virtual puppet.* For traditional puppets this is normally a result of the design of the steering device, for example, the strings of the marionette and through the resistance and flexibility of the material of which the puppet is made. In 3D animation everything has to be specified by the computer program and since the available 3D animation engines don't have pre-sets for this kind of features, it had to be specially designed.

3. *The difficulty in establishing a feeling of contact with and control over the virtual puppet in the projected image.* The fact that you can only grasp the object through a steering device is not new to the puppeteer, but the steering technique and the material are new. This challenge is related to the main thesis of the project – that the puppeteer is able to establish this relation intuitively even though the puppet is made out of light on a screen.

4. *The decision to work with "open puppet theatre", where the performer is visible acting on stage while playing the puppet, meant that we would have to develop two acting techniques that worked simultaneously; one for the puppet and one for the gestures of the actor.* In this way the actor/puppeteer would have to play the subtexts of two characters at the same time. This special acting technique is part of the formal training of puppeteers at the Ernst Busch school, but since it is closely related to the playing potential of a puppet, which were unknown at this point, it turned out to be the biggest challenge in the production. In practice, it had to do with integrating the cables in the image presented on stage.

5. *The mapping of the space on stage to the virtual space in the projections had to be different for each scene where a virtual puppet would appear, since the specific mapping configuration had to match the location of the performer.* Most technical performance animation solutions are meant for animation film, broadcast TV or computer games where the performer is hidden from the audience. The built-in virtual representations of the recording space in the studio are presumed to be static. When used for theatrical performances where the performer is visible on stage a lot of specific settings are necessary, since the performer does not use the whole stage all the time. Sometimes a little section of the stage would have to represent the whole virtual stage.

6. *The different media and the playing techniques had to be one unified whole.* The integration of high-tech solutions in stage performances often takes a lot of focus over the traditional elements. It was of great importance that the virtual puppets would be integrated as a new, unique and central expression, but it should not take all the attention.

9.4.3 Design of Virtual Puppets

Designing characters for performance animation is a new challenge for animators and puppeteers. To create a meeting point between the two traditions the animation director students would be given the same role as a traditional puppet maker whose task it is to design puppets for a production. As a group they represented the necessary skills within drawing techniques, character development and basic 3D modelling to make sketches for the virtual puppets. To develop a common understanding of puppet design for a theatrical performance the animators would meet and collaborate with the puppeteers who had to play the characters at an early stage in the design process. For this purpose a workshop was arranged where the teacher, Regina Menzel, and the four puppeteers from Berlin would visit the Film School in Copenhagen.

In this way the puppeteers would be part of the development of the prototypes for the virtual puppets as well as the characters for the play, before the actual rehearsals would begin two months later. The opening session of the workshop was a physical lecture in puppetry technique by Regina Menzel, followed by a session where puppeteers and animators would present their own work to each other.

The design session started with a screening of visual sources of inspiration from computer games, artistic 3D animation and films, followed by an introduction to the story and the characters, after which a lot of sketches were produced (for an example, see Figure 9.9). Most importantly it was decided that all the puppets had to have symbolic attributes, which had to be individually constructed (see the final design in Figure 9.17).

> **Father** a big hand – his false authority
>
> **Mother** wild flaming hair – emotion and aggression
>
> **Big sister** body like a swan and a snake* – power and ambition
>
> **Little sister** big eyes and pockets – openness, curiosity, truth

*this was gradually changed to hands and feet like knives when developing the prototypes.

In the following week the result was reported and uploaded to a website that would function as a mutual workspace for the project. This first workshop was very important for the production because a lot of decisions were made about the design of the prototypes, which otherwise would have been done by the animators and the research team without the influence of the puppeteers.

The first step towards functional prototypes was made in a 3D modelling and performance animation session at the University of Aarhus. In a week the animation directors would develop the sketches and make the first 3D models of the puppets in 3D studio Max with instruction from a 3D modeller. At the end of the session the 3D puppets would be connected to the motion-capture equipment and the software for real-time 3D animation, which was the Filmbox by Kaydara.

The motion-capture session was arranged as an open workshop, where the stage designer and dramaturge would also be present to discuss the development and integration of the prototypes in the performance. For this workshop the stage designer had prepared a model of the stage representing the council flat, into which the puppets could be projected (see Figure 9.10).

click > larger image

Comments

The features of the mothers are that of Gaia, the earth - big, sensual and round - and then the hair, which can get wild, flaming and threatening when she gets angry. The idea with the eyes on the ends of the hair is surreal and very interesting. The style is expressive and it catches the wild side as well as the sensual and protecting side of her. The perspective from above is good since it shows her as a planet - something which is stable and together.
I like the mix of 2D and 3D, which is unusual for realtime 3D animation.

Conclusion

The sensual and wild features are very good together and the edgy style fits with the character, but might be difficult to model in 3D.

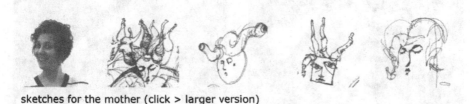

sketches for the mother (click > larger version)

Figure 9.9 Result from the character design workshop. Excerpt from the website. Sketches for the Mother made in collaboration between animation director Martin de Turah and puppeteer Claudia Engel.

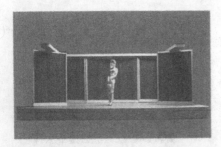
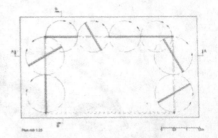

Figure 9.10 Model for the set design representing the council flat. The projection screens were designed as swinging doors, enabling the actors to walk "through" the walls of the flat. This feature was used throughout the play as doors (Figure 9.3) and symbolically in the surreal confrontation scene, where the attributes of the virtual puppets materialise as masks (Figure 9.5).

After presenting the model of the set and its functions in the play, we would discuss issues about the "virtual set" in the projections. A stage designer normally has decisive influence on the entire set design including the costumes and the lighting. This design task was different because the final visual appearance of the puppets, including the textures for their surfaces, would be done in collaboration between animators and puppeteers at the final puppet design session 5 weeks before the premiere. Until now the designer had designed the council flat as an empty projection space, with built-in movement possibilities for the actors. The visual appearance was left open. We decided that she would do the digital backdrops for the virtual puppets, which were going to be scanned wallpaper and that she would supervise the integration of the virtual puppets. At this stage we also agreed on a paper-like quality in textures for the puppets, since they were going to "live inside the wallpaper".

At this early stage of the project, when we were still working with models and prototypes, almost every member in the production team had been involved in the design of the virtual puppets. I believe this is one of the reasons that we succeeded in integrating the different elements to a whole. The value of the actual meetings and workshops cannot be emphasised enough. This gave the participants hands-on experience with the constraints in the actual equipment and a chance to meet the

Figure 9.11 The first functional prototype for two of the four virtual puppets; little sister and big sister.

team that would be responsible for operating it. It is not until the artist has a very physical and intuitive impression of the material and the people involved that the creative process takes off for real – before this everything is abstract ideas. Another important factor was that the fundamental elements in the story and the characters were designed for the available technical equipment and were outlined in the sketches and the script, which motivated and focused the development of the prototypes. As we will see further on in the evaluation (Section 9.6) this phase should have been extended before entering the actual production phase, ensuring that all members had an operational common language based on the actual possibilities – both technically and aesthetically.

9.5 Production and Rehearsals

9.5.1 Developing the Acting Style

In the production phase the virtual puppets and their playing techniques were developed stepwise as prototypes towards the final design along with the play. One important factor was the integration of the virtual puppets with the acting style of the puppeteers playing the family members (Figure 9.4 and 9.17). In the first rehearsals we would try out a naturalistic acting style, but it was difficult to combine naturalistic expressions with the 3D style of the puppets. This was especially problematic when we had to develop movements that both had to work for the character on stage and create movement for the puppet in the projection. Instead the puppeteers would develop humorist, stylised and absurd movement patterns which underlined the individual characteristics of the characters and the tragicomic nature of the play. This would allow the integration of non-naturalistic movement when animating the puppets and made it easier to develop animation techniques.

Figure 9.12 Developing stylised physical expressions for the characters on stage.

9.5.2 Developing Steering and Playing Techniques

The next challenge was the development of steering techniques for the puppets and the integration of them in the rehearsals. The magnetic sensors were attached to cables and would be visible on stage to the audience no matter how we tried to disguise them in the set. In the search for a natural way to integrate them on stage we decided to make them "built-in" features of the toys of little sister (Figure 9.7). In this way the person playing with the toys is controlling his or her virtual puppet. The next and closely related problem was how to map the movement of each sensor, now inside a toy, onto the virtual puppet and how the movement should affect the steering mechanism of the puppet. Another decision to make was how to work with the mapping of the physical space onto the virtual space in different translations.

These problems have two dimensions, one is the technical design of the steering mechanism and the other is the meaning and the dramaturgical function of it. Both had to be developed at the same time, since they are two sides of the same coin. This is a well-known challenge in traditional puppet theatre production, but knowing this did not prevent the main problems, because of the rather complex relations between software, hardware, virtual and physical space.

The Filmbox software by Kaydara offers a good GUI (graphical user interface) for representing the performer, the virtual character and the mapping of movement between them (Figure 9.13). The software is mainly designed for studio production concerning traditional animation for film and broadcast TV. In this kind of

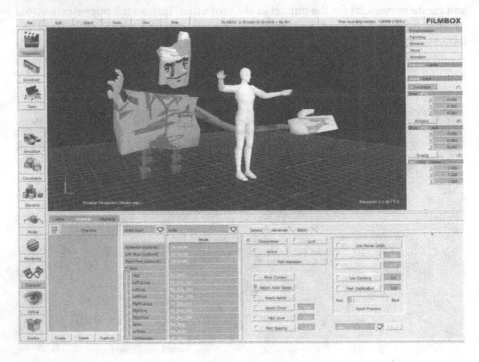

Figure 9.13 Representation of the virtual puppet as well as the actor in the Filmbox.

production the movements of the performer are hidden from the audience and have no meaning. The space in which he moves is normally a static square on the floor in the studio to which the sensors are calibrated.

In performance animation for puppet theatre, where the performer and the hardware through which he is playing is visible on stage as well as the virtual puppet, the gestures of the performer and the design of the hardware have meaning: Being a part of the presented image on stage, they are telling a part of the story. Furthermore, the relation between the physical space on stage and the virtual space has to be mapped towards the specific space in which the performer is actually moving at the time. This makes the design of the physical and virtual steering mechanism, the calibration of the sensors and the direction of the play a highly integrated process.

The Filmbox is specialised software for studio production of motion-captured real time and key framed animation, but very importantly it contains a spreadsheet for programming alterations to the pre-sets in the mapping and calibration of the captured motion. In praxis this meant that most of the features that we wanted to develop could be individually programmed.

This put very great pressure on the programmer and took a lot of focus away from the actual rehearsing sessions with the virtual puppets in the development of the play. One of the problems was that the programming language in the spreadsheet was a restricted high-level programming language, allowing only certain modifications of the features in the Filmbox. Another problem was that this task could only be carried out by the programmer, since there were no user-friendly GUI for what we wanted.

These were problems on the technical level, but they very soon became problems on the level of content also. The theatrical actions often had a hard time to match up with the steering mechanisms, manipulated by actors, who had to make sense out of playing with toys on the stage.

For a clearer understanding of the different types of movement and their meaning in the theatre it is useful to distinguish between the proxemic and the gestural movement of the puppet. The proxemic movement refers to the movement of the puppet through space, whereas the gestural movement concerns gestures and facial mimic of the puppet (Tillis, 1999). In traditional motion-capture studios for animation production the mapping between the performer and the animated character normally concerns the gestural movement. In this way the arm of the performer's hand can be calibrated and connected to the paw of a 3D dog, the elbow to the joint on the leg and so on.

As mentioned, we were introducing other techniques on this level by deconstructing the motion-capture equipment. The development of the gestural mapping techniques can be compared to the way puppet makers develop unique and sophisticated steering techniques for physical puppets by interconnecting the joints and attaching steering devices for the performer. These challenges are known in performance animation and supported by the tools in the Filmbox software and in the inverse kinematics skeletons in the 3D modelling programmes (Figure 9.13).

On the level of the proxemic movement, however, a difficult range of important mapping tasks emerged during the rehearsals with the virtual puppets on stage. Sometimes we wanted a small area on stage to represent the entire virtual stage – for example, moving the sensor a little bit on stage causes an enormous movement in the virtual space – sometimes we wanted the opposite (Figure 9.14).

The mapping and the calibration became important tools for the direction of the play, concerning the following questions: How do the characters move in space? From where do they enter the stage? What is the relation between the proxemic movement of virtual characters and that of the physical actors? In this way the new techniques offered a lot of dramaturgical possibilities and concerned important choices for the direction. These mapping techniques are unique to the theatre and were only indirectly supported in the Filmbox software, which meant that all of the important choices in the direction of the virtual puppets had to be individually programmed. This became one of the major challenges in the production, since the rehearsals and directing process became heavily influenced by technical issues and was constantly interrupted and delayed due to this.

Being problematic the development of the proxemic movement for the puppets also offered a lot of options known from film but new to the puppeteers because they are not possible with physical puppets. The movement of a magnetic sensor back and forth was programmed to "zoom" the puppet gradually from small to large. The movement across stage was thus programmed as a "pan" effect created by moving a sensor from side to side. Another technique developed was the "cut" from total to close up, which was done by turning a sensor 90 degrees as a kind of switch. In this way the puppeteer had to develop a technique for live film editing (Callesen, 2001), not playing the puppet directly but playing how it is framed. Some of these techniques are known from shadow theatre, where the movement of the puppet away from the screen causes it to grow in size (Schönewolf, 1968; Wilpert, 1982) but this application is completely new and far more sophisticated. The mapping technique for the gestural movement of the puppet concerning the articulation of

Figure 9.14 Mapping the space on stage onto virtual space in the projections. The surface of the little sister's table (20 cm) represents a zoom distance in the projection from barely visible (left corner of left picture) towards full size (right picture).

the gestures and the facial mimic also had to be specially programmed in the spreadsheet, since the Filmbox is designed for a 1:1 relation between the physical actor and the animated character. It is possible to make modifications in an easy direct manipulation interface – for example, letting the hand of the actor move the leg of the animated character – which, as mentioned, is useful if you have to animate a four-legged animal.

For the performance, the mapping task became complex and difficult to handle because we were using the deconstructed motion-capture technique to combine the gestural and the proxemic movement with special settings for each unique puppet.

The gestural movement used can be described as different combinations of inclination and rotation of the individual body parts, which derives from the techniques of Dalcroze. The proxemic movement was largely based on filmic techniques, such as the zoom, pan and cut, which in combination with the more traditional gestural techniques created a rather unique style of virtual puppet animation.

Through the development of the unique steering techniques the programmer became heavily involved in both the design of the puppets and also the direction of the play.

This role is somehow comparable not only to that of the puppet maker but also to that of the cameraman in the feature film, where the camera is the funnel through which everything has to move before it becomes actual (Seeger and Whetmore, 1994). The mapping of the proxemic movement in space from the actor's movement also involved the programmer heavily in the direction – having constantly to readjust the figures to the latest result. In this way the programmer had to communicate with the director, the character designer and the puppeteer, which meant understanding the intentions and work language of three different traditions. This obviously caused a lot of communication problems and too much responsibility for important artistic decisions.

During the rehearsals individual puppet animation training sessions were made with each puppeteer to develop the playing technique and allow the puppeteer to become familiar with the sensors and the particular puppet. The puppets would be played behind the actors most of the time, which meant that they had to play them

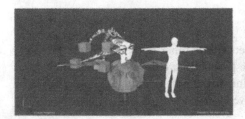

Figure 9.15 Programming the attributes of the mother; skeleton and steering techniques for her hair. Each strand of hair contained a skeleton, that was manipulated by a marker (the red boxes), centrally controlled by the rotation of the head. By introducing variations in the distance between the centre of the head and the markers a lot of dramatic effects could be created by rotating a single sensor.

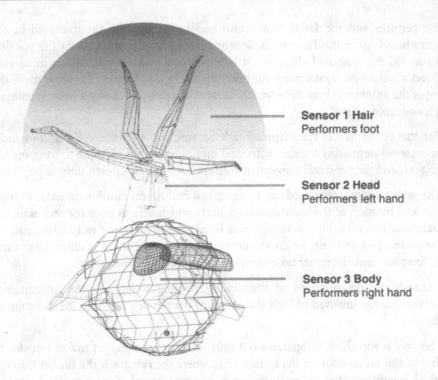

Sensor 1 Hair
Performers foot

Sensor 2 Head
Performers left hand

Sensor 3 Body
Performers right hand

Figure 9.16 Deconstructing the motion-capture equipment and combining gestural and proxemic animation techniques for each unique puppet. Sensor 1 was attached to the foot of the performer spreading the strands of hair when turned from 0 to 45 degrees; Sensor 2 was inside a toy and held in the performers left hand – it controlled rotation and inclination of the head; Sensor 3 was inside a toy in the performers right hand – moving the puppet in space through the zoom and the pan function (Callesen, 2001).

blindly – while facing the audience. To help them, the puppeteers would have a monitor situated above the audience, but still a lot of training was necessary to master this difficult task. At this point we were faced with the difficult task of balancing the development time, when the technician would use the equipment in order to finish the steering mechanism, and the rehearsing time, when the puppeteers would learn how to master it.

9.5.3 Putting It All Together

Parallel to the development of the puppets all the other elements for the play were created as in a traditional puppet theatre production: costumes, masks, trick films, sound design etc. In the process of combining all the elements a lot of ends had to be tied up and a lot of pragmatic solutions were necessary.

Since a lot of the elements were digital and worked on continuously by different people, the help of the graphic designer and digital media artist became extremely important. His experience with digital media production and work with tight deadlines helped us to get the best out of the produced material and to create a final

Figure 9.17 The final puppet design.

finish and a unified expression on stage. This work included the colouring of the textures made by the animators, digital blue screen montage of the trick films in the dream sequences and finally designing the poster and the programme for the performance.

A complicated part was to build control devices for different media. The virtual puppet could only be shown on one screen at a time, so we built a switching system that enabled it to be projected onto any of the four projection screens (Figure 9.20). When the virtual puppet was off, i.e. shown on another screen, it would be replaced by a digital backdrop showing the wall paper implemented as a Macro Media Director slide show.

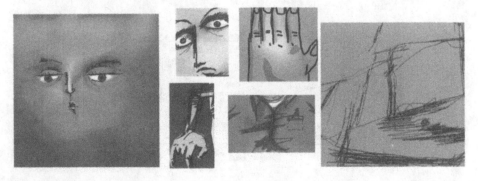

Figure 9.18 Some texture maps for the final puppet design.

Figure 9.19 Green screen recordings for the trick films showing family dreams. Excerpt from Gregor's (father) fishing trip feeding the family members.

With the VGA switches 1–4 we could shift between the virtual puppets and the digital backdrops. In this way we could place the virtual puppet on any screen we wanted, while the other screens would show digital backdrops controlled by the Macro Media Director. In the loading time for the virtual puppets, digital backdrops were shown on all four screens. VGA switch 0 allowed us to show a video sequence instead of the virtual puppet, which was used for the trick films in the dream sequences. The projectors were hidden under the stage floor to save space. The projections were then reflected back onto the screens by the use of mirrors.

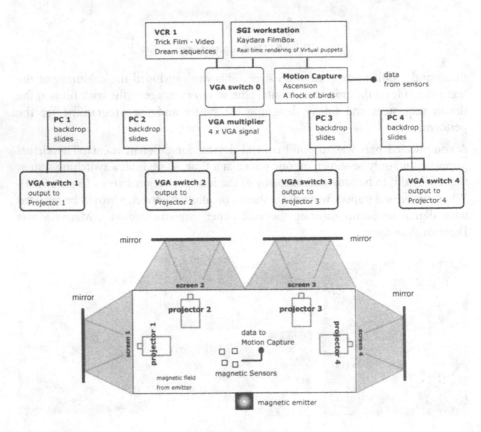

Figure 9.20 The technical set-up.

In the dream sequences the virtual puppet would be replaced by videotaped trick films shown on only one projection screen. During the trick film digital backdrops would appear on the three other screens, matching the background in the trick film. This meant that the technical crew had to shift digital backdrop every time the background changed in the trick film, which was a difficult synchronisation job that they had to rehearse several times.

The final process was very rewarding. It was fantastic to see so many different expressions from different genres coming to life on stage – trick films, 3D animation, digital backdrops, projection design etc., together with the traditional theatrical expressions – which showed that digital multimedia is very useful in this kind of theatre production.

9.5.4 The Result

The final result was a 50-minute performance in Aarhus, 28–29 April 2000, played four times in a theatre seating 40 people each time. The audience was a quite mixed theatre audience ranging from children to adults and naturally including interested researchers, puppeteers and animators.

It took a crew of three people behind the stage to control light, sound, digital backdrops, to load the virtual puppets and control the switchboard for the projections and another four people to help in fitting the masks on the puppeteer for the chaos scene.

9.6 Evaluation and Discussion of Methods

The evaluation of a theatre production or a film is normally carried out by critics, audiences and academics. In this production I had the twin role of scriptwriter and artistic director as well as researcher, which influences my analytical distance to the work.

I will leave others to judge the content and the artistic quality of the play and instead focus on a discussion of the play as a research result from the perspective of the participants and from my perspective as a researcher.

9.6.1 The Main Problem

As discussed in the introduction, the integration of a theatre production in a research project raises the question about how to evaluate a creative process with scientific methods and what function the production has for the research and vice versa.

In the planning of the research project and the actual production the division of labour within and between each field of activity were specified as outlined in Section 9.4. As the process went on, the borders became more blurred, exploring the new field between creative production in theatre and animation and methods from computer science and systems development. One of the big challenges was the development of a common language between the artist and the programmer/technicians and to define and invent new methods that were necessary to carry out the production.

I tried to explore the numerous reasons for this in the evaluation phase of the project. This was done by conducting qualitative interviews with the participants and by reviewing the large body of video documentation from the process. The footage was edited to a 50-minute documentary about the project on which the following assumptions are based (Callesen, 2001).

9.6.2 Interviews

Because of the many simultaneous activities and many different disciplines involved, creative productions in film and theatre are difficult to evaluate and describe. Furthermore, there are often personal questions involved about the relations between the participants, their artistic intentions and integrity.

A common way to gain insight about what happened behind the scenes in a production is through interviews with the artists and technicians involved, such as that done in the book by Seeger and Whetmore, *From Script to Screen: The Collaborative Art of Film-making* (1994).

Because of the experimental character of the project and the complicated combination of methods I chose to make video interviews with the participants, myself included, to reveal both the benefits and the problems of the project for the individual artists and the tradition they represent.

In the following part I have written out significant parts from these interviews, and in some cases commented on them. As the sentences are taken out of their actual context, some explanations had to be added.

Gunnar Wille

(Leader of the animation department at The National Film School of Denmark)

For the students of the animation department the project is a way to gain experience with a production involving performance animation and motion-capture techniques. Because the technology is so new, there is very little reliable production experience to draw from. Motion capture and performance animation are new crayons and pencils for artists to use – so why not use them!

In this project my students got the opportunity to design four characters for real-time animation with motion capture. Motion capture has a tendency of being used very naturalistically – but to make it work you have to make the movements simpler – and puppeteers know how to do that! The collaboration with puppeteers is interesting in this perspective. The puppeteer is trained to reduce the movement to what is necessary and sufficient.

During the process the puppets functioned well and as you would have expected. But because of the lack of technical resources only some of the potential of the puppets were used on stage. Therefore they did not work so well and that is a shame. It reduced the communication from stage a lot, and it is of course more satisfying to see that your product is completely finished.

Konstanza Kavrakowa-Lorenz

(Leader of the department for The Art of Puppetry, (Puppenspielkunst) at Hochschule für Schauspielkunst "Ernst Busch", Berlin)

Our wish to partake in the experiment came out of a curiosity about the meeting between two very different materials – linking a 3D computer animation to an act of theatre.

The meeting between the students and the new material was very interesting and showed a lot of new possibilities, the puppets were well designed, the story was well written and the scenic realisation well outlined.

Regina Menzel

(Teacher of puppetry techniques at the department for The Art of Puppetry, (Puppenspielkunst) at Hochschule für Schauspielkunst "Ernst Busch", Berlin)

In the beginning I had no positive feeling at all – computer animation to me was foreign to the theatre – it did not fit together. When I play puppet theatre I have my own time scale – I am not exact, I am not a machine. I therefore see possibilities when you animate virtual puppets live. The sensitivity of the motion-capture equipment is very high. You are actually forced to work through the eye only, and the transmission from the player to the material is different to that of physical puppets. Therefore you work on the mercy of the technology – you cannot interfere directly as with the marionette through the strings or even more directly with the hand puppet as an extension of your hand.

Comment

The two leaders of the more traditional form of education are both seeing the performance as an artistic event in the context of the known possibilities of their art form. They are finding it interesting, and they are both recognising the new possibilities. For the leader of the puppetry department the project was seen as a starting point for developing the aesthetics and dramaturgy of virtual puppets. Since performance animation is not planned to become an integrated part of their curriculum at the moment the technical integration problems were commented on with professional curiosity.

The teacher is naturally focusing on the skill needed, and realises the fine line between being controlled by or being in control of the technique. As a puppetry technique teacher she was able to give a very precise analysis of the problems concerning the development of training methods. She is aware that it will take a lot of specialised training to master this specific puppet technique, as it does with other puppets, for example, the marionette.

For the animation department of the Film School the project was an opportunity to gain experience within a field which will have major influence on the future development of their skills and tradition. The opinions about the actual developed animation techniques are naturally stronger and more critical.

To deconstruct the motion-capture equipment and develop live animation techniques for the stage introduced complicated programming tasks and prevented immediate results with the available equipment. It would have been more natural and relevant for them to let the puppeteer be hidden from the audience, only playing the puppet in the projection. This would definitely have meant another concept, another "story" for the performance to tell, but would have made the task easier for the puppeteer not having to play two roles at the same time, and be more like a "traditional" motion capture studio setting.

Kim Halskov Madsen

(*Leader, Multimedia Department, Aarhus University*)

In multimedia research you have to find new uses of the digital technologies. By doing so in practice, something will often show up. This is what happened here.

In this project we can see how important design and aesthetics is. Often technological approaches only focus on the technical aspects of motion-capture equipment. In this case it is actually not the technique giving life to the characters, but the character design in combination with the technique.

We have earlier done experiments with motion capture for dance and 3D animation and this shows yet other completely new and different uses of the technology. On the basis of these results we have to develop new scientific methods that integrate the practical knowledge and production methods of the artist from different genres and traditions.

Martin de Turah

(*Animation Director, the animation department at The National Film School of Denmark, second year*)

The idea was to design the character together with the puppeteers. They should be the creators of their puppets – we should be the tool for them to do it on the computer.

Because the control of the puppet is in their hands, they are bringing in a completely different dimension, as when you construct the movement frame by frame like in a traditional animation film.

One major problem was that what we wanted to do together in the first character design workshop was very far from what was actually possible, so we had to create it later in the process. We lacked the knowledge of the technical constraints and a technically developed language from the beginning.

It was all very exciting with the story, but we should have taken it much further – "you could lift a sensor and it would start to rain ..."

Nadia El Said

(Animation Director, the animation department at The National Film School of Denmark, second year)

One thing is to design the character – another is to model it. Perhaps the best method would be that some are designing and others are modelling. Maybe we should look at the division of roles in traditional animation and transfer it to this new field. As it was, everything was a bit mixed up. The techniques were not mastered well enough, which at times made the work process difficult. It takes many years of practice to master professional 3D modelling and we have just been introduced to it recently.

Christian Ballund

(Animation Director, the animation department at The National Film School of Denmark, second year)

The new digital tools seem to give a freedom – but it is a strange kind of freedom, because if all the new possibilities opened are not controlled very well things get out of hand. We should have had a clearer division of the roles – you do this, I do this. It could also have been very interesting participating in other parts of the production, such as the direction and the framing and staging of the virtual puppets. But I admit this would make the definition of roles even more complicated.

Rikke Hallund

(Animation Director, the animation department at The National Film School of Denmark, second year)

There was a very good connection between the actor and the animated alter ego – that came out very well – which I did not believe when we were making the sketches in the character design workshop. I think it ended up in harmony because the actors were present from the beginning, representing and defining the personalities of the characters.

Inka Arlt

(Puppeteer, Department for the Art of Puppetry (Puppenspielkunst) at Hochschule für Schauspielkunst "Ernst Busch", Berlin, third year)

This tendency in computer animation – more, quicker, better – is a contradiction to puppetry: here you are always working with the limitations of the actual puppet.

Perhaps it might be a good idea to have a supervisor in such projects between art and technology – one who knows both sides and can act as a kind of referee when problems occur and explain to both parties what is wrong. The technicians don't know how difficult it is to rehearse and we don't know how difficult it is to program the virtual puppets. The technical aspects and finding a way to talk about them consumed a lot of time. At points I was about to scream "I need a technician that understands me and I need him NOW!" In the end I had the feeling that there were different playing possibilities with the puppet and that I could establish contact with it, but this came far too late in the process.

Claudia Engel

(*Puppeteer, Department for the Art of Puppetry* (*Puppenspielkunst*) *at Hochschule für Schauspielkunst "Ernst Busch", Berlin, third year*)

The programmer, Peter, was nice. But it was difficult to communicate – you felt you had to ask all the time: "Please make my puppet do this". The rehearsals in the last days was very rewarding, I could play my part with the puppet and this as my specified task gave me a good feeling.

Comment

Common for the puppeteers is the problem of not understanding and not being understood at a technical level. They knew what they wanted intuitively but it was hard work finding a way of expressing it. The technician has to service the puppeteer, but does not know which point is crucial, and is not trained how to listen to the artist. What is expressed very clearly in one language is not understood in the other, and so the process can at times be a very fatiguing one, and is accumulating problems over time.

On the other hand, the puppeteers were very quick to adopt the techniques and playing possibilities, but they were also very critical towards the actual use of the virtual puppets. The big challenge was developing the techniques and expressions for the virtual puppets and at the same time finding dramaturgical motivation for them based on the story in the script. Sometimes the technical difficulties made this process a bit hard and a lot of interesting possibilities were rejected even though they were very promising. On the other hand it was very important, because it was through this process we developed the actual expression and made the final decisions.

The animators were to a higher degree concerned about the professional relevance and integration of the techniques in their own field of activity. The process revealed that performance animation for theatrical productions involves different problems and methods, but even so, they saw it as an important meeting with other professions with whom they will have to collaborate and find inspiration to develop their own methods.

Peter Skaarup

(Programmer, Multimedia Department, Aarhus University)

It was a great challenge to program the steering algorithms for the hair of the mother, but it was also one of the greatest successes, since it could not have been done in another way – using the motion-capture equipment so indirectly. Programmed animation is a funny art of programming. Suddenly the programmer becomes involved in the creation of the animations – finding out what does the puppeteer, what does the animator want it to do. Suddenly the programmer has to analyse the problem and evaluate if it is possible or not. There is definitely a communication problem – between theatre and the technology. Nevertheless the technology has to be adapted to human conditions – the other way round it is only interesting to the technician and not to the audience.

Comment

There are different ways to solve this problem, known from most creative disciplines employing programmers. One way is to educate programmers to become specially trained technicians who know the language of the creative personnel; another way is by teaching the creative personnel to use the tools themselves or to develop new and special tools based on their skills.

For this purpose a direct manipulation interface for mapping different stage areas onto the virtual material would have been a fantastic tool. With such a tool the mapping could have been done quickly and allowed easy integration with the stage direction, whereas it now has to be specified by the programmer, consuming valuable rehearsing time.

On a professional level the games development community have gained quite a lot of experience with this field, because in games you are also concerned with "programmed" live 3D animation, which brings the programmer into the core of the creative production process. Sometimes he is the one inventing new creative solutions within the domain of the character designer, at other times he is developing tools that facilitates his work and sometimes the character designer and the programmer is even the same person (Rollings and Morris, 2000, pp. 163-93). Mastering this balance is a completely new skill, which will have to be developed for the stage arts as it has been done within the games development community.

Signe Krogh

(Stage designer, Copenhagen)

I have always done "real" theatre settings. This one had to be an empty shell for projections. It is fun to solve a design task with another goal – the goal here was not to see it as I have done it but to see it for what it would be when the virtual puppets and their digital backdrops were projected onto the stage. But it is not convenient that some people are in Aarhus, some in Copenhagen and some in Berlin. You have to be there in the seconds when the decisions are taken. Otherwise the train has departed. You have to be far more involved in the other people's work. In such a process nothing belongs to anyone – nothing has to be finished before anything else – everything is developing continuously – you need another work process than the one I am used to.

Seen as a whole it was a true experiment – and I think it is very important to work in a way where the expression is unknown and unexpected, but the outcome has a purpose!

The Audience

The involvement of the audience in finding out whether prototypes or artistic pieces are understood and are pleasing or interesting is a difficult task from an artistic point of view, raising the question of artistic integrity. From a research perspective it is easier to motivate scientific analysis of the audiences.

The new conventions involving performance animation played by actors and even influenced by the audience themselves, might be so new and difficult to understand, that it would be a good idea to try out prototypes with the audience in test rooms. Another option is to conduct surveys after performances to find out what it actually means to them. I see this as an important source of information, but it was not carried out in this project due to a priority of resources.

9.6.3 Managing the Project

To make a performance was crucial for the whole idea of the experiment. From an artistic point of view it is the audience who evaluate the performance, they are creating the images in their minds and it is their response and experience that counts. The reactions indicated that it had the impact I had hoped for and sometimes something completely unexpected and very pleasing reflections turned up too. For me as a researcher/artist the process was very rewarding – the whole team was working to investigate my thesis and develop a play from my artistic intention, but it was also a great challenge and responsibility.

Sometimes I was criticised from all sides. I was moving into different professions with a goal to match the high level of artistic skills in the different fields. This of course was not possible, and not just because the academic research environment is not meant for artistic production.

In the course of the process it became obvious that my responsibility for the project as a project manager on the one side and the many different tasks – debut as a scriptwriter, artistic director – and at the same time researcher on the other side, was too big a challenge, and a reason behind some of the problems (e.g. the problem of not using the full potential of the virtual puppets). Thanks to the training, skill, independence and engagement of the puppeteers, they managed to create the performance with a minimum of actual "directing" from me. Furthermore, I had help from the dramaturge supporting the directing by the puppeteers and the management in relation to the development of the script with the puppeteers and me.

To make laboratory experiments with the new animation techniques is something other than an actual performance. First, when the experiments have been through the whole production process and are telling a story and meaning something for somebody you are able to see whether they possess any new and different qualities or not.

My goals as a researcher/artist were reached. First of all, the integration of the artistic means by the establishment of all the layers of the story through the media in a way that every part was motivated and had a function in the play. Secondly, the creation of the virtual puppets, which could be played by the acting puppeteer. Finally, the play allows us to experience the qualities and problems of integrating puppetry in performance animation on the premises of art.

As a researcher I will have to find means to prove it on the premises of science too, which raises another problem related to time management and planning of the research project. The production is very easily the full focus of the process, because it is very time consuming and the artistic staff require and deserve your full engagement in the production period. In this way it is very difficult to perform ongoing theoretical research while the production is running.

9.6.4 The Different Momentum in Artistic Production and Academic Research

In a project where the most important expression requires the development of new interdisciplinary methods and skills the momentum of an actual production motivates and forces the participants into a learning process exchanging practical knowledge and experience. Without the project the academic has no access to the knowledge and skills that are involved in the creative process. Nevertheless both the benefits and the problems in mixing the methods derive from the fact that an academic research process and an artistic production process not only have different goals but also a very different momentum.

A production process is, for the artist, driven by a mutual and emotional understanding of the goal of the project, which is to create the best expression to carry the message with the given resources. To reach that goal the artist uses methods specific to their discipline and tradition, which are often learnt through practice and therefore very intuitive and implicit. Within the time frame a lot of possibilities in the given material are tried out, leading to the decisive and crucial choices determining the final character and expression of the product.

A theatre and a film production is a large collaborative effort, where the whole team is involved in maintaining a flow supporting all the parallel processes. It is often described as a train you constantly have to catch and figure out what direction it is taking (Seeger and Whetmore, 1994). It is of great importance to underline that artists are trained to work with the material in a flow having a strong intuitive feeling of the direction it takes. When the product is finished, the work is done, the tension is released and all the rejected options might be used for something else, but this will be a new production – a new performance.

To the academic multimedia researcher and systems developer the performance might not be the only goal. It might be just as important to formulate thesis and theories about the meaning and nature of the work process, not only for the developed expression and its context but for the rejected options as well.

The research process has another momentum, which in this case started before the production and is resulting in an analytic discourse after the production is finished. This might result in a new product.

Based on the knowledge derived from this discourse the researcher is able to suggest uses of digital media, which are conceptually new, and to indicate how they might apply to a specific genre. That again can open doors that are closed to the practically oriented artist, explain complex technical and theoretical concepts and point in new interesting directions.

9.6.5 Methods for Bridging

The main problem with this kind of research is that the researcher is often satisfied with gaining an analytical understanding of the tools and the medium, whereas the artist wants to gain experience by using it.

Through actual use, the artist develops an implicit understanding which is often very different to the understanding of the researcher. To compensate for this difference, methods developed within participatory design and HCI, such as prototyping, mock-ups and analysis of the work process, can be used to create a mutual understanding between developer and user. This is a very useful and constructive approach for applications within office environments, homes, administration and production units. For the artist however the use of prototypes as an integrated part of the creative process is familiar. For the artist there is a very thin line between prototype and product, where a series of prototypes (in this case "rehearsals") normally leads to the final product. When the researcher gets involved with the artist's creation of prototypes, he or she will inevitably influence the artistic process and therefore be involved in the momentum of the production, which can be problematic because of the lack of talent and production experience.

Seen from the other side the researcher invents features and makes things explicit to point out new possibilities – both conceptually and technically – which is a part of the job, whereas the artist only wishes it done when necessary for the intentions of the production. The analytic praxis of the researcher can then be destructive to the creative process, because it disturbs the flow and opens too many new possibilities endangering the project never to end.

The challenge is how to balance experimental design methods developed by multimedia researchers with methods applied by the artists themselves. The "McPie" project (Horn et al., 2001) is a good example of applying systems development methods from participatory design and HCI (human–computer interaction) research to the production of an audience-controlled performance animation installation. Even though it was driven by systems developers and researchers and lacks the momentum of a production involving artists, it provides insight to the integration of useful methods such as mock-ups, design scenarios and video documentation of work processes. These methods are developed by multimedia researchers, but they might be useful for artists if they are modified and integrated in the artistic production process, for example supporting puppeteers and directors in developing a GUI for the Kaydara Filmbox, specially designed for the mapping and calibration of proxemic and gestural movement on the fly while rehearsing and directing.

9.7 Conclusion

The performance and the work processes behind it provide empirical evidence to at least three areas of interest within multimedia research.

1. The development of performance animation tools and production methods for animators and puppeteers.
2. The creation of new digital expressions for the performing arts.
3. The development of a theoretical framework to describe and explore the potential of performance animation and the use of virtual puppets and autonomous agents in mixed reality installations and other contexts.

As an art form performance animation is very promising but also very immature. Artistic research in performance animation for the stage arts can create an important meeting point between artists and scientists, because it involves so many different theoretical and practical aspects of real-time animation concerning theatrical, filmic and technological matters.

This experiment shows how an actual production can be such a meeting point and outlines its benefits and problems. It shows the importance of developing methods to create artistic evidence useful for the development of new techniques for the practically oriented production environment, which is also theoretically relevant to the scientific community. From a professional producer's point of view the production was too early and experimental regarding the prior knowledge and experience of the technology used.

Within artistic research, however, it is exactly this uncertainty which is a mutual task for the researcher and the artist to investigate. Through this process they might create outstanding artworks or interesting prototypes developing the art form. In my experience, therefore, both academic research methods and artistic methods are very relevant to develop new expressions in multimedia, but new methods have to be developed where the research process can be driven by the artist's intuitive investigation of the new material and development of the expression and not only by an analytical discourse about the process and the result, which is the norm in traditional HCI research. To do so academics and researchers working with multimedia need to know more about artistic production methods, and they need to respect and validate the intuitive "research" methods of the artist, who come from environments where skills and methods are often developed through practice. The work in developing a theoretical platform, using drama and puppetry theories for understanding the problems of the new media, has got valuable empirical evidence for further investigation, and is to be continued.

Acknowledgments

Information and Media Science, Aarhus University, Denmark – artistic director, concept and story: *Jørgen Callesen*; programming: *Peter Skaarup*; 3D modelling instruction: *Ruben Borup*; sound and slides: *Anders Brødsgaard*; production assistant: *Nana Benjaminsen*.

Hochschule für Schauspielkunst "Ernst Busch" Berlin, Abt. Puppenspielkunst, Germany – research: *Regina Menzel*; acting and directing: *Inka Arlt, Claudia Engel, Matthias Ludvig and Louise Danckert*.

The National Film School of Denmark, Copenhagen, Animation Instructors – character design and animated backgrounds: *Christian Ballund, Nadia El Said, Rikke Hallund, Kasper Kruse, Anders Morgenthaler and Martin De Thurah*.

Stage designer: *Signe Krogh*; Dramaturge: *Jette Lund*; costume designer: *Marie Halebro*.

Digital video editing/graphic design: *Jacob Tekiela*, Sampler-Copenhagen; 3D animation/post production: *Morten/Square one, Copenhagen*; English translation: *Andrea Earl*; documentation/editing of documentary: *Lise Jul Pedersen, Aarhus Film Workshop, Denmark*; evaluation/interviews: *Kim Halskov Madsen, Regina Menzel, Konstanza Kavrakowa-Lorenz, Gunnar Wille*.

References

Andersen, PB and Callesen, J (2001). Agents as Actors, in L Qvortrup (ed.), *Virtual Interaction: Interaction in Virtual Inhabited 3D Worlds*. London: Springer.

Barba, E, Savarese, N and Fowler, R (1992). *A Dictionary of Theatre Anthropology: The Secret Art of the Performer*. London: Routledge.

Bendazzi, G (1994). *Cartoons: One Hundred Years of Cinema Animation*. Indianapolis: Indiana University Press.

Callesen, J (2001). Virtual Puppets in Performance, in *Proceedings of the Marionette: Metaphysics, Mechanics, Modernity, International Symposium*, University of Copenhagen, 28 March–1 April 2001.

Hooks, E (2001). *Acting for Animators: A Complete Guide to Performance Animation*. Portsmouth, NH: Heinemann.

Horn, B, Svendsen, EH and Madsen, KH (2001). Experimental Design of an Interactive Installation, in L. Qvortrup (ed.), *Virtual Interaction: Interaction in Virtual Inhabited 3D Worlds*. London: Springer.

Kaplin, S (1994). Puppetry into the Next Millennium, *Puppetry International* 1, 37–39.

Kaplin, S (1999). A Puppet Tree: A Model for the Field of Puppet Theatre, *The Drama Review* 43 (3), New York University and the Massachusetts Institute of Technology.

Layborne, K (1988). *The Animation Book: A Complete Guide to Animated Filmmaking – From Flip-Books to Sound Cartoons to 3-D Animation*. New York: Three Rivers Press.

Lund, J (1995). *Die fiktive Wirklichkeit – und die wirkliche Fiktion; Elemente zur Theorie des Puppentheaters*. Masters thesis. Copenhagen: University of Copenhagen, Institute of Art History and Theatre Research.

Lund, J (2001), Puppets and Computers, in *Proceedings of the Marionette: Metaphysics, Mechanics, Modernity, International Symposium*, University of Copenhagen, 28 March–1 April 2001.

Rollings, A and Morris, D (2000). *Game Architecture and Design: Learn the Best Practices for Game Design and Programming*, Scotsdale, AZ: Coriolis.

Schönewolf, H (1968). *Play with Light and Shadow: The Art and Techniques of Shadow Theatre*. New York: Reinhold Book Corporation.

Seeger, L and Whetmore, EJ (1994). *From Script to Screen: The Collaborative Art of Filmmaking*. New York: Henry Holt & Co.

Tillis, S (1999). The Art of Puppetry in the Age of Media Production, *The Drama Review* 43(3), New York University and the Massachusetts Institute of Technology.

Wilpert, CB (1982). *Schattentheater*. Hamburg: Hamburgerisches Museum für Völkerkunde.

Video

Callesen, J (2001) The Family Factory: Drama and Performance Animation; Producing a Play with Virtual Puppets. In collaboration with Aarhus Film Workshop.

Films

Antz (1998) directed by Eric Darnell
Jurassic Park (1993) directed by Steven Spielberg
Life is Sweet (1990) directed by Mike Leigh
Toy Story (1995) directed by John Lasseter

Computer Games

Final Fantasy VII (1998) Eidos Interactive

10

The Evolution of Computer Bugs: An Interdisciplinary Team Work

Ole Caprani, Jakob Fredslund, Jørgen Møller Ilsøe, Jens Jacobsen, Line Kramhøft, Rasmus B. Lunding, and Mads Wahlberg

Ole Caprani is associate professor in computer science. He has used computer controlled LEGO models for many years in teaching at all levels from school children to university students.

Jakob Fredslund has a PhD in computer science and is an excellent LEGO builder and the designer of several embodied agents, for example, a LEGO face that shows feelings.

Jørgen Møller Ilsøe has a Master's degree in computer science and is a master LEGO builder. As one of the few master students of computer science, he brought a huge LEGO model for his Master's exam.

Jens Jacobsen, an engineer, has designed and implemented an interface for interactive dance and other electronic devices for artistic use.

Line Kramhøft, a textile designer, has concentrated on the production of textiles, scenography, costumes and textile art using three-dimensional surfaces.

Rasmus B. Lunding, a musician and composer, has played as a soloist and in groups, has published two solo CDs as well as toured and presented compositions at an international level.

Mads Wahlberg is a light designer and electrical technician. He has designed and produced a number of technical gadgets for use in theatre.

10.1 Introduction

An investigation of robots as a medium for artistic expression started in January 2000. As a result, insect-like LEGO robots, *Bugs*, have been created, that through movements and sounds, are able to express what to an observer seem like emotions, intentions and social behaviour. To enhance the perception of Bug behaviour as

Figure 10.1 People watch life in the Jungle Cube through peepholes in the black cloth.

aggressive, hungry, afraid, friendly or hostile, an artificial world has been created for the Bugs, an environment with a soundscape, dynamic lighting and a scenography of biologically inspired elements. This installation is called "The Jungle Cube". Figure 10.1 shows the Jungle Cube from the outside. Through peepholes the audience can watch the life of the Bugs inside the cube.

Figure 10.2 shows a Bug inside the cube. In front of the Bug is a tuft of straws that the Bug can sense with its antennas and interact with, as if the Bug is eating from the straws. The life in the Jungle cycles through four time periods: morning, day, evening and night. There are two kinds of Bugs in the Jungle, *Weak Bugs* and *Strong Bugs*. During the day, the Weak Bugs are active, e.g., wandering around, searching for food, or eating, while the Strong Bugs are trying to sleep. During the night, the Strong Bugs are active, hunting the Weak Bugs while the Weak Bugs are trying to sleep. Strong Bugs search for a place to sleep in the morning, whereas the Weak Bugs search in the evening. When Bugs meet, they react to each other; e.g., when a Strong Bug meets a Weak Bug, the Weak Bug tries to escape and the Strong Bug attacks.

From a *technical point of view*, the installation can be described as a collection of computer-controlled elements as shown in Figure 10.3. The computer platform for an eight-channel cubic soundscape is a PowerPC computer; the rest of the elements are controlled by the LEGO MindStorms RCX computer, an Hitachi H8/3292 micro-controller embedded inside a specialised LEGO brick. Each Bug is controlled by a single RCX; the plastic straws can be moved whenever LEGO motors under the tufts are activated from an RCX-based Straw Controller. The lighting is controlled

Figure 10.2 A Bug, an insect-like LEGO robot, in a biologically inspired environment inside the cube.

by a collection of RCX computers, each controlling three spotlights; and finally, an RCX-based Co-ordinator broadcasts infrared messages to the other RCX computers with information about the current time period: morning, day, evening or night. By means of these messages the Co-ordinator synchronises all RCX computers with respect to time period, and hence makes life happen in the Jungle Cube, cycling though the four time periods.

The Jungle Cube has evolved over a period of almost two years. Different versions have been presented to a general audience during that period. First at the NUMUS Festival for Contemporary Music in Aarhus, April 2000; then at the opening of the Center for Advanced Visualization and Interaction (CAVI) in Aarhus, March 2001; at the NUMUS Festival, April 2001; and most recently at the Nordic Interactive Conference, November 2001, Copenhagen (NIC 2001). One of the experiences from the presentations is that robots can indeed be perceived as autonomous creatures, and interaction among the robots creates an illusion of life-like behaviour in the artificial world of the installation. The main reason for this achievement is that people with different skills have been involved in the project: four people with *technical skills*, one engineer and three computer scientists; and three people with *artistic skills*, a composer, a scenographer and a light designer. This chapter describes how the multimedia installation, The Jungle Cube, has evolved as a result of the work of this *interdisciplinary* project group.

At the beginning of the project we were inspired by the robots of Grey Walter (1950, 1951), Machina docilis and Machina speculatrix. With very few sensors and actuators controlled by simple mappings from sensory input to actuator output, these robots could produce behaviours "resembling in some ways the random variability, or 'free will,' of an animal's responses to stimuli" (Walter, 1950). Furthermore, we learned that autonomous, mobile LEGO robots can be made to behave like the robots of Grey Walter or the simple vehicles of Braitenberg (1984),

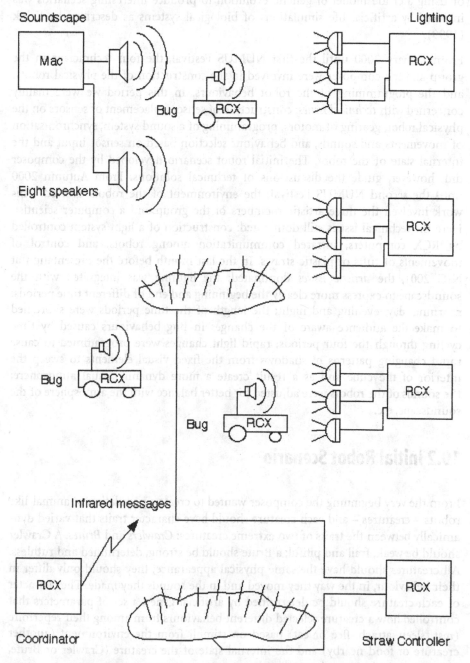

Figure 10.3 A technical view of the computer-controlled elements in the Jungle Cube.

and that a population of such LEGO robots interacting with each other and the environment can generate a great variety of behaviours, or scenarios, that are interesting for an audience to watch for quite some time. Based on this knowledge, the composer came up with an idea for a *robot scenario* with a population of animal-like robots that evolve through mutual exchange of artificial genes. The idea of using a crude model of genetic evolution to produce interesting scenarios was inspired by artificial life simulations of biological systems as described by Krink (1999).

From January 2000 until the first NUMUS Festival, the four technicians in the group and the composer were involved in the construction of the physical robots, and the programming of the robot behaviours. In this period we were mainly concerned with *technical issues*: construction of sensors, placement of sensors on the physical robot, gearing of motors, programming of a sound system, synchronisation of movements and sounds, and behaviour selection based on sensor input and the internal state of the robot. The initial robot scenario developed by the composer did, however, guide the discussions of technical solutions. From Autumn 2000 until the second NUMUS Festival, the environment of the robots evolved. This work involved the three artistic members of the group and a computer scientist. Here the technical issues still dominated: construction of a light system controlled by RCX computers, infrared communication among robots, and control of movements of tufts of plastic straws. In the last month before the presentation at NIC 2001, the *artistic issues* dominated: the lighting was integrated with the soundscape to express more clearly the beginning and end of different time periods: morning, day, evening and night; the length of the time periods were shortened to make the audience aware of the changes in Bug behaviours caused by time cycling through the four periods; rapid light changes were programmed to cause rapid changing patterns of shadows from the fixed visual elements to sweep the interior of the cube and as a result create a more dynamic visual atmosphere; the sounds of the robots were adjusted for better balance with the atmosphere of the soundscape, etc.

10.2 Initial Robot Scenario

From the very beginning the composer wanted to create a population of animal-like robots – creatures – and each creature should have character traits that varied dynamically between the traits of two extreme creatures: *Crawlers* and *Brutes*. A Crawler should be weak, frail and pitiful; a Brute should be strong, determined and ruthless. All creatures should have the same physical appearance; they should only differ in their behaviour, in the way they moved and in the sounds they made. The character of each creature should be determined by artificial genes, a set of parameters that controlled how a creature selected different behaviours from among their repertoire (rest, sleep, attach, flee or eat) based on stimuli from the environment (another creature or food nearby) and the internal state of the creature (Crawler or Brute, hungry, aggressive, scared or content).

The creatures should exist in an environment where they should move around looking for a place to sleep, for the other creatures, or for food. When the creatures met they should interact, and a transfer of genes between the interacting creatures might take place. As a result the artificial genes of the interacting creatures would change, for example, through a crossover of the genes of the interacting creatures. Hence, the character traits of the creatures should change through interaction, and different scenarios would evolve depending on the character traits of the initial population and the patterns of interaction: All creatures might end up as either Brutes or as Crawlers or maybe some steady state might be reached with a few Brutes, a few Crawlers and a varying number of creatures with both weak and strong character traits.

The idea of artificial gene exchange was not realised in the Weak and Strong Bug scenario, but the idea of robots as creatures with different character traits was, as we shall see, realised in the Bug scenario.

10.3 From a Mobile Robot to a Bug

The four technicians on the team had previous experience with construction of physical LEGO robots controlled by programs running on the RCX. It was decided to construct the creatures of the initial robot scenario out of LEGO with the RCX as the controller platform: through sensors (touch or light sensors) connected to the input ports, the creatures could perceive the environment, and through actuators (motors or lamps) connected to the output ports, the creatures could act in the environment, while the infrared transmitter/receiver could be used to exchange artificial genes between the creatures.

After the choice of LEGO and RCX the immediate challenge was to build an animal-like creature out of LEGO bricks and develop programs to make them move and sound like animals. The result of these initial efforts looked very much like the robots of Figure 10.4. The advantage of the choice of LEGO was that the physical robots could be easily rebuilt to change the appearance of the creatures, to change the mechanical mode of operation, and to make them mechanically robust. Several small changes have since been made to the robots in Figure 10.4. The two-wheel base has been changed to a four-wheel base with two passive front trolley wheels, making it possible for the robots to move more suddenly and abruptly; and the stalk holding the speaker in the rubber tyre protruding from the top of the Bug was shortened to change the vibrations of the speaker resulting from the moves of the robot. In order to change the appearance of the robots dramatically when the ultraviolet light was turned on during the night in the Jungle Cube, the colour of the Bug eyes was altered and special red tape was put onto the coloured carapace around the robots. Additionally, the movement of the two eyes resulting from the robot movements was constrained so that the eyes moved to the left or right almost simultaneously.

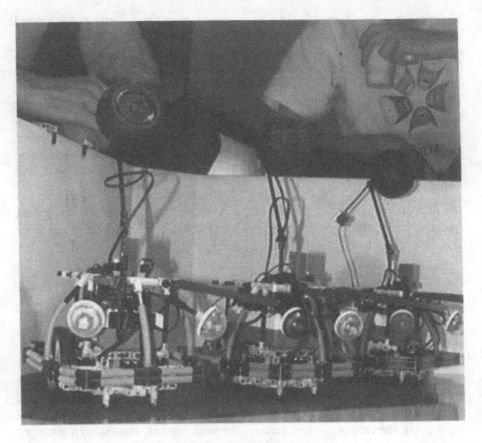

Figure 10.4 The Bugs, NUMUS 2000.

However, the choice of the RCX had its drawbacks:

- the RCX has only three independent input ports, and only primitive touch, light, temperature and rotation sensors are provided by LEGO;
- the RCX has only three independent output ports and only motors and lamps are provided as actuators;
- the sound from the built-in speaker is very weak, and bandwidth is limited;
- there is limited memory space, less than 32 k bytes;
- the programming tools that LEGO offers have limited features for data structuring and only allow slow and limited access to the 8 bit micro-controller embedded inside the RCX, the Hitachi H8/3292.

Because of this we decided:

- to develop a few customised sensors;
- to implement a sound system based on a customised speaker; and
- to use the general-purpose language C as the programming language.

10.3.1 Sensors and Locomotion Actuators

Figure 10.5 shows the resulting customised sensors: two antennas, based on bend sensors, and four independent bumpers, mounted on LEGO touch sensors. A push on a bumper is registered by a touch sensor. Since there are only three input ports, we had to connect several sensors to one input port. For an observer it is not easy to distinguish between a bend on the right or left antenna, so the two antennas were connected to the same input port. On the other hand, to an observer it is obvious on which side the robot encounters an obstacle, so the robot should be able to distinguish activation of each of the four bumpers. To achieve this, the resistors inside the LEGO touch sensors were changed to have distinct values. This made it possible to register activation independently on the different bumpers, even though the four touch sensors were connected to the same input port. Two LEGO light sensors were also used: one underneath the Bug to sense the colour of the floor, the other on top of the Bug to sense the ambient light level in the room. A light sensor and the four touch sensors can be used independently even if they are connected to the same input port. In total, we managed to have seven independent sensor inputs on three input ports. Through the antennas and the bumpers the Bug can sense obstacles; through the light sensors the Bug can sense coloured areas on the floor and day/night light in the room.

The movements of the Bug is accomplished by two wheels driven by two independently controllable LEGO motors. The rotation speed of the motors is also controllable. Hence, the Bug can be controlled to perform a variety of manoeuvres, for example, a very slow sneak forward or a fast wiggle.

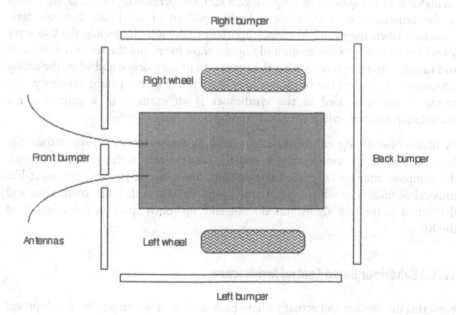

Figure 10.5 Sensors and actuators connected to the RCX of the Bug.

10.3.2 Sound Actuator: Square Wave Synthesiser

An electromagnetic speaker connected to an output port of the RCX can be turned on and off under program control. As a result, the diaphragm of the speaker will move back and forth between its two extreme positions. This is the basis for the sound generation system of the Bug. As an example, a tone with frequency 100 Hz will be generated if the speaker is repeatedly turned on for 5 msec and off for 5 msec, since 1000/(5 + 5) Hz = 100 Hz. Using the accurate timers of the RCX to control the on and off periods of the speaker, a software synthesiser has been programmed, see Figure 10.6. The synthesiser has two oscillators, a *tone oscillator* and a *gating oscillator*. The basic waveform of the tone oscillator is a double square wave consisting of two consecutive single square waves. The sum of the four time periods that define the on and off periods of the double square wave determines the frequency of the tone. The timbre of the tone is determined by the relationship between the four on/off periods. The double square wave was chosen as the basic waveform because the timbral possibilities increase significantly with four time periods instead of the two time periods of a single square wave: keeping the sum of the four periods constant while adjusting the relationship between the four periods creates a tone with a surprising variation in timbre. This was already discovered and used in the late 1950s as described in Manning (1985, pp. 72–74).

The basic waveform of the gating oscillator is a single square wave. The on/off periods of the gating oscillator is used to modulate the tone by turning the tone oscillator on and off. The usage of a gating oscillator to modulate a tone oscillator also goes back to the late 1950s. The result of the gating depends on the relationship between the frequencies of the two oscillators: When the frequency of the gating oscillator is in the sub-audio range (e.g., 5 Hz), the periodicity of the gating results in the generation of a rhythmic pulse-like pattern of the tones from the tone oscillator; when the gating frequency approaches the tone frequency, the two wave forms merge into a triple- or multiple square wave form, and the result is drastically and rapidly changing tones with a rich spectrum of harmonics; and when the gating frequency gets higher, the result is a tone determined by the gating frequency. The gating modulation used in the synthesiser is an example of a general signal modulation method, called amplitude modulation, Roads (1996).

By means of short algorithms that change the six parameters of the synthesiser (the four periods of the tone oscillator and the two periods of the gating oscillator), the composer managed to program algorithms that generated a variety of insect-like musical sounds. The advantage of this sound system is that the synthesiser and the sound generating algorithms do not take up much space in the memory of the RCX.

10.3.3 Behaviour-based Control Architecture

Now that the sensors and actuators have been described, we turn to the development of the *Bug control program*. Through a number of experiments we found a way of

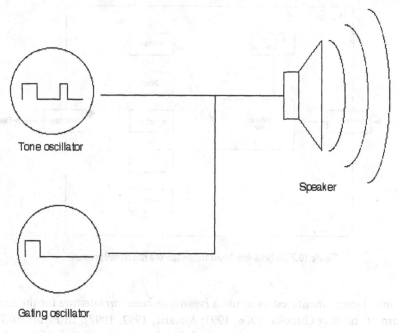

Tone oscillator

Speaker

Gating oscillator

Figure 10.6 The square wave-based software synthesiser.

controlling the two motors so that the resulting movements of the Bug make it appear like an insect wandering around: first the Bug goes forward for a random period of time, between 100 msec and 500 msec; then it stops abruptly by braking the two motors; afterwards it waits for a random period of time; then by a small random angle it turns in-place left or right; and finally, it repeats this sequence of actions by going forward again. Randomly chosen speeds are used each time the motors are activated. The perception of an insect wandering around is not only caused by the Bug movements but also the accompanying insect-like sounds and the physical appearance of the Bug while moving, e.g., the way motor activation and motor braking cause the eyes, the antennas and the speaker stalk to move. Our next series of experiments were concerned with Bug reactions to obstacles. Through the bumpers and antennas, the control program gets information about obstacles encountered. There is, however, not much information about what kind of obstacle the Bug has encountered, whether a passive obstacle like a wall or another Bug. At first, we did not care much about this but tried to program two kinds of reactions: avoid the obstacle, or attack the obstacle. Furthermore, we wanted the reaction to an obstacle to be instantaneous: stop the current movements and sounds immediately and start to avoid or attack the encountered obstacle, while signalling this by generating sounds. In the beginning, we could only make the Bug look like a car bumping into an obstacle in front and then backing up with an alarm-like tone. As a result, the illusion of an insect was broken and the robot was seen as a car. Later, the composer made melodic insect-like sound sequences to accompany the movement, so instead of a car, the robot was perceived as an insect being surprised, afraid, curious, or aggressive when encountering an obstacle.

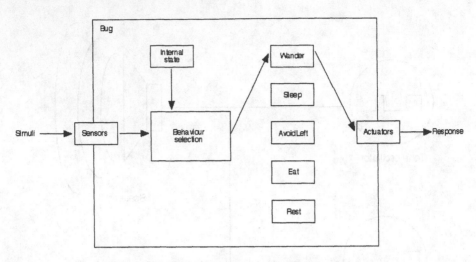

Figure 10.7 The behaviour-based architecture of a Bug control program.

These initial experiments led us to use a *behaviour-based architecture* for the control program of the Bug (Brooks, 1986, 1991; Mataric, 1992, 1997). In Figure 10.7 the behaviour-based architecture is shown. Each Bug has a repertoire of different behaviours: wander, sleep, avoid-left, etc. Each *behaviour* consists of two independent program modules, a *locomotion module* and a *sound module*. When executed, each module generates a sequence of simple instantaneous actuator actions. Locomotion modules start or stop the motors, sound modules start or stop one or both oscillators that control the speaker.

At any given instance, only *one* behaviour is active. The two modules of the active behaviour are executed concurrently: the locomotion module moves the Bug around, while the sound module generates the accompanying sounds. Triggered by external stimuli like a bumper being pushed, or triggered by changes in the internal state, e.g., an avoiding behaviour that finishes, the active behaviour is terminated and a new behaviour is selected to be the active one. Hence, the *behaviour selection* depends on external stimuli and the internal state as shown in Figure 10.7. The selection mechanism itself is based on the concept of *motivations* (Krink, 1999). At any given instance, each behaviour is associated with a *motivation value*. The behaviour with the highest motivation value is selected to be the active behaviour. Motivation values are calculated every 50 msec by means of *motivation functions*, one for each behaviour. The motivation functions use sensor values resulting from external stimuli, and the internal state to calculate a motivation value: during the day the motivation value for the behaviour "wander" is high, during the night it is low. The opposite applies to the motivation value for the behaviour "sleep"; the motivation value for "avoid-left" is higher than the value for wander or sleep when the left bumper is activated and the value stays high until the avoid-left behaviour ends. One of the consequences of this behaviour selection mechanism is that the reaction to obstacles is delayed at most 50 msec and is perceived as immediate reaction.

10.3.4 Behaviours

In the above description of the behaviour-based architecture, the word behaviour has been used to denote two different things. On the one hand, it denotes an *internal mechanism* of the control program, that is, the locomotion and sound modules that generate time-extended sequences of actions to the motors or the speaker. On the other hand, it denotes an *external interpretation* of the Bug enacting these actions. During the development of the Bugs, these two aspects of the behaviour concept turned out to play a central role. To make the creatures of the initial scenario more concrete we simply tried to figure out what the creatures should do in the different situations they might be put in. As a result, the composer came up with a list of named behaviours with a description of the conditions for the different behaviours to be enacted (sleep at night, wander around searching for food during the day, go forward when bumped into from behind, etc.). Then the technicians programmed these behaviours one by one as program modules and added them incrementally to the control program. Hence, the description of the initial robot scenario was *decomposed* into a list of desired behaviours and these behaviours were then *built up* from the primitive actuator actions.

Programming the locomotion and sound modules was accomplished by developing *levels of abstract commands* to bridge the gap between the primitive low-level actuator actions and the high-level descriptions of the desired behaviours. It turned out that only one level of abstract commands was necessary to express all the desired locomotions as simple program modules. These commands were: GoForward, TurnLeft, TurnRight, and Brake. Each has an obvious implementation in terms of the primitive motor actions. The names of these commands correspond to the observed, resulting movement of the Bug when such a command is executed by a locomotion module. The introduction of these commands was not only a means to simplify the programming but also a means to develop a common language among the technicians and the composer in discussing locomotion.

The development of levels of abstract commands to program the sound modules was much harder and time consuming than the development of the one level of abstract locomotion commands. In fact, only one of the sound modules programmed for the NUMUS 2000 presentation was re-used in later versions of the Bug. There were several reasons for the slow development of the sound modules. The technicians had had no experience with programming sound generation at this low level; the composer had had no experience with square wave synthesis. Furthermore, the composer experimented a lot with individual animal-like melodic sound effects for each Bug, and sound modules that made Bugs perform small melodic pieces of music in concerto. For example, a small piece of music for three Bugs was composed to accompany the three Bugs on their way home. It was, however, difficult to make sure that all three Bugs joined in at appropriate times, because the Bugs might not be on their way home simultaneously. Finally, during autumn 2000, one of the computer scientists and the composer finally managed to find useful abstractions for sound module programming. It turned out that two levels of abstractions were enough to program all current sound modules. The lowest level is the square wave synthesiser of Figure 10.6. The synthesiser is controlled by a set of commands that start and stop the two oscillators: StartPlaying, StopPlaying, StartGating, StopGating. The commands at the next level are all expressed in terms of musical concepts: PlayNote, PlayNoteGlissade, PlayTimbreGlissade. The first has an obvious meaning, the next plays an up or down glissade of intermediate notes between two notes, and the last command plays a glissade from one square-wave form of a note to another wave form of the same note. All commands have a simple implementation in terms of the lower level commands. At the start of this sound module development, the computer scientist wrote a number of sound modules in terms of the abstract commands; the composer listened and suggested changes. Through these experiments, we found that sounds generated by using the gating commands together with glissade commands yielded a rich variety of sound material, which were immediately useful as insect sounds. Later, the composer managed to program all the sound modules in terms of these two levels of abstract commands.

Synchronisation of movements and sounds is accomplished in two ways. The first way is to start the locomotion and sound module of the active behaviour simultaneously and to execute the two modules concurrently. The result is that, e.g., the sound accompanying the Avoid-Left movements starts immediately when a Bug bumps into an obstacle and the Avoid-Left sounds are heard while the Bug is turning away from the obstacle. The second way is to turn the speaker on and off from within a locomotion module. This can be used, e.g., to turn on the sounds accompanying the Sleep movements only during the short periods while the Bug is wiggling in its sleep.

10.4 Evolution of the Bug Scenario: From Crawlers and Brutes to Weak and Strong Bugs

A month before NUMUS 2000 we were still far from a realisation of the initial scenario of Crawlers and Brutes. The behaviour-based architecture had been programmed and tested with the locomotion modules for wander, hunt, avoid and attack behaviours. However, we were still struggling with the corresponding sound modules. The character traits expressed by enacting the implemented behaviours resembled the desired Crawler and Brute traits. Unfortunately, though, we had not yet implemented a parameter mechanism to change the behaviour selection or to control the behaviours dynamically. Hence, there was no way of changing the character traits of the creatures by mutual exchange of parameters. At the peak of this crisis, the composer came up with a revised scenario in which only two kinds of creatures exist: Weak Bugs and Strong Bugs. These creatures were to have *fixed* character traits. The Weak Bug should be like a Crawler; a Strong Bug like a Brute. In the initial scenario, the overall dynamics originate in changing character traits of the creatures between Crawlers and Brutes. In the revised scenario, the overall dynamics result from both the explicit passing of time through day and night and the spatial placement of home locations and food areas for the creatures. The Weak Bugs are active during the day; the Strong Bugs are active at night. Both the Weak and the Strong Bugs have a home where they sleep at night or day. The homes of the Weak and the Strong Bugs are situated in different locations in the environment. Close to the home of the Strong Bugs there is a food area which the Weak Bugs search for during the day. When they find the food, they eat a meal.

The composer described the revised scenario as a list of Weak and Strong Bug behaviours similar to the original Crawler and Brute behaviours. Moreover, most of the locomotion modules already implemented could be used in the revised scenario. Two new behaviours, GoHome and Eat, were the only behaviours we had to implement from scratch. As described in the introduction, the idea of Weak and Strong Bugs with fixed character traits are still used in the present version and so are many of the locomotion modules implemented for NUMUS 2000.

10.5 Evolution of the Bug Environment: From a Box to a Cube

In the description of the initial scenario of Crawlers and Brutes, we only had vague ideas about the environment of the creatures and these ideas had not been developed any further before the introduction of the revised scenario. At that point, we began to think about how to realise a *physical environment* for the Weak and Strong Bugs. The physical environment should enable the Bugs to move around and it should include elements that the Bugs could perceive through their sensors, such as day/night, food and home. An environment along these lines was constructed for NUMUS 2000 (see Figure 10.8).

Figure 10.8 People watch the Bug life in a box environment, NUMUS 2000.

The environment was an open wooden box measuring $1.7 \times 1.0 \times 0.4$ m. The floor had a flat, smooth surface, so that the locomotion actuators could move the Bugs around. Two spotlights were placed above the box, a yellow and a blue one. Yellow on, blue off signified day; yellow off, blue on signified night. The duration of day and night periods was controlled by an RCX that periodically turned the two spotlights on and off. The light sensor on top of the Bug, the ambient light sensor, was used to sense the day and night light. The food area, the Weak and Strong Bug homes, and paths to the Bug homes were laid out on the floor as coloured areas (see Figure 10.9). The colours were chosen so that the light sensor underneath the Bug, the floor light sensor, could be used to distinguish the different locations. The two different coloured paths along the walls were used by the GoHome locomotion module to navigate the Bugs to their home area: when a Bug comes close to a wall it uses the path colour to decide which way to turn to head for the right home.

At the NUMUS 2000 Festival there were three Weak Bugs and three Strong Bugs. The two spotlights were controlled to yield a 10-minute overall time cycle with 5-minute day and night period.

Table 10.1 shows an overall model of the Bug responses to the stimuli from the elements of the NUMUS 2000 environment. The table contains a list of what we considered to be the main stimuli that the Bugs should react to. Also listed are the sensors the Bugs use to sense these stimuli; how the Bug control program interprets the received sensor values, i.e., how the stimuli are perceived by the Bugs; and the behaviours that are either activated or influenced by the stimuli. This list of behaviours is, on the one hand, a list of the control program modules that generate the low-level responses to the stimuli in terms of sequences of movements and sounds. On the other hand, the names in the list describe the intended external

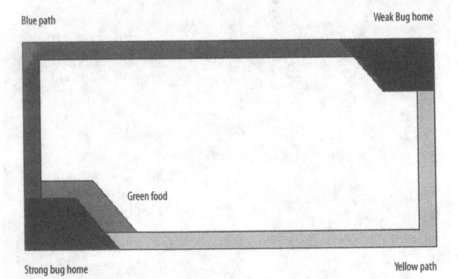

Figure 10.9 The coloured areas of the floor in the box environment, NUMUS 2000.

Table 10.1 Bug responses to stimuli from the box environment.

Stimuli	Sensed by	Perceived as	Perceived as activate or influence behaviour in Weak/Strong Bug
Bump into wall	Touch sensor/antennas	Obstacle	Avoid/Attack
Bump into Bug	Touch sensor/antennas	Obstacle	Avoid/Attack
Yellow light	Ambient light sensor	Day	Wander/GoHome or Sleep
Blue light	Ambient light sensor	Night	GoHome or Sleep/Hunt
Green area	Floor light sensor	Food	Eat/–
Blue area	Floor light sensor	Path	GoHome/GoHome
Yellow area	Floor light sensor	Path	GoHome/GoHome
Black area	Floor light sensor	Home	Sleep/Sleep

interpretation of the low-level responses to the stimuli. Hence, the stimuli/response list is not only a model of the mapping from sensors to actuators performed by the control program, but also a model of the intended perception by an audience in terms of causality: when a Weak Bug bumps into a Strong Bug, the Weak Bug tries to avoid the attacking Strong Bug; when a Weak Bug detects food during the day, it eats; when night turns into day, the Strong Bugs search for their home and when home, they sleep.

What actually happened in the box at NUMUS 2000 was in many ways different from the intentions modelled in Table 10.1. When the spotlights were turned on and the Bugs started, the audience saw six animal-like LEGO robots moving around with no purpose, swiftly and abruptly, while avoiding and attacking each other or the walls. The audience heard a steady, high intensity animal-like sound mixed with melodic fragments. Although it was obvious that the sound came from the robots, it was impossible to locate the origin of the different sounds. The enacted scenario was perceived as disturbed creatures which were either in panic, afraid or simply confused. This emerged from frequent Bug-wall interactions and Bug-Bug interactions as a result of the wander, hunt, avoid and attack behaviours. Because of several flaws in the day/night light detection, the floor colour detection, and the behaviour selection, these four behaviours were active most of the time. The sleep, go home and eat behaviours were only activated occasionally and only for short periods of time – actually, for so short periods that activation of these behaviours was not perceived as a consequence of the day/night light or the food colour on the floor.

Even though the Bug behaviours were not enacted as intended, and hence were not perceived as part of the scenario described by the composer, we were encouraged to continue our efforts, partly because of the positive comments from the audience, and partly because several people did watch the Bugs for quite some time. During the following few months we fixed the flaws in the control program so the day/night stimuli had an obvious impact on Weak and Strong Bug activities. Furthermore, the Bugs could indeed find their way home, they slept at home, and the Weak Bugs ate on the green area. However, because of the limited physical space, the perception of the individual Bugs was still disturbed by the frequent activation of avoid and attack behaviour.

In the beginning of the summer, 2001, two of the computer scientists and the engineer left the project; the composer and a computer scientist continued to discuss how to improve the environment of the Bugs. During September 2001, the composer came up with an idea for a new Bug environment: *a closed cube*. The idea was, first of all, to make enough room on the cube floor for the Bugs to move around without frequent collisions. Second, peepholes in the cube should enable an audience to watch the Bugs in a jungle-like environment created in the interior of the closed cube. The composer and the computer scientists designed a physical cube together with a local theatrical design and production company. In November, the company finished the physical cube.

10.5.1 The Cube

The cube measures $3 \times 3 \times 2$ m. It is constructed as an iron skeleton covered with black cloth containing peepholes for the audience. At CAVI 2001 and NUMUS 2001 we used a cloth with holes positioned, so the audience had to stand up to put their heads through the holes (Figure 10.10). In the present version, NIC 2001 (Figure 10.1 and Figure 10.11), the holes are positioned so the audience can sit more comfortably on cushions around the cube. Furthermore, the audience gets a better view of the Bugs from the head positions closer to the cube floor. Also added to the NIC 2001 version are two TV monitors outside the cube. Video on the monitors show the Bug life inside the cube. Two static cameras inside transmit the video to the monitors.

Figure 10.10 The Jungle Cube, NUMUS 2001.

Figure 10.11 The NIC 2001 Cube with cushions and two TV-monitors.

In the first version of the black cloth, two holes for the arms were positioned below each peephole. The idea was to enable the audience to influence the activities of the Bugs and other elements inside the cube. Through the armholes the audience should be able to reach for an electric torch hanging down inside the cube, switch it on and point it at, e.g., a Bug to make it react to the light.

It turned out that we did not make any use of the armholes. The reason was that we could only think of panic as the Bug reaction to torch light, and if most Bugs were panicking because of torch lights pointing at them, it would prevent the audience not using an electric torch from experiencing the rest of the Bug behaviours. The armholes caused some confusion at the CAVI and the NUMUS presentations: people thought that waving arms through the hole had an influence on the Bug behaviours and children thought it was meant to enable them to touch the Bugs.

10.5.2 The Scenography

At first, only the composer and the computer scientist discussed the appearance of a jungle-like environment inside the cube. We imagined a mix of natural and artificial elements like stones, plants and RCX controlled, non-mobile, animal-like LEGO elements with movable speakers. We also began to work on non-mobile elements such as a speaker built into an angular, plastic tube.

After these initial discussions and experiments, the composer suggested involving a scenographer. At the first meeting with the scenographer, we used a demonstration of the Bugs in the box and a video from NUMUS 2000 to initiate discussions about the scenographer's involvement in the project. Based on this and the revised scenario, the scenographer came up with a model of the interior of the cube (see

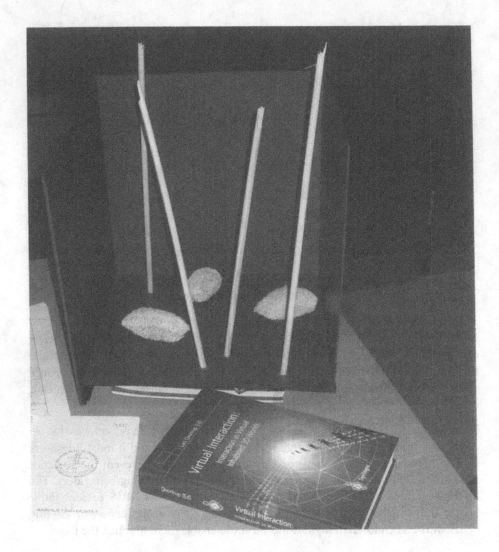

Figure 10.12 The scenographer's model of the cube interior.

Figure 10.12). The idea was that the cube should only contain artificial elements with an organic appearance to enhance the insect-like appearance of the Bugs. Furthermore, there should only be elements that the Bugs could sense and that seem natural to an audience as something the Bugs can react to.

First of all, the model gave us a shared understanding of the scenographer's conception of the visual appearance of a jungle-like environment inside the cube. Secondly, the involvement of the scenographer directed our focus from the single Bug behaviours onto the design of an environment in which these behaviours would make sense to an audience. At the beginning of the discussions, the scenographer only had a vague understanding of the Bug sensors and the possible Bug perception of an environment through the sensors. Hence, the scenographer simply accepted that there should still be, as in the box environment, coloured areas on the cube floor, and these areas should still be perceived by the Bugs as home and food locations. Also accepted was the idea of navigating the Bugs to home and food locations by means of coloured pathways on the cube floor.

10.5.3 The Lighting

As can be seen from Figure 10.13, the visual appearance of the elements depends on the light setting. The scenographer did not have the technical skills required to set up and control the light inside the cube, so a light designer with experience in stage-lighting control was involved in the project. The primitive on/off RCX control of the yellow and blue spotlights of the box environment inspired the light designer and the computer scientist to experiment with a similar autonomous RCX-based light control mechanism, but with numerous theatrical spotlights and the conventional stage-light fading mechanism instead of the crude on/off control of the two box lights.

The control of the light intensity of a spotlight by a program on an RCX turned out to be quite a technical challenge. The spotlights need a 12 V power supply, the RCX output ports can supply 9 V. This means that the power to the spotlights had to come from a 12 V power source controlled by signals from the RCX output ports; a signal of carefully timed on and off periods on the output port was sent to an electrical circuit that used the signal and a 12 V power supply to turn on a spotlight with intensities ranging from almost dark to full light; and the intensity is controlled by the relationship between the duration of the on and off periods of the

Figure 10.13 Model of cube interior with light setting.

RCX signal. The light designer built the electrical circuits, while the computer scientist programmed the fading algorithms and the overall control of the cube light from the RCX-based Co-ordinator and Light Controllers (see Figure 10.3).

The overall control of the light setting is expressed in light control concepts known to the light designer: For each time period there is a table of light cues and time intervals between cues; for each cue, the table contains up and down fading times common to all spotlights and the target light percentage for each spotlight. The entries are used by each Light Controller to fade up or down a single spotlight depending on its current light percentage and the target percentage. After implementation of the light control system, the light designer simply filled in and edited the four tables with light cues, fade up and down times, and light percentages to test different jungle light settings. Besides the spotlights, the light designer also installed on/off controllable ultraviolet neon tubes to be used during the night period.

10.5.4 The Soundscape

The composer's jungle-cube idea included a soundscape as part of the jungle-like environment inside the cube. The acoustics of the closed cube covered with cloth made it possible for a person with both ears inside the cube to spatially position sounds from differently located speakers inside the cube. A speaker was placed in each of the eight corners in the cube. The composer used the eight speakers to create an eight-channel soundscape in which sounds can be positioned in each of the eight corners or sounds can be moved around inside the cube. To create the musical material for the soundscape, the composer used Max/MSP to manipulate sounds and to spatially position the sounds, and the composer used ProTools to assemble the musical material into a soundscape, and to control the playback of the soundscape. These platforms run on the PowerPC and they are well known to the composer.

To integrate the soundscape with the insect-like Bug sounds and the organic visual appearance inside the cube, the composer chose sampled insect sounds as the basic sound material for composing the soundscape. The resulting soundscape has some resemblance with a natural jungle soundscape, although none of the individual sounds are immediately recognisable as natural sounds.

10.5.5 Co-evolution of Bug Scenario and Cube Environment

The Bug scenario and the cube environment evolved through the three presentations at CAVI, NUMUS and NIC, e.g., the visual appearance changed as illustrated in Figures 10.14–10.16. The three presentations represent stages in the process of integrating the scenography, the lighting, and the soundscape to create a jungle-like visual and sonic atmosphere inside the cube. The three presentations also represent stages in our attempt to integrate Bug behaviours and cube environment so the Bug behaviours enacted in the cube environment make sense to an audience.

Figure 10.14 The floor of the Jungle Cube, CAVI 2001.

Figure 10.15 The floor of the Jungle Cube, NUMUS 2001.

Figure 10.16 The floor of the Jungle Cube, NIC 2001.

After the internal cube had been modelled (Figure 10.12), and after the overall structure of the technical platform had been designed (Figure 10.3), there were numerous discussions about the Bug scenario in the new environment, mainly between the composer and the computer scientist. As a result, the composer refined the Bug scenario. The main change was the addition of the two time periods, morning and evening. This explicit time separation of the day, with active Weak Bugs, and the night, with active Strong Bugs, was intended to enhance the difference between the two kinds of Bugs. The composer also suggested having four Weak Bugs and two Strong Bugs. This emphasises the two Strong Bugs as lonely hunters, and the flock of Weak Bugs as the hunted. Furthermore, the introduction of four instead of two time periods was also intended to make it possible to exploit the dynamics of the lighting and the soundscape to express the passing of time more precisely than the crude yellow/blue light on/off periods used in the box environment. Each of the four time periods could then be expressed with different visual and sonic atmospheres.

10.5.6 Integration of Scenography, Lighting and Soundscape

Design and creation of a scenography, light setting and composition of a soundscape are well-known to the three artistic people. As a consequence, the visual and sonic atmosphere presented inside the cube already at CAVI communicated a jungle-like environment to the audience. The lighting was, however, not well integrated with the scenography and the soundscape. The reason was that the time-consuming development of the technical platform for the light control prevented the light designer from spending enough time with fine-tuning of the light tables. As a result, the lighting was too stationary: only the ultraviolet light was used during the night period, even though the soundscape clearly expressed different sonic atmospheres within the night period; the spotlights used in the morning period were too constant and too bright so changing shadows from fading spotlights illuminating the fixed elements of the scenography were not used to express, e.g., a sunrise.

Unfortunately, the light designer did not have time to change the lighting until we started working on the NIC presentation. At that time, the scenographer and the light designer made a thorough change in the visual appearance, as can be seen in Figure 10.16. They integrated the colours and the shapes of the scenographic elements with the lighting: coloured filters and cardboard with patterns of holes were placed in front of spotlights. Furthermore, a dynamic visual atmosphere was created by having periods of rapid light changes causing rapid changing patterns of shadows to sweep the interior of the cube, and these periods were integrated with the soundscape. For example, the sunrise in the jungle morning was expressed as yellow and red spotlights fading up, accompanied by soft, high-pitched and calm sounds, while the jungle night was expressed as a short period of down fading and flashing spotlights focused inside plastic pipes accompanied by low-pitched, raw sounds moving slowly around in the eight speakers, followed by a long period of only ultraviolet light accompanied by sounds moving fast around the top four speakers like the sound of a storm.

At the CAVI and the NUMUS presentations, the audience had to spend 15 minutes with their heads through the peepholes to experience the four time periods. Because of several minutes with almost no Bug activity in the CAVI and the NUMUS scenarios, and because of the stationary lighting, most people spent only a few minutes watching the jungle life. At the NIC presentation, the time periods were shortened so people only had to spend 6 minutes to experience all periods of the jungle life, and these 6 minutes were made comfortable by the cushions outside the cube. Furthermore, the TV monitors outside the cube and the sonic atmosphere coming from the Bug sounds and the soundscape inside the cube were meant to stir the curiosity of people passing by so they would put their heads into the Jungle Cube.

10.5.7 From Path-controlled Navigation to Random Search

On the floor at CAVI (see Figure 10.14), coloured pathways were used for navigating the Bugs to their homes or to food. A lot of experiments were performed to choose appropriate floor colours. On the one hand, they should be chosen so they could be distinguished by the Bug control program through the floor light sensor and perceived as different locations; on the other hand, they should be part of the colours of the scenography. Five colours were used on the CAVI floor: a black ground, several green areas to signify Weak Bug food locations as well as Strong Bug homes, dark grey areas as Weak Bug homes, and two-coloured pathways of pale grey/white lines connecting green areas and dark grey areas. The two-coloured pathways made it possible for the Bugs to choose direction either towards home or towards food. To distinguish five colours was, however, just on the edge of what could be reliably perceived with the floor sensor. As a consequence, the path navigation did not work: when Bugs started on the pathways by following the coloured lines they simply turned off the pathway shortly after, and found neither home nor food.

The floor was changed for the NUMUS presentation, as can be seen in Figure 10.15. The main difference was that the pipes and the tufts of straws were now used, instead of green areas, to represent food. In the middle of the floor a large dark grey area represented the Weak Bug home, and the two-coloured pathways now connected the home with the three tufts. The Strong Bugs had no home; they simply slept somewhere on the floor. The reduction of the number of colours to four instead of five, made the Bug colour interpretation more reliable than on the CAVI floor. As a result, a Bug could use the pathways for reliable navigation. Unfortunately, it did not look very insect-like when it followed a pathway. It looked more like a car driven by a drunken driver.

From the very beginning, the scenographer did not like the two-coloured pathways because they dominated the visual appearance, and they only made sense to the Bugs, not to an audience. After all, there are no two-coloured Bug pathways in a jungle. So when we started working on the NIC presentation, the composer suggested to leave out the pathways and use only coloured areas to represent the homes: two large dark grey areas as Weak Bug homes, and several small, pale grey areas as Strong Bug homes. Instead of path navigation, home and food were searched for by random walk. It turned out that random walk was just as efficient as the NUMUS path navigation for the Bugs to find their homes and food. The small size of the Strong Bug homes made sure that the two lonely hunters also slept alone, whereas the large size of the Weak Bug homes had the effect of gathering the Weak Bugs for the night.

10.5.8 From Obstacle, Colour Sensing to Making Sense of the Environment

At CAVI, the Bugs avoided or attacked not only the walls and each other but also the pipes and the tufts. The behaviour that emerged from Bug interaction with the straws and the pipes could be perceived as a Bug eating a meal. After CAVI, the scenographer and the computer scientist discussed how to change the environment so that the Bugs could sense the pipes and the straws as food. A very simple solution was found. We prevented the antennas from touching the walls by placing a low barrier along the four walls. This barrier could be sensed through the front bumper without touching the wall with the antennas. As a consequence, the antennas could be used for sensing tufts, pipes and other Bugs. In order to distinguish tufts and pipes from Bugs, infrared communication was used: whenever an obstacle is sensed through the antennas and the obstacle identifies itself, it is a Bug; otherwise it is a tuft or a pipe. The combination of front bumper sensing, antenna sensing and communication made it possible for the

Bugs to react differently to walls, tufts and pipes, and other Bugs. At NUMUS, the Weak Bugs interpreted the pipes and the tufts as food and enacted an eat behaviour, moving the antennas from side to side in the straws of a tuft or scratching a pipe.

The space of possible sensor values resulting from external stimuli is called the *sensor space* of a Bug. The values in the sensor space are interpreted by the control program to make sense of the environment. The space of possible interpretations is called *perception space* of a Bug. For example, in the box, the perception space included day/night and home. The infrared messages from the Co-ordinator make sure that the current time period is available to the Bug. Infrared messages are also used to identify another Bug encountered in front. Since this use of communication can be considered a substitution for sensors, we also include the current time period and the identity of an encountered Bug in the perception space of the Bug.

The perception space of a Bug has changed a lot since the box environment. In the box, for instance, a Weak Bug could perceive (day/night, food, home, path to home, front/left/right/back obstacle). In the NIC environment the perception space has been enlarged to (morning/day/evening/night, food, home, wall, Weak Bug in front, Strong Bug in front, left/right/back obstacle). The enrichment of the perception space has been achieved by engineering the environment by placing a barrier along the walls. A well-known biological assumption is that animals adapt to the environment. The Jungle Cube might be said to have evolved the other way around: the environment has been adapted to the Bugs. The changes to the environment have always been made with the audience in mind: *the perception and the subsequent reaction of the Bugs should be meaningful to an audience.*

10.6 Discussion

The initial robot scenario of Crawlers and Brutes has acted as a framework for our investigation of robots as a medium for artistic expression. Within this framework, we have experimented with robots enacting animal-like behaviour. Hence, we relied on biomorphism to trigger associations in the audience which made the robot behaviour meaningful.

In our experiments we were inspired by behaviour-based artificial intelligence (Brooks, 1991). This line of research within artificial intelligence takes inspiration from biology. Around 1984, Brooks proposed "looking at simpler animals as a bottom-up model for building intelligence", and "to study intelligence from the bottom up, concentrating on physical systems (e.g., mobile robots), situated in the world, autonomously carrying out tasks of various sorts". This research has resulted in a variety of mobile robots, also called agents, and flocks of mobile robots or multi-agent systems (Maes, 1994; Mataric, 1997). These agents and multi-agent systems produce what in the eye of an observer is intelligent behaviour. The behaviour emerges from interaction of primitive components that can hardly be described as intelligent:

> It is hard to identify the seat of intelligence within any system, as intelligence is pro-
> duced by interactions of many components. Intelligence can only be determined by the
> total behaviour of the system and how that behaviour appears in relation to the envi-
> ronment (Brooks, 1991).

In the mind of an observer, the behaviour-based approach to robotics creates an illusion of intelligence when robots are carrying out tasks like navigation in an office or collecting empty soda cans. Our first aim, within the initial scenario framework, was to create the illusion of animal-like behaviour in LEGO robots. It turned out that the behaviour-based approach, with motivation functions used for behaviour selection, were fruitful in creating the illusion. At our first presentation, NUMUS 2000, the Bugs were indeed perceived as animal-like robots by the audience. Furthermore, the curiosity of the audience was stirred by the fact that small, autonomous and mobile LEGO robots could enact several situations where they were perceived as fighting, mating or searching. Bug–Bug and Bug–box interactions produced these situations. They were not produced by any particular behaviour module, but *emerged* from rapid switching between modules within each Bug, and the dynamics of the interaction of the individual behaviour modules with the world in which the Bug was *situated*. Hence, the explanation for the observed intelligence of a soda can-collecting robot also applies to the observed aliveness of the Bugs in the box. But there is more to it. Collecting empty soda cans is a well-defined task; it is easy to tell whether the robot succeeds. Creating animal-like behaviour is not as well-defined a task as the tasks researchers normally make their agents do. It turned out that the combination of movements and sounds was crucial in our effort to express animal-like behaviour and to create the illusion of creatures with goals, intentions, and feelings. If the speaker is disconnected the illusion almost breaks down.

Our next choice was to investigate how *traditional media of artistic expression* like scenography, lighting and soundscape can be used to create an environment in which the Bug behaviour appears as more meaningful to an audience than in the box environment. In the CAVI and the NUMUS 2001 presentations, we tried to make the robots enact the intended Weak and Strong Bug scenario with the con-frontations of Weak and Strong Bugs as the main generator of dramatic situations. At first, the confrontations were expressed as abrupt and sudden movements accompanied by almost annoying, high-pitched Weak Bug sounds and low-pitched Strong Bug sounds. The result was very dramatic. The number of confrontations taking place could, however, not be controlled. As a result, a sequence of frequent confrontations was annoying both to watch and listen to. Later, we expressed the confrontations less dramatically with the result that the conflict between the Weak and Strong Bugs was not perceived by the audience. As an alternative, we considered using the idea of a central Stage Manager (Rhodes and Maes, 1995), to monitor the number of confrontations and to command the Bugs to express these confronta-tions more or less dramatically depending on the current confrontation frequency. We abandoned this approach in order to investigate *randomness and emergence as generators of interesting situations.*

Before the NIC presentation, we had a few discussions on how different artistic intentions might be expressed by the Bugs in the cube. We finally abandoned the idea of expressing the conflict between the Weak and the Strong Bugs and of regarding this as the main element of the scenario to communicate to the audience. Instead, our choice was to balance all the expressive elements in the Jungle Cube to create an installation of an ambient, visual and sonic atmosphere – the mimesis of insect life in a jungle. Each of the elements can attract attention from the audience, for example, when the straws start to move, when the soundscape starts the storm, when the lights flash rapidly in the pipes, or when a Weak Bug suddenly sounds scared and lonely because it cannot find a home for the night.

Bøgh Andersen and Callesen (1999) have drawn on "literature, film, animation, theater and language theory" , to describe the idea of using agents as actors "that can enact interesting narratives". In our framework, we have chosen biology and ethology as inspirations for the scenarios. Instead of telling stories, as suggested by Bøgh Andersen and Callesen, we have used behaviour-based control programs with a simulation of biological behaviour selection as the generative system producing the situations that the audience watches.

Other people have used biological models as a generator of artistic expressions: when Felix Hess created *Electronic Sound Creatures* he was inspired by the sound of frogs (Chadabe, 1997). Hess created small machines with a microphone listening, a little speaker calling, and some electronics. He created the machines so they "react more or less to sounds the way frogs do". For Hess, "it was a synthetic model of animal communication". To other people "it was art".

10.7 Conclusion

In an essay on agents as artworks, Simon Penny (1999) has discussed two different contexts in which production of artworks based on agent technology has taken place: an artistic context and a scientific context. Penny argues that the two different contexts will inevitably lead to two different approaches to agent design, "the approach to production of artworks by scientifically trained tends to be markedly different from the approach of those trained in [visual] arts". As a case example of the different approaches, he compares two works in the Machine Culture exhibition at SIGGRAPH 93 (Penny, 1993): *Edge of Intention* by Joseph Bates and Luc Courchersne's *Family Portrait*. Penny generalises the difference in approach:

> (with apologies to both groups): artists will klunge together any kind of mess of technology behind the scene because coherence of the experience of the user is their first priority. Scientists wish for formal elegance at an abstract level and do not emphasise … the representation schemes of the interface.

Furthermore, Penny discusses "the value of artistic methodologies to agent design" and describes how artistic methodologies seem "to offer a corrective for elision generated by the often hermetic culture of scientific research".

In our project, we have tried to avoid the two extreme approaches described by Penny. Throughout the whole project, artistically and scientifically trained people have been involved. As a consequence, we have avoided the two pitfalls of klunging together "any mess of technology", and of neglecting the audience. The technicians of the team used their mechanical, electrical and programming skills to come up with robust and re-usable technical platforms: the mechanics of the LEGO robots only required minor changes after the first NUMUS presentation; the electrical components in the customised sensors, the robot speaker, and the 9 V to 12 V power converter were not changed after initial testing; and the behaviour-based architecture and the motivation selection have acted as the architectural pattern for the control program since the first NUMUS presentation. Furthermore, we did emphasise "the representational schemes of the interface". By involving artistically trained people we have managed to integrate scenography, lighting, soundscape and the Bug movements and sounds in the Jungle Cube installation to conjure meaning in the mind of the observer.

The development of different installations, as carried out in this project, might be called *artistic prototyping*: We have tested the potentials for artistic expressions made possible by the technical platforms – for example, the robots – by creating scenarios and environments as installations based on the platforms; and, as usual in artistic practice, the installations have been presented to a general audience. The reaction from the audience has clearly indicated that robots can indeed be used for artistic expression. Whether the latest prototype, the NIC Jungle Cube, can be described as art is for other people to decide.

Acknowledgment

The Jungle Cube was sponsored by Kulturministeriets Udviklingsfond and the Center for IT-Research.

References

Bøgh Andersen, P and Callesen, J (1999). Agents as Actors. In L Qvortrup (ed.), *Virtual Interaction: Interaction in Virtual Inhabited 3D Worlds*, London: Springer.

Braitenberg, V (1984). *Vehicles: Experiments in Synthetic Psychology*. Cambridge, MA: MIT Press.

Brooks, RA (1986). A Robust Layered Control System for a Mobile Robot. *IEEE Journal of Robotics and Automation*, RA-2, 14–23.

Brooks, RA (1991). Intelligence without Reason. In *Proceedings, IJAI-91*, 569–95, Sydney, Australia.

CAVI, Center for Advanced Visualization and Interaction: www.cavi.alexandra.dk.

Chadabe, J (1997). *Electric Sound*. Englewood Cliffs, NJ: Prentice-Hall.

Krink, T (draft). *Motivation Networks: A Biological Model for Autonomous Agent Control*.

Krink, T (1999). *Cooperation and Selfishness in Strategies for Resource Management*. In *Proceedings MEMS-99, Marine Environmental Modelling Seminar*, Lillehammer, Norway.

LEGO MindStorm: www.mindstorms.lego.com.

Maes, P (1994). Modeling Adaptive Autonomous Agents. *Artificial Life Journal*, 1(1–2).

Manning, P (1985). *Electronic and Computer Music*. Oxford: Clarendon Press.

Mataric, MJ (1992). Integration of Representation into Goal-driven Behavior-based Robots. *IEEE Transactions on Robotics and Automation*, 8(3), June, 304–12.

Mataric, MJ (1997). Behavior-based Control: Examples from Navigation, Learning, and Group Behavior. *Journal of Experimental and Theoretical Artificial Intelligence*, special issue on Software Architectures for Physical Agents, 9 (2–3), 323–36.

Penny, S (1993). Machine Culture. In *ACM Computer Graphics SIGGRAPH93 Visual Proceedings,* special issue, 109–84.

Penny, S (1999). Agents as Artworks and Agent Design as Artistic Practice. In K Dautenhahn (ed.), *Human Cognition and Social Agent Technology*, John Benjamins Publishing Company.

Rhodes, B and Maes, P (1995). *The Stage as a Character: Automatic Creation of Acts of God for Dramatic Effect*. Working Notes of the 1995 AAAI Spring Symposium on Interactive Story Systems, Stanford: AAAI Press.

Roads, C (1996). *The Computer Music Tutorial*. Cambridge, MA: MIT Press.

Walter, WG (1950). An Imitation of Life. *Scientific American*, May, 42–45.

Walter, WG (1951). A Machine that Learns. *Scientific American*, August, 60–63.

11
Artists in the Virtual Studio

Morten Constantin Lervig and Kim Halskov Madsen

Morten Constantin Lervig is a composer and has held the position of musical director for a range of major multimedia events. A primary focus in his work has been the use of music as an element in holistic performances.

Kim Halskov Madsen holds a PhD degree in computer science and his research interests are design studies and human–computer interaction.

11.1 Introduction

The virtual studio is a video technology that makes it possible to combine video of physical objects, such as people, with video images generated in real time from digital 3D models. Virtual studio technology is commonly used for television productions that can be broadcasted directly or taped live with only a limited amount of editing. One of the main qualities of digital 3D scenography is that it can be dynamic, which can, for instance, be utilised in election broadcasts, where election results can immediately be visualised as 3D graphics, and in viewer polls, where the results can generate elements which are part of the digital 3D set.

Virtual studio technology has thus been used in TV broadcasting, but in the same way that artists have begun to work with computer and video as their working materials, it is obvious that they also may use virtual studio technology as artistic material. This chapter explores the work of three artists in the virtual studio. The theme thus becomes that of digital art, but where most research in this area is focused on the works of art, the focus here is on the creative process involved in making the works.

The chapter is based on three cases where artists work with a project group whose participants' professional background is in architecture and digital 3D scenography. Based on the work with the three productions, we identify aspects of significance for the work process that takes place when this type of artistic activity is carried out in a virtual studio. These aspects are identified with the aim of gaining insight into, and a better understanding of the process, including reflections on how such processes can be planned.

The analysis of the production processes is based on Alexander's (1977) idea of patterns, as he has developed it in the professional field of architecture. The focus in this chapter is on what happens in the work process in the virtual studio – the elements and concepts at play and in what ways. By following and analysing the work process, these elements and concepts will be revealed, along with their importance to the progress of the work. Since we are working with new technology here, not to mention new, artistically oriented use of this technology, our pattern language will take on a different aspect than Alexander's, for while Alexander searches for patterns in the entire history of human architecture, giving him access to a huge mass of empirical material, our empirical field is not very large. This task's ambition is not to create a comprehensive pattern language for the work process when artists and technicians work together in the virtual studio, but by analysing the empirical material, in all modesty simply to identify elements that seem to be important to the work process and to generalise them, so they can be understood in a broader context. These elements are described in a manner strongly inspired by the way in which Christopher Alexander describes his patterns, meaning a stringently uniform form that both describes, contextualises, evaluates and finally operationalises central aspects of the process.

Considerable scientific work is available in the area of digital art, but most of it by far is oriented toward the analysis of the finished product. Here, we will instead attempt to investigate the work process that takes place during the genesis of the product, so that this task more closely resembles what happens in the field of system development.

The next section of this chapter begins with a brief introduction to the most important of the technologies involved in the virtual studio, followed by a section introducing Christopher Alexander, whose theory forms the basis of the work with the empirical material. After this, there is a description of the investigative method used, a summary of the three cases and the patterns developed and finally, a conclusion based on the results achieved.

11.2 The Virtual Studio

The virtual studio is a video technology that makes it possible to combine video of physical objects, such as people, with video images generated in real time from digital 3D models, see (Moshkovitz, 2000). A production method resulting in productions that can be broadcasted directly or taped live with only a limited amount of editing, at the same time allowing for real time interaction between the TV-viewer and the studio in which the filming of the physical objects is taking place. This can, for instance, be used in election broadcasts, where election results can immediately be visualised as 3D graphics, and in viewer polls, where the results can generate elements which are part of the digital 3D set. In spite of the delay of from 1–5 twenty-fifths of a second for calculations and synchronising, the virtual studio is said to operate in real time.

The virtual studio opens up for new production methods in the professional TV world. On the introduction of this technology, the arguments for launching it have usually been economic – produce more for less money – but apart from this cost benefit perspective, there are obvious aesthetic opportunities which are far more wide-reaching than simply making sports studios, game shows and election broadcasts where the scenography can be quickly and cheaply replaced.

For years, TV broadcasts have utilised blue screen technology, e.g., in presenting weather reports, where the studio host stands in front of a blue or green surface, and this monochrome field is replaced by a weather chart in the final TV picture. The limitation of this classic blue screen construction is that it is impossible to zoom or move the camera. The virtual studio offers a solution to this problem in its 2D versions, and goes even further in its 3D versions.

The 2D versions mean that it is possible to put a flat background, in the shape of a two-dimensional image, behind the physical objects, and that a fixed camera can zoom, pan and tilt when filming. In principle, it works as shown in Figure 11.1.

The 3D versions mean that it is possible to work with a spatial model on the virtual set, where one can put the camera on one's shoulder or on a tripod, and move around in the virtual scenography; see Figure 11.2.

In principle, the technology works like this: physical objects, including people, are filmed in a monochrome, usually blue, TV studio. The positions of the cameras and the adjustment of focus and zoom are registered by a tracking system. This information is sent to the computer that handles the virtual scenography in the shape of a 3D model, so that it can match the virtual camera in the virtual model to the physical camera in the monochrome studio, and from this virtual camera position render out a picture identical in position and zoom to the picture the

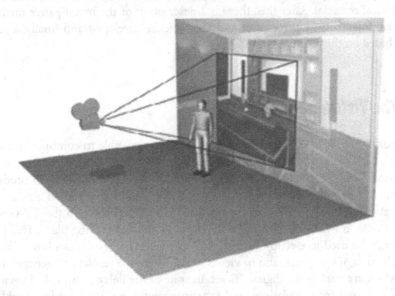

Figure 11.1 Schematic diagram of a 2D virtual studio.

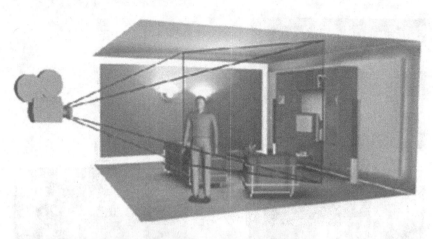

Figure 11.2 Schematic diagram of a 3D virtual studio.

physical camera is taking at the same time. We now have two pictures in the system: one taken by the real camera in the monochrome studio, and one generated by the computer, based on a camera position replicating that of the real camera. These two pictures meet in the keyer, where the background colour in the picture from the monochrome TV studio is removed and replaced by the computer-generated picture; see Figure 11.4.

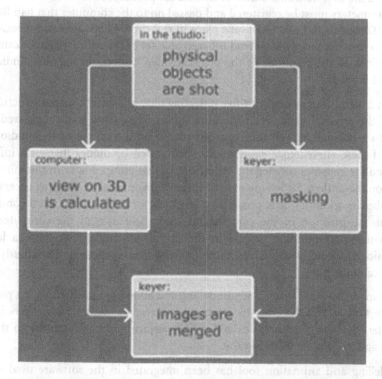

Figure 11.3 Schematic diagram of the technology of the virtual studio, on a component level.

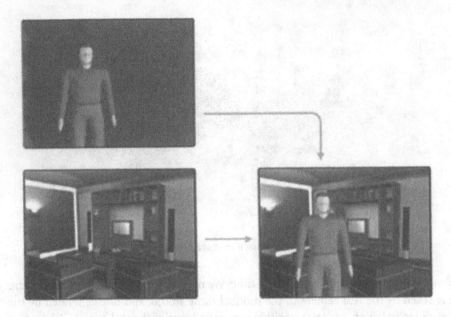

Figure 11.4 How the keyer works.

As can be seen in the above, it is a prerequisite for the virtual studio that the physical camera in the monochrome studio is tracked for position, zoom and focus. That is, these parameters must be registered and passed on to the computer that handles the digital 3D model, and this must take place in real time. There are various solutions for this, where the most widespread is based on a set of special surveillance cameras' observations of the positions of the physical video cameras in the blue studio, see Figure 11.5.

There is a metal framework with five reflecting blue globes in a spatial structure on each of the physical cameras in the blue studio. These antlers are registered by a total of six infrared surveillance cameras placed on the ceiling of the studio. The lenses of these surveillance cameras are surrounded by diodes that emit infrared light, and the cameras register the reflections of this infrared light in the mirroring globes on the antlers. By having at least three of these infrared cameras observe the five globes in an antler, it is possible in less than a frame – 1/25 of a second – to calculate the position of the camera and send these data to the computer that renders the corresponding picture in the digital 3D model. The camera lenses' mechanical tracking of zoom and focus delivers data on these synchronously with the optical tracking.

The 3D model is made using a 3D modelling and animation tool, which is a piece of software that allows the user to create and treat own digital 3D models in the computer, give them texture, i.e., add visible surfaces, and add lighting to the 3D models and to animate them in time.

A modelling and animation tool has been integrated in the software used in the virtual studio in this project (VIZ), which has been created and optimised for use in

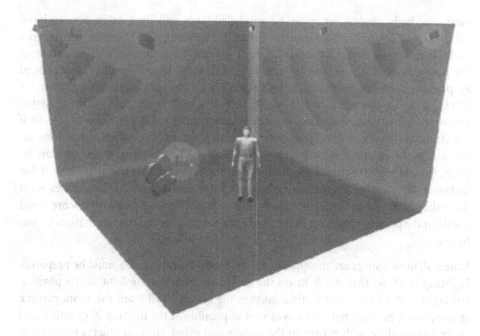

Figure 11.5 Illustration of tracking.

connection with a virtual studio. That means that this tool can be used to create models and animations that do not require much calculation – necessary to meet the need for real time rendering – and at the same time, a large amount of ready-to-use material is available in the shape of functions and attributes not normally seen in a 3D program, but which are practical in a situation where time is of the essence.

The demand for simple calculation has been met by simplifying the models for use in the virtual studio, limiting details, so that lighting calculations are not particularly involved. Furthermore, use of the built-in ready-to-use material fosters a tendency to make products with a specific expression of TV aesthetics, namely the most widespread use of the technology at the moment: for news and sports programs.

However, the program can also, with certain limitations, import models and animations from more advanced 3D programs, so that more advanced things can be constructed outside of the VIZ, and then imported into it, although this does not eliminate the limitations with regard to calculation weight.

Production in the virtual studio requires considerable preparation. First, the production process is planned; this can be in the shape of a classic storyboard, giving an overview of the course of the production. In addition to the descriptions of the production process resulting from a storyboard in a conventional TV or film production, consideration must be given to the fact that the virtual studio offers components capable of real-time interactivity. It is therefore necessary to write a description, not of what happens, but of everything that may possibly happen. A systematic review of this description will reveal all the preparations that must be carried out before the production can go on the air.

First, the basic digital set must be modelled; this will, just as in conventional scenography construction, require detailed knowledge of camera movements and the action, so that the model can meet the situations that arise in the course of the production. Next, all possible interactions must be identified and pre-produced as possible animations that can be controlled by the producer. This might, for instance, be an elevation of the studio, where a quiz contestant enters a virtual elevator on the digital set and the virtual scenography is animated so it looks as if the studio is sinking as the elevator continues to the next floor, where the movement stops and the studio host can leave the elevator. This type of sequence can be prepared and ready to use, without, however, any certainty that it will be used. If, for instance, we imagine a quiz where how well the contestants do determines what floor they are on, then a specific occurrence – a contestant getting a high score – will result in the person changing floors, and only in this case will the animation be put to use.

When all these things are pre-produced, the monochrome studio must be prepared. Lighting is set, so that the light on the digital set matches the light in the physical studio, and the keyer, which distinguishes the background from the monochrome studio, has to be adjusted to do so as well as possible in the lighting in question and as well as possible with regard to the people and other physical objects involved in the production. There must be cues for the participants, in the form of marks on the floor or something similar, and they must be able to see themselves on monitors in the monochrome studio, so that, for instance the quiz contestant in the above-mentioned elevation can see where he enters the elevator. Not until all these preparations have taken place can the production be put into on-air mode and produced, whether it is broadcast directly or taped on a video tape-recorder as a live-on-tape production

11.3 Christopher Alexander

Christopher Alexander is an architect working with theories of architecture, and in the trilogy (Alexander, 1975, 1979; Alexander et al., 1977) he has created a theoretical and methodical fundament for architecture. While *The Timeless Way of Building* describes the fundamental nature of the task of creating buildings and cities, and *The Oregon Experiment* exemplifies the method, in *A Pattern Language*, Alexander et al. create and describe a pattern language consisting of individual patterns which together embrace the entire field of architecture.

> The elements of this language are entities called patterns. Each pattern describes a problem which occurs over and over again in our environment, and they describe the core of the solution to that problem, in such a way that you can use this solution a million times over, without ever doing it the same way twice (Alexander et al., 1977, p. x).

Alexander's goal is to create an operative tool, where it is possible at any point to go in and look up any problem, find out in what larger sets of problems it is inscribed, gain an understanding of the problem, find an operative solution in the form of an instruction and, finally, see what other problems are embedded in it. The patterns in the language are thus mutually organised in something resembling a hierarchical structure. In spite of the somewhat pretentious goal of creating a universal pattern language, Alexander et al. (1977) emphasise that one of several possible pattern languages is created, and that this takes place in a dynamic process of change, arising from new knowledge gained through application.

We can gain more insight into this if we use an example to investigate the structure of Christopher Alexander's patterns: Pattern no. 99, Main Building, (Alexander et al., 1977, pp. 485ff). On the front page of the pattern we first see the title, and under it there is a picture of a main building, or at least a building which, with its symmetry around a central part, its good condition and the controlled growth surrounding it, signals precisely *main building*. The picture acts as a kind of poetic, mood-creating approach to the problem. After the title and the picture, there is a section that sets the context for this pattern and how it may relate to other larger patterns; in this example it says: "once you have decided more or less how people will move around within the **building complex (95)**... showing that pattern no. 99 refers back to pattern no. 95, which is about *building complex*". Next, there are three diamonds, indicating that the description of the problem starts here, and these are followed by a headline in bold print, describing the essence of the problem in one or two sentences. In the case of pattern no. 99, it says: "**A complex of buildings with no center is like a man without a head**". After this headline, there is a description of the problem, its empirical background, the proof of its validity, the extent of the ways in which it can manifest itself in a building, etc. In no. 99, for instance, it is argued that the main building in a building complex is important as a signpost in the mental landscape that we use to orientate ourselves when finding our way, and further as the functional heart of the purpose of the building complex. Following this, again in bold print, is the solution to the problem, always presented as an instruction, so we know precisely what to do using this pattern. For pattern no. 99, it says among other things: "**For any collection of buildings, decide which building in the group houses the most essential function – which building is the soul of the group, as a human institution. Then form this building as the main building, with a central position, higher roof ...**" and this instruction is followed by a diagram or a sketch, in this example some roughly sketched buildings, with one centrally placed building being taller than the others. An arrow points to the highest roof, saying *high roof*, another arrow saying *main function* points to the body of the building under this roof, and finally, under the body of the building, it says *central position*. Another three diamonds follow, indicating that the description of the problem ends here, and, as the final component of the pattern, a section linking the pattern in question with all the lesser patterns in the language which contribute to the perfection of this pattern. For instance, it says: "Build all the main paths tangent to the main building, in arcades or glazed corridors, with a direct view into its main functions – **Common Areas At the Heart (129)**", showing that there is a special relation between the main building and the main paths in the building complex.

Thus the structure of Christopher Alexander's patterns is:

1. The name of the pattern.
2. A picture showing an archetypical example.
3. The context of the pattern.
4. A headline describing the essence of the problem.
5. A description of the problem.
6. The solution to the problem in the form of an instruction.
7. A sketch or diagram, also showing the solution.
8. The link between the pattern in question and lesser patterns making it up.

While Alexander's idea of patterns for the description of very different problems was shaped from a desire to describe, evaluate and operationalise sets of problems in architecture, the basic structure of his pattern language has gained a foothold in other areas. Gamma et al. (1995) have established a pattern language that includes design patterns for reapplicable object-oriented software.

> A design pattern names, abstracts, and identifies the key aspects of a common design structure that makes it useful for creating a reusable object-oriented design. The design pattern identifies the participating classes and instances, their roles and collaborations, and the distribution for responsibilities. Each design pattern focuses on a particular object-oriented design problem or issue. It describes when it applies, whether it can be applied in view of other design constraints, and the consequences and trade-offs of its use (Gamma et al., 1995 pp. 3ff).

In this way an attempt is made at creating a pattern language, with the clear idea of revealing, gaining insight into and an overview of design strategies that can contribute to understanding and choosing the most suitable way of solving a given task and at the same time contextualising it, so potential reapplications can be identified.

Kjeldskov and Nyvang (2000) have been inspired by Alexander's pattern language method to create a fragment of a pattern language for Computer Supported Collaborative Work (CSCW), based on a review of a large number of CSCW research results. The material presented in this chapter is more closely related to Kjeldskov and Nyvang's application of pattern language than to that of Erich Gamma et al. The latter has a clear, very direct application-oriented use of the idea of pattern language. Kjeldskov and Nyvang's application has as its goal to gain insight into an area of investigation that can both create an overview of concepts, sets of problems and subjects in the area, but at the same time can also contribute solution models on a number of different levels.

While Alexander's own pattern language is based on a number of architects' practical experience and observations, and in addition utilises the entire history of architecture as empirical material, the present application is solely based on the three cases described, and can therefore only be expected to result in a fragment of a pattern language. Alexander's pattern language has been chosen as inspiration for a model for the presentation of the knowledge acquired. The form seems advantageous for a collected presentation of a heterogeneous sum of results, where the knowledge acquired can be expected to be inspiring and operative for others in similar circumstances.

Common to Alexander and Gamma as well as Kjeldskov and Nyvang is that they look at patterns of *products* – buildings, software and CSCW applications respectively – where in contrast this chapter treats patterns in *processes*. The focus here has been guided by Donald Schön's (1983) studies of design processes, in which he has documented the importance of earlier examples, experiments and the use of design materials, as well as the importance of contemplating the language domains utilised in the design process. Schön defines design processes very broadly as processes in which an existing situation is to be altered to a desired situation. Specifically of the artistic process, he says: "Artists make things and are, in this sense, designers" (Schön, 1991, p. 42).

11.4 Investigative Method

The empirical basis for shaping an outline of a pattern language has been the three cases which were briefly presented in the introduction. The production process was organised with meetings between the artists and the project group as its axis, with these meetings being well-defined windows to the process, through which insight into the process was made possible. These meetings provided a long series of different documents, reports, notes and production sketches, and these, as well as e-mail communication between artists and project group, have been a source of insight into the progress of the process. The most important empirical material has, however, been video-recordings, primarily from meetings, secondarily from practical work situations in the blue studio, the control room, or in front of the computer.

The analysis of the video material is based on principles of interaction analysis as described by B. Jordan and A. Henderson (1994, p. 1): "Interaction Analysis as we describe it here is an interdisciplinary method for the empirical investigation of the use of human beings with each other and with objects in their environment."

Before the collaborative projects with the artists began, a number of focal points were formulated, and later used in the video analyses. These foci were excellent and operative for identifying points in the meetings where something of importance to the development and direction of the process took place, and are clearly inspired by:

- The material presented, understood in the broad sense as place, equipment, technology, productions, inspiration. What materials play what role.
- What the artists tell about their earlier work that is or is not relevant to this situation.
- The ideas put forth about production/experiments, and by whom.
- The professional/technical/aesthetic/social domains at play.
- The role played by the various people, what is expected of them to begin with.
- The characteristics of the situation and how it is organised.

The analysis itself is based on what Jordan and Henderson (1994, p. 19) call ethnographic chunks, which are delimitable ethnographic units in interaction, with the advantage that it allows for a review of quite a large amount of material, thus ensuring a good basis for the results.

In the first review of the video material, such chunks were identified and registered, after which a second examination resulted in notes about the individual chunks. In the third review, concepts, subjects and problems that appeared in these chunks were isolated, and it was attempted to find a balance between those that were too general and those that seemed to be too case-specific. Along the way, the video material was revisited, so that the analysis took on the character of an iterative process. This preparatory work for a pattern language is in accordance with Christopher Alexander's way of understanding a pattern language, as something in which where there is a continual development of the pattern language itself.

All in all it can be said that the empirical material has been treated, supported by Jordan and Henderson, with theoretical reference to Alexander Schön, in an effort to find subjects, concepts and sets of problems making up patterns in a pattern language created according to Alexander's model.

11.5 Overview of Cases

11.5.1 Martin Bigum

Martin Bigum is a pictorial artist who uses a classic painting technique in which he works in layers upon layers with a very high degree of detail in the material, but he has also earlier used blue screen technology in connection with the production of a video with himself as the main character. Martin Bigum demonstrated his experience in film production shortly after the initial contact between him and the project group by sending a sketch of a storyboard, which was gone over in detail at the first meeting and which came to form the basis of the production. In addition to the storyboard, Martin Bigum sent a number of sketches and copies of his own pictures in various formats previous to the first meeting. Some of these were intended to give the project group an idea of what he does as an artist, but most were intended as part of the storyboard, as well as the basis for modelling and as textures in models.

The first meeting with Martin Bigum took place as a presentation of the participants in the project, and an introduction of the technology involved, using examples of productions, both earlier partial results of the overarching research project, and material in the shape of demo-tapes from the producers of virtual studio equipment. Later it was agreed to use the storyboard we had received as a starting point, and the rest of the meeting became a review, primarily from a practical production point of view, of how Martin Bigum's ideas could be implemented in this technology. Naturally, the aesthetic expectations for the project were also launched in this perspective.

On the background of this first meeting, the project group prepared a first sketch, attempting to implement the ideas contained in the storyboard. This material was sent to Martin Bigum in the shape of a videotape. He reacted with a number of requests for changes, most of which arose from an interest in having the project appear sufficiently professional to be shown in connection with exhibitions of his pictures.

Work on the production continued until Martin Bigum came for a second meeting, where the actual video production was to take place. Martin Bigum was to take part in the video production as pianist and actor. On this occasion, it was clear that he was uncertain whether the impression, so vital to him, of a professional product could be achieved. The project group was unable to finish all the shooting that day, and the rest of the planned shots were done on the following days, using a stand-in for Martin Bigum. The resulting videotape was then sent to him.

Martin Bigum's reaction was to send the project group a new storyboard, in which he sketched a number of preconditions for the continuation of the project, stressing among other things the necessity of using the technology so as, without demanding an unreasonable effort, to meet his requirement of not breaking the illusion in the work. This gave rise to a discussion in the project group of whether or not to continue. The arguments for stopping were based on concern as to whether the project group was capable, in the framework of the available resources, of producing anything satisfactory to Martin Bigum, at the same time as the project had moved from being production-specific in relation to virtual studio technology to being more capable of being advantageously implemented in post-production. After some discussion between Bigum and the project group, the collaboration was discontinued, after which the part of the production based on Martin Bigum's storyboard was done with a stand-in.

11.5.2 Ingvar Cronhammar

Ingvar Cronhammar is currently of great interest with his gigantic sculpture project, *Elia*, which just on the strength of its budget of over ten million Danish kroner is one of the most important contemporary works in Denmark. During the past 15–20 years, Cronhammar has become more and more prominent on the Danish art scene as the creator of unique monumental works on the borderline between sculpture and installation. With works like *The Gate*, *Syvende Søjle* (the Seventh Column) and *Stage*, which are now all in public collections, Ingvar Cronhammar has found his unique form of expression, often combining natural materials with artefacts from the indus-trialised world and with detail and volume giving rise to an unparalleled textural effect.

As far as we knew, Ingvar Cronhammar had not worked with video, apart from what might be required for his ordinary work, such as documentation of his own works. So contacting him in connection with this project was contacting a proficient artist who could not be expected to be technologically proficient in the area of virtual studio technology.

Because of the pressure of work on *Elia*, Cronhammar was not able to prepare a new project, but he did have a project that he had worked on for an exhibition, and which he thought might possibly be used. The project is called *Blodrummet* (The Blood Room) and is in its sculptural form a model of an imaginary vehicle.

At the first meeting with Ingmar Cronhammar, he presented his work, *Blodrummet*, in the shape of 2D computer drawings, and there was a thorough discussion of the detail of this object, in the shape of materials, construction, colours, light, lighting, etc. Cronhammar's idea was simply to make a 3D staging of this work, which could perhaps be presented and run as a video loop in connection with an exhibition of the physical work. At this meeting Cronhammar was introduced to the technology of the virtual studio, to which he reacted with a certain distant curiosity. On the one hand, he claimed to be the kind of person who does not understand and is not interested in understanding digital technology; on the other hand, there was nothing to indicate that he would not accept or use it.

The first meeting ended in agreement that the project group would construct a model of *Blodrummet* (Figure 11.6), and explore various ways in which people could pass through this space. Cronhammar wanted the production to be as underplayed as possible, and he suggested doing this by means of an investigative camera, which, although hand-held, would calmly explore the object.

A videotape of the result of the experiments was sent to Cronhammar. The tape contained a sequence of a 3D model of *Blodrummet*, filmed with a hand-held camera, and a series of sequences where various persons pass through the object, with added delay effect, meaning that the person who goes through the picture leaves a trace, in that the image of this person is only gradually toned out.

Cronhammar's reaction to this film was primarily that it shouldn't be people, but a dog, in that the purpose is only to add scale to the object; that the shots composing the video should be almost orthogonal on the object; that the camera shouldn't be hand-held; and that the style should be *cool*. Furthermore, the object should be painted with glossy paint (like a car), the nipples (tiny sources of light on the object) should be smaller, and the light in the window should be left on the whole time.

At a following meeting with the project group, it was very clear that Cronhammar was interested in a visualisation of his sculpture as he imagined the work implemented. He wanted the production to appear cool, or in other words, that the

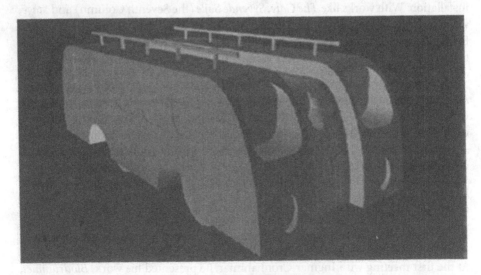

Figure 11.6 The first 3D model of *Blodrummet*.

visualisation be objective, registering, almost cynical, in contrast to subjective. This is expressed, for instance, in the fact that Cronhammar no longer wanted a hand-held camera, which, as he had discovered during the process, gives a certain interpretative, subjective impression. In the final part of the production process, work was done directly on the virtual studio's software, after which Cronhammar was shown the technological possibilities and limitations in the form of sketches, at the same time as the solutions were implemented in the model of the object.

11.5.3 Superflex

Superflex is a group of three artists, Rasmus Nielsen, Jacob Fenger and Bjørn-Stjerne Christiansen. Like a number of other young artists, Superflex has thrown itself into productions and forms of productions that can best be grouped under conceptual art. Their approach to the concept of art challenges the concept of the work of art; for instance they are responsible for a project where they have designed and implemented a low-tech bio-gas plant for use in developing countries. Others of their projects can be seen on their website: www.superflex.dk.

The joint project, as sketched at the first meeting, came to be based on two of Superflex's other projects, *Karlskrona 2* and *Superchannel*.

The *Karlskrona 2* project is a virtual world, which to a certain extent mirrors the real Swedish town of Karlskrona. Briefly, the idea is to create a virtual world on the Internet, where the citizens of Karlskrona, using an avatar, can meet, chat and construe in 3D. According to Rune Nielsen (2002), *Karlskrona 2* can be used as a tool for discussing the field of tension between the modern city's demand for contemporaneity and the fact that Karlskrona has been inscribed as part of UNESCO's world heritage, which ties the city to history. One of the central ideas in the original *Karlskrona 2* concept was to set up a window between the virtual and the real world in the form of a giant screen erected in the center of Karlskrona. It has not been possible to implement this screen in the current Beta version of the system, so the window between the real and the virtual world in this version exists only in the shape of the PC at which the user sits.

Superchannel is a low-end system that can stream video production onto the Internet close to real time. At the same time, a chat can take place on the website the streaming is shown on, and via this chat, the viewer can also send messages directly to the video studio, in order to possibly influence the current production. In addition to this technology, there is a joint server on which earlier productions can be seen. On the *Superchannel* website, http://www.superchannel.org, the portal for all the different (approximately 20 at the time of writing) *Superchannel* channels with associated studios can be found.

At the first meeting with Superflex, the parties involved introduced themselves to each other, and the Superflex group was shown the technology and facilities. At this point, Superflex really had no ready-to-use idea of what they might do with this technology; it was clear that they were more interested in principles and conceptual possibilities than in actually doing a production as a work of art.

At one point, Bjørn-Stjerne asked: *This is live equipment, but you are not using it, what happens when it really comes alive?* Based on this question, a long series of ideas, all circling around this theme, were explored, and naturally enough, *Karlskrona 2* was repeatedly brought into play, since it is precisely a virtual world that functions in real time. The meeting ended with a decision to attempt to have *Karlskrona 2* streamed in as video-feed in the virtual studio, while a model of *Karlskrona 2* was being constructed for the scenography in the virtual studio. The aim was to achieve the effect of having real people, and possibly other objects in *Karlskrona 2*. This was then to be streamed out over a *Superchannel* in real time, so people from *Karlskrona 2* and everyone else could interact with the real people in the blue studio via the chat.

In the following period various technological possibilities for implementation of the desired set-up were explored, forming the basis for a two-day meeting with Superflex. At the beginning of the meeting, it was clear that they expected to be able to walk around via the avatars in the model used for the blue studio. This would be fully implemented if *Karlskrona 2* in real time could be the model used in VIZ. This is impossible for two main reasons: (1) the VIZ is locked against changes when it is in broadcast mode, and *Karlskrona 2* would not be implemented, if changes cannot take place; (2) the software used for *Karlskrona 2*, supplied by *RealWorlds*, is a closed standard. It does, however, support the implemented system to the extent that a studio host can walk around with the avatars.

The set-up that was implemented functioned as follows: Digital scenography was constructed in the VIZ software in the virtual studio, imitating parts of the *Karlskrona 2* scenography, where it was possible to stream a video signal in real time, generated from *Karlskrona 2* in real time, and place it on the surface of an object in the VIZ, thus allowing this video stream to act as a screen in the VIZ, where *Karlskrona 2* was running in real time, see Figure 11.7.

The video stream coming from *Karlskrona 2* is pictures generated from a camera which is the eyes of an avatar. In the experiments with the set-up, the person whose avatar's eyes generated the stream, was present in the studio with his computer. This had the obvious advantage that it was possible to talk to this person and ask him to have his avatar move, thus controlling the "eyes", or in other words, the camera generating the stream.

The video produced from the VIZ in real time was – likewise in real time – streamed out onto the Internet via Superflex's system, *Superchannel*, and could then be accessed as a TV program on *Superchannel*.

This set-up allowed *Karlskrona 2* users, qua their presence in *Karlskrona 2*, to become visible on *Superchannel* as part of the picture from *Karlskrona 2* that was streamed into the virtual studio and from there out onto *Superchannel*. A precondition for this was that the users were logged on to *Karlskrona 2*, and at the same time had turned on the program on the *Superchannel* net channel that was sending the program – this also allowed them to communicate with others logged on to *Karlskrona 2* via its chat.

After a brief introductory discussion between the project group and Superflex, everyone went into the studio and began working with the possibilities of the

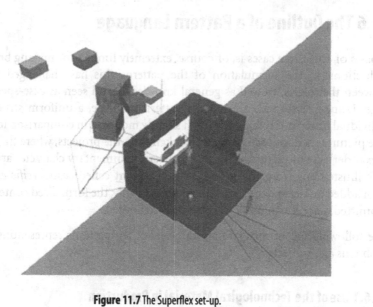

Figure 11.7 The Superflex set-up.

implemented system. Superflex made use of the space, and carried on the discussion of what they wanted to do and what the system was capable of, and it is worth noting that at this point there was still a *conception* of a great difference between what Superflex wanted to achieve and what the set-up could deliver. However, in the practical situation, when Superflex and the project group tested the set-up, it appeared that there was good compatibility between Superflex's wishes and the potentiality of the set-up. By narrowing down the field in working with the set-up, two prototypical events that could be attempted were identified in the course of the day, and a message was sent out to a small hand-picked group of faithful and curious *Karlskrona 2* users, saying that a test would be run the next day.

The next morning started with a summing-up or production meeting, where the two ideas were presented:

1. To prepare a space in *Karlskrona 2* where the avatars were encouraged to build the scenography, and to let a studio host perform in the blue studio, with *Karlskrona 2* as the dominant background. The studio host could then talk to the avatars by way of *Superchannel* and get their answers through the *Karlskrona 2* chat. Here, the studio host could ask them what they had done.

2. Likewise, with the same pre-prepared space in *Karlskrona 2*, but now as a video-feed on the wall of the virtual studio. The studio host could interact with the participating avatars as mentioned above, but the idea was now that the avatars could build something in *Karlskrona 2* that could be copied into the virtual studio. The latter could be done in advance by making copies of the simple objects that the avatars built in the virtual world.

The two events were broadcasted, and in both cases the communication between the studio host and the avatars worked well, in spite of the technical problems the set-up had in this regard.

11.6 The Outline of a Pattern Language

A basis of only three cases is, of course, extremely limited for making broad general deductions. In the formulation of the patterns this has challenged the balance between the results, viewed as general knowledge, and seen as case-specific knowledge. Using Christopher Alexander's pattern language, a uniform structure of the individual patterns is retained, though slightly modified in comparison to Alexander. The pictures used for each pattern are taken from the projects, where the relations to Alexander's use of pictures with a very general commentary character appear as specific illustrations from the cases. Further, a point called *case-specific examples* has been added to Alexander's pattern structure. Finally, the formalised contextualisation is omitted, since the number of patterns is so limited.

The following subsections contain the total of ten patterns representing significant problems and subjects.

11.6.1 Use of the Technological Material in Production

The Essence of the Issue

The hard-and-software of virtual studios is a complex material process, which, when used experimentally creatively, can contribute to the implementation of the project.

Figure 11.8 Superflex tests the technology.

Description of the Problem

In collaborations where both aesthetic and artistic capacities are present and working with virtual studies software, it is possible, by direct interaction with the software, to influence the aesthetic expression. By assessing, evaluating and criticising concrete uses of the technology on the screen and immediately changing these or making suggestions for how they can be changed, production can be furthered in spurts, and the design choices made have great authenticity because they are made on the basis of direct interaction with the material.

It is difficult to understand the limitations and possibilities of a complex technological construction like the virtual studio. An overview of and insight into the virtual studio's technological material in the shape of the technologies involved can be created by working with its set-up. This provides experience with the inherent possibilities of this material and creates an understanding of how the individual technologies' components depend on each other.

Practical experience with the systems' software in direct interaction, where both artistic and technological capacities are represented, is thus a very operative way of furthering the process.

Case-specific Examples

Interaction with material in the form of the hardware and software of the set-up gives rise to design-decisions in all three projects. Martin Bigum notes that the three planes of the landing approach of his project have a visible edge and expresses dissatisfaction with this, whereupon Rune Nielsen suggests a way of avoiding it. This method is used in the final production.

Ingvar Cronhammar follows Andreas Lykke-Olesen's attempt to meet the request for *Masarati glans* in the surface finish of the vehicle. Cronhammar doesn't give up until Rune Nielsen has suggested a solution that involves using a certain reflection-map, which Andreas Lykke-Olesen immediately attempts to implement.

Superflex only delimitated a number of aesthetic spaces of possibility by implementing a specific technological construction prior to the final meeting. Here, the first day's interaction and work with this set-up is decisive for the two prototypical productions that are developed and tested during and after this meeting. Many of the decisions that led to the two current applications of the set-up were made in situations where the set-up was investigated and tested.

Therefore:

Use the virtual studio's hardware and software experimentally.

11.6.2 Aesthetic Materials Used in Production

The Essence of the Issue

Aesthetic materials can be used directly in production in the shape of choice of colours, pictures and video used as textures in the 3D models.

Description of the Problem

The use of aesthetic materials in the production makes it possible to bring the results of work in other professional disciplines and situations into a production in the virtual studio, just as there will often be a certain fabrication of aesthetic materials specifically for use in a production. With the use of previously produced aesthetic materials, the production takes on the character of a kind of montage, where materials can have surprising effects in this new connection. When artists use materials from previous productions, strong aesthetic references are often created between the new production and the artist's earlier productions, so that a strong sense of identity with the artist is created. At the same time, the use of pictures as texture contributes to more rapid attainment of a greater degree of completion than otherwise possible.

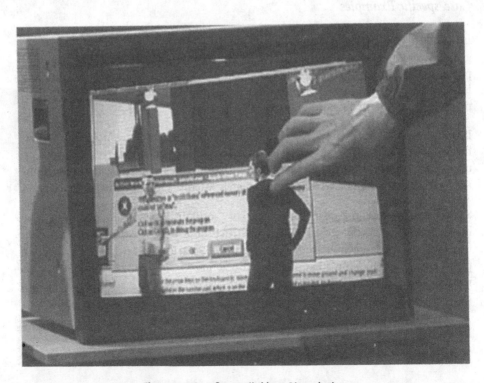

Figure 11.9 Superflex uses *Karlskrona 2* in production.

Case-specific Examples

Martin Bigum's production makes use of pictures that he has drawn or painted as texture on spatial models. This contributes to a great degree to identifying the finished production as being by Martin Bigum, just as it adds – in certain areas – a very high degree of completion to the production. In the case of Superflex, live-streaming from the virtual world of *Karlskrona 2* is used as textures on spatial models, with the result that *Karlskrona 2* becomes a direct participant in the production, at the same time as *Karlskrona 2* as an aesthetic expression comes to appear as part of the production.

Therefore:

Use aesthetic materials from previous artistic projects by participating artists.

11.6.3 Aesthetic Materials as Examples and Inspiration

The Essence of the Issue

Aesthetic materials used as examples and inspiration function particularly well in the process of describing the aesthetic properties of the project.

Figure 11.10 A discussion with Ingvar Cronhammar, based on a drawing of *Blodrummet*.

Description of the Problem

Materials used as *examples* are used in order, through the material, to point out the concrete attributes that are to be transferred to the project. Materials as *inspiration* are used when there are attributes of the material that can form a *jumping-off point* for work on the project. It is not possible to clearly define the difference between aesthetic materials serving as examples and serving as inspiration, since this is a question of the two extremes of a continuum. Aesthetic materials used as examples specifically state the effect a component of the production is to have, and how it is to be achieved. As inspiration, materials can serve to isolate and describe more general characteristics of a production.

Case-specific Examples

Martin Bigum's project has images that serve as inspiration for the graphical universe to be implemented. Especially in connection with one picture, where Martin Bigum's little figure, Art, is lying in the bottom of a boat, the question is whether or not the surface of the water in the picture is to be "photo-shopped" in the production in the virtual studio – meaning whether it is to be used directly as material for the production after being treated in the graphic program called Photoshop – or if it is only the effect that is desired. To this, Martin Bigum answers that it is the effect that is desired, and the material therefore acts as inspiration for work with the real water surface, and as such enunciates a great deal, in the sense that it is cartoon-like, has a specific colour, etc. Martin Bigum stands up at a meeting on his project, grabs a chair and points at the leather, saying: "This is the effect I want the figure rising through the grand piano to make on the surface!" This shapes a common frame of reference that the project group can use as basis for the texture to be applied to the figure.

In order to gain insight into and understand the characteristics of the Superflex project, the project group together watch *Superchannel* on the Internet. In this way they see the aesthetic context of the project, and it is clear that the fact of seeing and trying it quickly creates this understanding.

Cronhammar says: "The vehicle is to be surgical green. You know the colour surgical green, don't you?" This is a very precise description of the colour, which requires matching fabric from a hospital gown.

Therefore:

Drag lots of aesthetic materials into projects.

11.6.4 A Common Space of Reference as Line of Sight

The Essence of the Issue

Common spaces of reference contribute to the identification of an overall line of sight for the project.

Description of the Problem

A main part of the description of a project in the virtual studio is identification of the goal of the production. This delimitation can take place by pointing to desired directions for the production, but it can also take place by pointing to unwanted effects for the project. The common space of reference can have a direct influence on the work process, as when participants in the process experience a feeling of accord on the universe, the mood, the feeling to be sought after in general or in a specific segment of the production.

Case-specific Examples

In a commentary on one of the demo-videos provided by the producer of the virtual studio, Martin Bigum says: "I like it a bit more tame, otherwise there's too much marble…" He hints at a common space of reference as he looks around and his statement is affirmed by those present. Another example is when Martin Bigum, at one of the first meetings tells the group about the effect he wants the real video production to have when it is seen at an art exhibition: "so, if you arrive at an art exhibition … and you think: 'Damn, it looks like he's lying there', so that could be a goal, that you like, that nothing stops you from meeting it …". Here, Martin Bigum creates a common space of reference around how the video is to be experienced, and the contexts in which it is to be experienced. When Superflex's Bjørn-Stjerne describes their *Superchannel* project at the Trapholt art museum, where a number of school classes were invited to make suggestions as to what a TV studio should look like, it is also a common space of reference.

Figure 11.11 Using a metaphor, Rune Nielsen explains how the set-up works.

Therefore:

Note how common spaces of reference can contribute to the focus and progress of the project.

11.6.5 Experiments

The Essence of the Issue

The artistic production in the virtual studio is implemented through experiments.

Description of the Problem

Most experiments in the blue studio begin with the group agreeing to try some implementation or alteration in the current sketch of the production. Next, the project group attempts to carry out what was agreed on, after which the result is evaluated, both in the project group as the work is taking place, as well as by producing a video sequence showing the result, which is then evaluated by individual participants. This form is used in working with series of experiments making up segments or partial segments of the production, and in single experiments based on a simple problem. These are experiments where a specific effect is sought through a certain action. The evaluation of the result of the experiment applies not only to the question of whether

Figure 11.12 Bjørn-Stjerne Christiansen from Superflex caught in *Karlskrona 2* in an experiment with keying of pictures generated from *Karlskrona 2*.

the desired result was attained, but whether the changes – expected or not – caused by the experiment on the whole are desirable or not. Another type of experiment in the virtual studio is when we try to find out if a given version of the set-up can provide a fruitful situation, allowing investigation of its characteristics in detail. That is, a type of experiment with a concrete aim, but where the goal is to create the possibility of further experimentation.

Case-specific Examples

Right from the first meeting, the work methods of both Martin Bigum and Ingvar Cronhammar are very much that things decided upon in consensus are tested by the project group. During this phase, local experiments are carried out; in Invar Cronhammar's case, they test whether a certain video effect might fulfil the expectations for the production. This is first evaluated by the project group alone, and if the result is found satisfactory, it is sent for further evaluation by Cronhammar, who turns it down (or accepts it). So in these productions there is a sequence that says: agreement is reached on the experiments to be carried out; the project group carries out the experiments and has its own evaluation in this process; the results are presented to the artists, who evaluate, and after this another consensus can be reached on the experiments to be done.

In Superflex, the prototypical production does not really begin until the second meeting. Previous to this, the production set-up has been described by Rune Nielsen, and implemented by the project group. The meetings with Superflex are mostly about delimiting a kind of tool-like use of the virtual studio, which also involves two of Superflex's other projects, namely *Karlskrona 2* and *Superchannel*. In this way the discussions primarily come to treat the possibilities offered by various versions of these set-ups. Previous to this second meeting, Superflex has built up an expectation of what the system can do in the set-up described – an expectation that apparently cannot be met. But through experiments with the set-up, it is seen that the system actually is fully capable of meeting Superflex's needs and wants. Generally speaking, this is an experimental test of a hypothesis, and it is seen in evaluation that the experiment was successful to a great degree, but not completely, since there is not complete agreement between what Superflex wanted and what the system was finally capable of doing.

Therefore:

Deliberately plan the process as a series of experiments.

11.6.6 Aesthetic Competence

The Essence of the Issue

Aesthetic competence is of definitive importance.

Description of the Problem

If a finished production has a significant aesthetic dimension, then aesthetic competence naturally plays an important role. Aesthetic competence comprises, among other things:

- competence in 3D modelling and animation;
- digital 3D scenographic competence and classic TV scenography in the virtual studio where both work together in the total impression;
- competence in film-aesthetics, including camera work, cutting between cameras, lighting, the effect of sound and sound recordings, video effects, etc.
- media-aesthetic competence in the use of the virtual studio for live broadcasting with real time interaction;
- pictorial aesthetics, the combination of video recordings and computer-generated images.

From the beginning of the individual production, there was an aesthetic goal for the production, which has been introduced and maintained by the artist throughout the production. This goal is described in words, and illustrated by references, examples and materials. Through a discussion of various ways of implementing the goal, a decision is made as to how to do so, after which the aesthetic experiments can begin. This must necessarily be the case, because the aesthetic limitations of the set-up are so varied, and in many cases unpredictable, that experimenting with materials is the most operative way of making progress in the process.

Figure 11.13 Ingvar Cronhammar.

Case-specific Examples

Ingvar Cronhammar's aesthetic goal for the production was to create a visualisation of *Blodrummet*. In the situation where Cronhammar realises that the camera work is being interpreted, namely when his own idea of a hand-held camera is put into effect, and the production thus begins to tell a story, he turns strongly against it, and asks for a camera that *scans* the object, so the production is given a cool, almost cynical expression.

In Superflex's production, the fact that it was possible to use this technology for real-time interaction between TV viewers and the studio comprised the media-aesthetic perspective that seems to be fundamental for their aesthetic decisions throughout the process. The focus was on how to make this interaction meaningful, and their other aesthetic competences were subject to this perspective.

Therefore:

It is especially important that the aesthetic goal is explicated, thoroughly evaluated and maintained throughout the project.

11.6.7 Technological Competence

The Essence of the Issue

Apart from general competence in studio technology, a number of competences specific to the virtual studio are required.

Description of the Problem

Competences in the various technologies in the virtual studio include:

- Competence in traditional video production, including camera technology, sound technology, lighting, producer functions, stage management, production planning, use and maintenance of video equipment, an understanding of video and audio set-ups, and many other things.
- Competence in 3D modelling and animation, in particular including experience with transfer of files from other formats and low-polygon modelling.
- Competence in the use of tracking technology.
- Competence in the use of real-time keying.
- Competence in general computer support and maintenance, including networks and graphics.

The technological competences needed to use all the equipment for virtual studio production are an understanding of the individual technologies and especially of the

Figure 11.14 Andreas Lykke-Olesen explains a detail from *Blodrummet*.

way they interact. That means that knowledge of how information and video signals are exchanged between the individual components is necessary in order to understand and correct problems in these flows. In addition, competence in the use of virtual studio software is necessary.

Case-specific Examples

Svend Erik Søfelt, Andreas Lykke-Olesen and Rune Nielsen's technological competences came into play in the review of Martin Bigum's first storyboard, in the solution-oriented evaluation of the course of events sketched by Bigum. The aesthetic demands are met by technological competences in a solution-oriented process that brings competences in film and video technology, modelling technology, graphical technology and the virtual studio into play. The result is an outline of how technological competences are to meet the aesthetic expectations of the production. Later in the process it was seen that the technological competences and technology were not able to meet these expectations to the degree envisaged by Martin Bigum. The aesthetic goals both challenge and develop the technological competences, while at the same time the limitations of technology are revealed.

Therefore:

The necessary technological competences must be present in the project, and those lacking must be externally available.

11.6.8 Interaction Between Aesthetic and Technological Competences

The Essence of the Issue

Both the aesthetic and technological domains are decisive for implementation of the production. At the same time, it is clear that the aesthetically formulated projects challenge and develop technological competence.

Description of the Problem

The virtual studio is a complex technology, developed with focus on certain production situations. This focus has been important for a number of technological properties, including having definitive influence on the aesthetic possibilities of technology. This is the case for obvious things like the fact that the final output is a video signal, and therefore has a relatively low resolution, as well as for easily comprehensible things like the fact that there are calculative limitations in living up to the real-time character of the system. Similarly, the artistic competence represented in the form of an artistic idea plays a definitive role in the development of the project, and has a definitive influence on how the technology is used.

In the work process there is a tendency to focus on the limitations technology puts on aesthetic possibilities, and it is very important that this technological

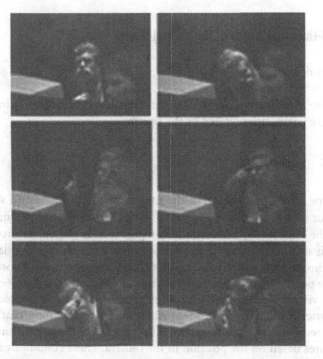

Figure 11.15 Ingvar Cronhammar and Andreas Lykke-Olesen working together.

competence is transferred to the field of aesthetics, but it can be seen that there is also considerable movement in the other direction. That is, the expectations and goals based on aesthetic competences are capable of developing technological competences by challenging the use of technology to a degree that alters it.

Case-specific Examples

In Bigum's case, a cone of light was to *end* in a certain way in the scene around a grand piano. It was necessary to experiment with various lighting and animation effects in order to find a final solution. In the case of Cronhammar, the need for a certain stream of light through the windows of the vehicle did not seem to be possible, but the problem was solved by giving the windows a slightly larger surface in the model, where a transparent pattern was added, giving the impression of light streaming from the windows. Superflex's desire to build interactivity into the model while broadcasting from the situation seemed impossible, but it could nevertheless be done by carrying out a so-called "illegal" activity by broadcasting while in modelling mode.

Therefore:

Note that the effect of the transfer of aesthetic competence to the technological field can be most fruitful, contributing both to solving current problems but also to developing technological competence.

11.6.9 Real-time Attributes of the Virtual Studio

The Essence of the Issue

The real-time attribute is central. This characteristic is of definitive importance to the expressive possibilities offered by the system.

Description of the Problem

The real-time attribute is central to the understanding of the virtual studio, and is aspired to for several reasons. The alternative to a real-time production, if one wants to achieve the same illusion of combining digital worlds and objects from the physical world, is to film the objects in monochrome surroundings and later combine keyed versions of these with renderings of digital scenographies in a post-production process. The possibilities for editing in post-production are much greater, but in contrast to the virtual studio, there is no possibility of interaction between the digital and the physical world. The real-time attribute is particularly important to two of the links in the sequence, the identification of the position of the camera and the rendering of pictures based on the position of the camera. These conditions have a strong influence on the possibilities for aesthetic expression.

Figure 11.16 Bjørn-Stjerne Christiansen from Superflex watches himself communicate with an avatar from *Karlskrona 2* on the monitor.

Case-specific Examples

Superflex's use of the virtual studio takes advantage of the real-time interaction between the studio host and the viewers who are watching the direct broadcast on *Superchannel*.

Therefore:

A strong awareness of the real-time attribute is a prerequisite for a successful project in the virtual studio.

11.6.10 The Technology of the Future in the Virtual Studio

The Essence of the Issue

What expectations can we allow ourselves to entertain for the technology of the future; in what areas will there be changes of importance to artistic productions in the virtual studio?

Figure 11.17 Rune Nielsen in the virtual room in the virtual studio, constructed of elements copied from *Karlskrona 2* in real time.

Description of the Problem

For some years now, there have been great expectations for developments in the computer field, yet even so, developments have astonished us again and again. In what areas will greater computer speeds and lower hardware prices influence the virtual studio? The following offers some suggestions as to the importance of development in central areas. More TV production companies will be able to afford to invest in virtual studio technology. At present technology is dependent on the presence of super-computers, but the first PC-based solutions are expected to be launched in the relatively near future. Also, developments in hardware and software in the field of image-generation will mean that the models used to generate pictures can become more complex, as can calculative models for things like light and shadow.

The technology of the virtual studio will thus be improved. These improvements will more or less solve the problems encountered by technology today, so there is no harm in attempting to press present technology to the utmost limits of its ability. Experience will presumably also be valuable in the future, where it will be possible to implement artistic ideas and concepts, which at present can only partially be put into effect. In the light of all this, a more detailed analysis of expected developments in technology can give us an idea of where the greatest changes will come, and where less change can be expected.

Case-specific Examples

The way Superflex uses the technology demonstrates a kind of outline of what it will be capable of in the future. For instance, when the project was carried out, it could not support modelling in real time, as was done in Superflex's second prototypical broadcast, where Rune Nielsen as studio host had Andreas Lykke-Olesen transfer models by copying those from *Karlskrona 2* to the virtual studio. This feature is, at the time of writing, partially supported by the newest version of the software.

Therefore:

Do not allow the development of aesthetic ideas to be hampered by current technological limitations.

11.7 Discussion

The outline of a pattern language presented in the previous section revolves around both social and technical issues related to artists working in the virtual studio. The themes and issues of the ten patterns quite naturally have strong similarities to the vast knowledge about the nature of practices in the domain of design of computer applications for work settings, but there are also some differences.

When designing computer applications for the workplace, one of the dominant paradigms has been that this is a co-operative effort where the designers learn about the work practice of the users and the users learn about potentiality of the technology (see, for instance, Bjerknes et al., 1986). Bødker et al. (1986, p. 254) puts it in this way in the context of a project about computer applications for graphical workers: "This makes a process of *mutual learning* possible in which e.g. graphics workers learn about the technical possibilities of computers, bit-mapped displays, lasers, etc., and the computer professionals learn about the computer professionals in question." Along the same tradition, co-operative prototyping (see Bødker and Grønbæk, 1991), puts strong focus on integrating technical knowledge and knowledge about work practice by communicating knowledge about new technology to users in terms of prototypes, which the user is able to relate directly to his or her current work practice.

In the cases discussed in this chapter there is a strong focus on the technical issues as reflected by patterns 11.6.1, 11.6.7, 11.6.9 and 11.6.10, whereas the concern for work practice obviously has been replaced by aesthetic issues, see patterns 11.6.2–11.6.6. While knowledge about current work practice is *the* essential starting point for the design of business applications (see, for instance, Greenbaum and Kyng, 1991; Beyer and Holtzblatt, 1998), aesthetic materials play the role of sources of inspiration or as a way to identify specific qualities aimed at (see pattern 11.6.3). The co-operative nature of the design of computer systems in general (see Greenbaum and Kyng, 1991; Schuler and Namioka, 1993), becomes even more essential when it comes to the production of digital art (see patterns 11.6.4 and 11.6.8). An essential element of co-operative design activities has been design by doing, which implies that design ideas emerge during practical hands-on experience (see pattern 11.6.5).

References

Alexander, C (1975). *The Oregon Experiment*. New York: Oxford University Press.

Alexander C (1979). *The Timeless Way of Building*. New York: Oxford University Press.

Alexander, C, Ishikawa, S and Silverstein, A et al. (1977). *A Pattern Language*. New York: Oxford University Press.

Beyer, H. and Holtzblatt, K (1998). *Contextual Design: Defining Customer Centered Systems*, San Francisco: Morgan Kaufman.

Bjerknes, G, Ehn, P and Kyng, M (eds.) (1986). *Computers and Democracy: A Scandinavian Challenge*. Brookfield, VE: Gower Publishing Company.

Bødker, S, Ehn, P, Kyng, M, Kammersgard, J and Sundblad,Y (1986). A Utopian Experience: On Design of Powerful Computer-Based Tools for Skilled Graphic Workers. In Bjerknes, Ehn and Kyng (1986, pp. 243–69).

Bødker, S and Grønbæk, K (1991). Design in Action: From Prototyping by Demonstration to Cooperative Prototyping. In Greenbaum and Kyng (1991, pp. 197–218).

Gamma E, Helm, R, Johnson, R and Vlissides, J (1995). *Design Patterns: Elements of Reuseable Object-Oriented Software*, Reading, MA: Addison-Wesley.

Greenbaum, J and Kyng, M (eds.) (1991). *Design at Work: Cooperative Design of Computer Systems*. Hillsdale, NJ: Lawrence Erlbaum Associates.

Jordan, B and Henderson, A (1994). *Interaction Analysis: Foundation and Practice*. Palo Alto, CA: Institute for Research and Learning (IRL 94-0027).

Kjeldskov, J and Nyvang, T (2000). *Lessons from Being There*. Aalborg University, Denmark.

Moshkovitz, M (2000). *The Virtual Studio*. Woburn, MA: Focal Press.

Nielsen, R (2002). Collaborative spaces: Inhabiting Virtual 3D Worlds. In L. Qvortrup (ed.), *Virtual Space: The Spatiality of Virtual Inhabited 3D Worlds*. London: Springer.

Schön, D (1983). *The Reflective Practitioner*. New York: Basic Books.

Schön D (1991). *Educating the Reflective Practitioner*. San Fransisco: Jossey-Bass.

Schuler, D and Namioka, A (eds.) (1993). *Participatory Design: Principles and Practices*. Hillsdale, NJ: Lawrence Erlbaum Associates.

12

Morgana: From Vision to Visualisation

Marie Christensen and Bettina Lamm

Marie Christensen holds a degree in communication from Roskilde University and has taught production planning and creativity techniques at a Multimedia Design College in Copenhagen for three years.

Bettina Lamm holds a degree in landscape architecture. She has worked as a designer in traditional landscape firms and as a project developer for a web firm. She is currently pursuing a PhD on spatial vocabularies in virtual reality art at the School of Architecture in Copenhagen.

Process is more important than outcome. When the outcome drives the process we will only ever go to where we've already been. If process drives outcome we may not know where we're going, but we will know we want to be there.

(An Incomplete Manifesto for Growth, Bruce Mau, 2000).

12.1 Introduction

12.1.1 How It All Began

When we initially met in 1998, we both found contemporary computer games boring and single dimensional. The majority of computer games that we encountered were testosterone-driven and targeted at a male audience. Where were the feminine, the poetic, the value-oriented or the aesthetically pleasing? We missed content and we missed being challenged by interesting concepts and stories that were meaningful and relevant to us.

This led to discussions about whether we were just naive in our ideas that it could be different or, whether it were true, what many people in the game business said: "Women don't play computer games", and "Games have to be competitive to be interesting". A natural follow-up question was then: "If we were to play a computer game, then what would that be?"

Morgana is an attempt to offer our personal answer to this question. We have now completed a demo version of Morgana.

12.1.2 Focal Points

In this article we have chosen to focus on the driving motivation and the visual expression as two focal points that together illustrate Morgana as a concept and a development process.

We will describe some key elements in the working process that illustrate how a project development can be driven entirely by personal involvement and vision. Our aim is to inspire other developers and to exemplify ways of running a loosely structured project. We have identified some main milestones in the working process that we think can be of relevance to others involved in similar projects.

Our second focus is the development of the visual expression and graphical techniques. We concentrated on specific corners of the Morgana environment and thereby defined an overall visual expression. In the investigation of different methods, techniques and graphical results, some key points have arisen, which we think can have a wider use in bringing the visualisation of ideas into concrete form.

We would like to emphasise that the following description is not a scientific documentation of a working process. We have not systematically recorded our moves and choices as we developed the project. Nor has our work on Morgana been based on any specific quantitative methodology. What is written here is our personal recollection of how we experienced the process and our reflections about what drove the project forward. Our hope is that we can inspire others working with multimedia development and production. Also we hope that people involved in the academic analytical field within digital media can get a glimpse of what a creative working process can be.

But before going into reflections and evaluations of specific areas of the working process, we think it is relevant to present a more general description of the Morgana concept.

12.2 Morgana

12.2.1 The Concept

Morgana is an inner voyage of discovery, mediated via a digital multimedia universe. In Morgana you play to explore, relate and grow. Entering Morgana is a spiritual and poetic journey into a landscape charged with symbolic meaning and fairytale atmosphere. The experience is not driven by violence or competition, but by the desire to learn about your own self.

A visit to a fortune-teller frames your inner journey. She will ask you to write a personal question that you wish to explore. You enter the Morgana landscape through her crystal ball, and her voice will guide you as you travel. She will help you realise your inner stories.

In Morgana, you journey through a living universe inhabited by mythological creatures and symbolic objects. You will encounter deserts and lava landscapes, gardens of paradise and deep forests; you will perhaps climb mountains and investigate hidden crystal grottoes. You explore the universe moving and interacting freely led by your own intuition. Your interaction with the characters, objects and puzzle-scenarios in the landscape creates a montage of stories. As you unfold the scenarios, you will bring life to the Morgana landscape.

All your moves and choices are tracked. When combined, they reflect your temperament and your potential. The outcome is an answer to your personal question and a decoding of your present state of mind. As your question and choices change from game to game, so does your experience and the outcome. Morgana is non-competitive and non-linear. There is no right or wrong way to play. You travel around freely, exploring the world and thereby yourself.

Morgana is an experience-based, adventure-like voyage. There is no competition and the goal lies not at the end of the voyage but within the process. It is your ongoing choice that is decisive. On the other hand, there is a clear objective and reward in the form of the prophecy. The divination offered in Morgana is not a revelation of the future, but a light in which to see the present.

12.2.2 The Environment

The Morgana environment is a landscape charged with symbolic meaning. Morgana consists of four landscapes based on the elements fire, water, earth and air (Figure 12.1). The inspiration comes from the medicine wheel, an ancient Native American symbol of earth astrology (Sun Bear, 1992). In the East lies the land of fire. The land-

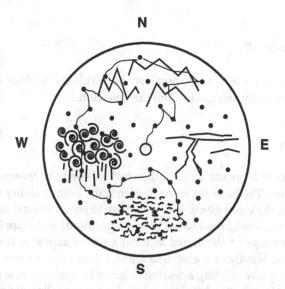

Figure 12.1 Diagram of the Morgana landscape with its four areas. Clockwise from top: Earth: forest; Air: cool mountains; Fire: volcanoes; and Water: lush gardens. Scenarios are connected by paths in the landscape.

scape is evolved from a foundation of lava, and hides an underworld of volcanic power. In the West a deep forest represents the earth element. The trees create a closed space, around the process of growth and destruction. In the North is the air landscape of snow-covered mountains, where the wind howls and the clear sound of crystals fills the air. The water world with its fruitful gardens is in the South. Strange and beautiful sea creatures inhabit its deep waters.

When moving through the Morgana landscape, the spatial sequence and rhythm tell their own story. The narrative is created in the investigation of places and events. The journey ties the story together and links the events that the participant meets on her way. The spatial structure makes up a connected whole, in which the participant can move around freely. Events are associated with places in the landscape and it is the interaction with these, which creates the prophecy. Each sequence, each series of actions in the individual realm, encircles and interprets the voyage's objective: to see a reflection of oneself.

You venture into Morgana through the fortune-teller's crystal ball and your starting point is Morgana's central node. From there you enter a network of connected paths and your journey can begin. Because the physical movement of the traveller has a symbolic meaning and is used in the divination, it has to be based on intuition and coincidence. Therefore there will be no map to guide you. You will never get stuck in a dead end, but it is possible to get lost. The sequence of actions is not important, but it is important that the participant travels widely around to collect the objects spread all over the landscape.

Each area in the landscape has four puzzles whose theme relates to the quality of the element, giving 16 puzzles altogether. Every puzzle can be solved by four different objects, one from each area. The theme of each puzzle is related to the area in which it can be met.

12.2.3 The Experience

The experience and user motivation can be divided into four central themes: personal gain, curiosity, interaction and identification.

Personal Gain

The driving force in Morgana is our human compulsion to be recognised and to elicit personal response. The basis for identification is the human ability to read personal significance into the input given. It is our ability to see a personal message in nearly every form of prophecy (from tea-leaves to star positions) that is applied in Morgana. The personal message or the sacred sign has a strong appeal to many women, not because it is used blindly as a guideline for all actions, but because it is a source of inspiration. It is a way to bring attention to issues by applying new evaluation positions. The trivial lines in the daily horoscope give you a small frame of mind in which to recognise the present mood and the day's event.

The point system, that defines the prophecy, is hidden and not important for the traveller. However, the creatures, places and objects that you favour are all given a value in a system that gives you a special profile at the end of each game. The texts describing the elements are based on a custom-made psychological analysis carried out by the Jungian psychologist Pia Skogemann. We have made two pre-tests so far, whereby she travelled through a scenario, analysing the symbols and the interaction. These analyses will be a tool for shaping the written divinations. Since this part is crucial to the user's experience of Morgana, it has to be professional in both content and form.

Curiosity

We have asked about 100 women whether they played computer games and if so, what kind of games they played and it seems that short puzzles like Tetris and Solitaire are very popular. Women seem to prefer challenges that take some thinking, but not too much time. Each of Morgana's 16 puzzles represents a certain notion connected to the given element. In the Earth landscape, for instance, the themes are "To Protect", "To Create", "To Give" and "To Seed". When interacting with the scenery, the notion is brought into action and the intent is to transfer the symbolic meaning to the user, so that she herself feels "Protecting", "Creating", "Giving" or "Seeding".

The puzzles are neither obvious nor easy, so the user will have to try different possibilities before the action succeeds. Sometimes a solution is found fairly easily, but the action itself is then hard to complete. In both cases the reward plays an important role. Some puzzles end with a small animation that completes the scenario. In that way the user is told that her interaction has been successful and the scenario is fulfilled. A fulfilled scenario, however, is still interactive; the user can return many times just to play with the sounds, shapes or movements.

Interaction

The interaction can be described through its frequency degree, meaning and feeling. A product can feel very interactive without having a very high degree of interactive possibilities. This feeling can either come from the consequences of the interaction or from the personal associations created in the user while interacting. The interaction degree is very high in Morgana. The cursor icon is used in very many variations and that gives an array of tools and objects to use within the world. Also, the way the mouse is used is significant for the experience of a high degree of interaction. For example, you have come to a pool where a large orange fish is swimming about. By using specific objects with a circular, slow movement the fish will dive; on clicking slowly it will jump; and by clicking fast it will splash. As regards the interaction frequency, the goal is to offer possible interaction at every step of the journey. Because the landscape is filled with realistic objects and creatures, it is also natural to expect that these will react to your touch. It is an important goal that the universe will be experienced as living and dynamic.

Identification

In Morgana the user interacts as herself and the screen is her window to the Morgana universe. All her actions are, on an abstract level, directly connected to her own personality. She is told to travel in her own subconscious and that she will encounter her own inner landscape. She knows that the journey will end with a personal answer to her question, which is related to this precise moment and situation. With these parameters we intend to create a close identification with the universe and that will be the most important step in creating the feeling of interactivity and meaning.

12.3 The Working Process

The development of Morgana is driven by dreams and enthusiasm. Our vision is to develop a concept that connects technology with emotional growth and insight. The vision is based on our personal curiosity and commitment. Morgana is therefore a highly idealistic project.

So what does it take to bring ideals into reality?

12.3.1 The Driving Motivation

Motivation is obviously important if you want to bring a project from idea to completion. A large part of our motivation was based on a continuous learning and experience process. Such a motivation will eventually lead to new insight that will change the defined goal and plans. When the project changes direction and maybe also content, how can you keep up the energy and motivation to continue? In our experience the "vision" is an efficient tool, as it has enabled us to navigate among unforeseen difficulties, new knowledge and changes of plans.

A vision is not necessarily realistic. It is not founded on the possible or the likely. The vision is only grounded in what we think is good or what we think ought to be realistic. A vision is based on qualities we can dream about, not specific goals we can plan towards. Because it deals with qualitative dimensions, a vision can remove the pressure of reality and release energy and resources that might bring the project further than what was actually realistic to start with.

Our vision was founded in a longing for interactive games that we wanted to play. The vision was also based on some questions that we wanted to investigate. Hence, the process of developing the Morgana concept was an investigation of possibilities within interactive digital entertainment. The first question was: is it possible to create a game where I play as my self? In so many games one had to identify with an avatar, a character. We wanted personal involvement. We secondly asked: is it possible to use a spatial structure of a symbolically charged landscape as a narrative frame? Many game developers battled with the apparent contradiction between narrativity and interactivity. We thought we might be able to solve this through a spatial structure. We also asked: is it possible to create a game targeted towards a female audience? We wanted to find out if the preferences of men and women really were so different. Finally we asked whether it was possible to make a spiritual experience and a divination system that seemed meaningful. It was not about truth or prediction but about supplying input to a personal situation.

Our shared vision has served as a leading star towards the first goal – the creation of the Morgana demo. It has been important that the vision could be expressed in a few qualitative lines such as: "We want to approach a female audience by bringing emotions and personal growth into CD-ROM entertainment". This is a very abstract vision with lots of room for individual interpretation and ideas, but it is not precise enough to make the link to the actual interface and interaction design. To raise adequate funding and attract professional co-workers, more concrete goals had to be set, so that the continuous learning process could go on. Our solution has been to put the question: "*How* can this vision be fulfilled"? The *how* forces one to become concrete and to focus on possible solutions. With the *how* things must be given a form, an expression.

We had some goals that focused on what kind of experience the protagonist should have in Morgan. We want to give the user freedom of movement within a fictive landscape. We wanted to provide a tactile experience of manipulating objects in a highly responsive environment. We wanted the visual atmosphere to be rich, complex and organic; the computer graphics had to be supplemented with texture mappings from original objects. We want to reach a new target group: by researching the target group's game habits and possible wants, by researching similar existing products (astrology and Tarot CD-ROMs, angel cards, new-age literature etc.) with appeal to the target group and by using parameters like meditation, intuition and personal profiling.

The point is to distinguish between goals at different levels and not to set any restrictive goal too early in the process. As described, the vision is the abstract leading star at the top level, to reach down through the goal levels we ask *how* and to get back up again we ask *why*. In that way we could distinguish between practical assignments and future hopes.

12.3.2 Milestones on the Way

Another motivation lies in actual, practical milestones, such as concept presentations for multimedia companies and deadlines for funding applications. These milestones have forced us to re-evaluate the quality of the project, the content of the scenarios, the user experience and future goals for the project. Without an external client it can be hard to keep up speed and motivation. So to force the project forward, we found it very productive to set up meetings both with possible users and production companies. Every time we had to communicate the project to others we became clearer about the central concept. Also we received valuable feedback that gave us new ideas to work with.

We wrote funding applications to the EU MEDIA II Programme and to the Danish Ministry of Cultural Affairs and it forced us to clarify our ideas in writing. The EU application also had a number of very specific questions about the product that they wanted answered in short and concise writing. These were, for example: "In which ways is your project particularly suited for a interactive multimedia format?", "What kind of experience will the user have?", "How does the navigation work?" and "What is the look and feel?" Those kinds of questions force one to make conceptual choices.

The descriptions were very useful to us when we later needed to communicate our vision to the team involved in the project. We were also required to deliver a budget along with our application for developing the demo of Morgana. Therefore it became necessary to be very specific about what needed to be done, how it would be done, who would participate and what each step would cost. These elements are of course natural parts of a traditional project plan, but since our project structure was very loose, this milestone became a valuable alternative.

12.3.3 Intuition as a Tool

The third important motivator has been intuition. To examine new ideas, we have found inspiration within the spheres of the magical. With the Tarot we have explored various perspectives of potential decisions and alternative solutions. Intuition has proven to be a strong tool, perhaps especially because of the nature of the project and our working style. According to the American Heritage Dictionary definition, "intuition" means "the act or faculty of knowing or sensing without the use of rational processes or a sense of something not evident or deducible; an impression". Intuition is, however, not an act of random decision-making. Rather it has to do with knowing without logical reasoning, when something seems right in relation to the overall concept. Intuition can be described as an immediate perception of a whole or of relations without prior logical thinking. Through intuition one senses when a problem is solved and whether the right solution has been reached.

Because Morgana is more closely related to an art project than to any kind of science, intuition is an acceptable source of knowledge and can be justifiably used for making important decisions. In broader terms we can call it inspiration and association and in our opinion, most creative and innovative development must involve these sources in its work process. The difference, for instance, between a systematic and an intuitive process would be that, in a systematic process, one would follow several ideas and then compare and choose the best of them, whereas an intuitive process would slowly encircle one theme guided by an idea. An intuitive working process could be defined as associative and circular.

Intuition can also have to do with starting a process without knowing what the exact outcome is. The quote from Bruce Mau at the beginning of this chapter has almost been a manifesto for us, making us focus on one step at a time, without immediately pouncing on the solution. As he says, you can only come up with new things, if you dare venture into the process without constantly trying to picture the final result. One important thing in the creative process seems to be to feed the mind with material that can ignite new thoughts and visions. Materials like images, objects, books, stories, keywords, and games can open up associations and hence start ideas rolling. The Tarot cards (Crowley) with all their symbols and themes, were useful because their typology is closely related to the subject matter of Morgana.

In our opinion it is important to make room in the plans for evaluation and also for the actions that this may recommend. After working a whole year with a certain line of ideas, we felt that the project was losing energy and we had a lot of loose ends in the concept. After an evaluation, where we used a PMI method (a list with Plus, Minus and Interesting factors), we decided to throw the old system away and start all over again with a much simpler and more universal system – the four elements. When the demo was completed we did yet another evaluation of Morgana. We invited four people from the field whose opinions we regarded highly to an input workshop. It was deliberately called an input workshop, as we wanted to stay focused on the possible solutions rather than on the problems. Hence, the core question for the group was "what will it take to make the scenarios fun, the divination relevant, and the target group motivated". It can be very hard to find time and money to do this re-evaluation in commercially driven projects, but, on the other hand, these sessions widen the possibility of success; we, as a developing team, kept our motivation and work speed and the concept improved.

12.4 Visualising the Vision

Visualisation is all about giving shape to a vision; about giving ideas a concrete form. In this process, we have used models of various fortune-telling systems. The Morgana universe is inspired by the Native American medicine wheel. It is based on the four elements, or "temperaments", air, water, earth, and fire, also found in astrology, in Tarot cards, and in the archetypes of Jung. Each element is a symbolic expression of a temperament: thoughts, emotions, reason and spirituality.

12.4.1 Collaging Expressions

Through discussions and readings of books about the medicine wheel, we translated each of the four elements into their most apparent landscape counterpart. Water is related to emotion and fertility. We wanted a watery place, but also some place where water helped other things grow. Water gardens with lush bright colours, fruits and flowers seemed to be appropriate. Earth is related to the physicality and cyclic experience of life. The forest with its materiality and brown colours was an obvious choice. For air that represents the thought we wanted something fresh, light and clear. Snow-covered mountains with a fresh breeze and a far-reaching vision were chosen to represent this element. Fire was the most difficult element to pinpoint. The element refers to energy and will, but it also means spirituality. An obvious choice was a volcanic landscape but we also wanted to avoid creating the impression of a dry desert. These interpretations of elements into landscape features are entirely our own translations and not something directly related to the Native American medicine wheel or Jung.

By making collages, we were able to approach a visual expression of the Morgana landscape that matched the four psychological temperaments. With a large paper collage of images from magazines and books, we worked towards framing the atmosphere and expression of the four landscapes (see Figure 12.2). This helped us define textures, colours and elements significant to each area. Rather than expecting all ideas to come directly from our own imagination, we used pictures from other sources to foster inspiration and associations. This process also helped us communicate and share our own inner, vague ideas of how we each imagined the atmosphere and moods of Morgana. At this point in the process we had not yet scripted the specific scenarios. We only knew that we wanted to create a landscape filled with symbolic meaning and atmosphere that reflected the four elements. First we created the environment, and then we created the events that would take place within that environment. Lisa Lopuck (1996) suggests that in multimedia projects one should design places rather than screen shots. When creating her own storyboards, she described the environments prior to writing the stories related to them. This confirmed that we were on the right track.

The same method of working with collages was continued on the computer. In PhotoShop we created images that could be an example of scenery that one would

Figure 12.2 Paper collage of the four Morgana landscapes. Clockwise from top: Air, Fire, Water and Earth.

meet when journeying through Morgana. There are many photo databases on the Internet and by searching these we found images that could be associated to our environment. We trimmed and rearranged elements from images and assembled them into possible Morgana landscape vistas (see Figure 12.3).

(a)

(b)

Figure 12.3 (a) Fire landscape collage; (b) Earth landscape collage; (c) and (d) *Continued over page.*

(c)

(d)

Figure 12.3 (c) Air landscape collage; (d) Water landscape collage.

The goal was to visualise the atmosphere of the environment rather than make an exact description. When confronted with actual material, it becomes much easier to approach a definition of what the places could consist of, than it would have been, by trying to imagine it all within the mind. We had inner associations and images, but they were vague and non-communicable. Hence, making the collages was both a design process as well as a visualisation of an atmosphere. It is difficult to say what the exact criteria of selection were. Our choices were motivated by the question "What kind of elements could I meet in Morgana?" In the design process one is merely focused on what seems to work and therefore those elements, which do not, are quickly discarded and forgotten.

The method of using photographed images in the working process has definitely had an impact on the mode of the final visual expression. With photographs one works with elements that somehow already exist physically in the world. The images are photo-realistic; the abstraction comes from how the elements are assembled. The result is close to a surrealistic expression of recognisable objects in strange and unexpected constellations. We did not necessarily strive for photo-realism in the sense that a scene in Morgana could not be distinguished from a view in the primary world. Still, we wanted complexity, texture and detail, something that can be difficult to get in images made from scratch on a computer.

12.4.2 Mapping the Manuscript

Combining the collages with a basic model for the fortune-telling scenarios, we began creating the events that would take place within the landscape. Thus, atmosphere, place and structure were developed before the interactive elements. Switching from manuscript to a visual process and back again was a cyclic experience. The images not only helped us pinpoint and share the expression of the Morgana environment, it also fostered ideas for the manuscript. Pictures of strange animals and objects gave ideas about the beings who might inhabit these landscapes we had created, and the elements suggested some of the scenarios we were about to create. Both for the visual expression and for the scenarios our main goal was to approach the essence of the four elements. What was really their concern in terms of atmosphere and as themes for events?

The script-writing process was long and tedious. We needed exciting stories with a clear symbolic content, but we also needed a structure that was manageable for an interpretation system to work. After having spent many hours building complex story lines and symbolic interactions inspired by concepts from the Tarot, we discarded it all. Our interactive scenarios were interesting, we thought, but we soon realised that if we wanted to track the protagonists moves and choices within Morgana and use these choices as a foundation for a fortune-telling system, we had to make them manageable in a systematic way. Before we could make stories with scenarios, we had to make a structure or system for these scenarios. So we cleaned everything off the table and started all over again. This was a difficult step to take because, after working for months, one is suddenly left with nothing. Back to scratch! "Kill your darlings!", to quote a famous saying. Our experience is that sometimes one gets so fixated on a singular idea that it gets in the way of evolving the concept. Rather than being a step back, it can be a great leap forward.

We still had our landscape with the four elements represented and an idea that small puzzles in the landscape would provide an outcome in terms of a divination. As

Figure 12.4 A map describing landscape features and relations between narrated scenarios.

soon as we had cleaned the table and re-evaluated what was the essence and core concept of Morgana, a very clear model appeared to us making it possible to structure the many scenarios that we wanted in the game.

Once we had narrated each scenario, we created a large map placing them into a landscape with paths and areas (see Figure 12.4). The person travelling through Morgana would never encounter this map but we wanted to create the experience of a coherent world. The traveller journeys through a world with four distinct but connected landscapes. On her way she encounters events and riddles in the landscape that she can engage in. The map helped us orchestrate the relation between the scenarios and at the same time outline the local environment related to each of them. The map in a way became both the flowchart and the foundation for designing the visual expression. For the demo we had decided to focus on three of the scenarios that belonged to three of the four landscape types.

1. East/Fire – The Steam Plain – To Control. You walk through a dry, reddish landscape and arrive at an eroded plain full of holes. Small clouds of steam spurt out of the holes. If you block one of them, the steam underground will be compressed slightly and the pressure will send a small lizard up out through the hole. If you find the right combination, you will be able to compress the steam enough for larger animals such as chameleons and salamanders to fly up through the holes. The greater the pressure, the more animals you bring into the world.

2. West/Earth – The Flowering Fence – To Fertilise. A raven sits in a tree in the forest. In its beak, it has a butterfly chrysalis. If you bring out a shiny object, the raven

will dive down and take it. When it opens its beak it drops the chrysalis and a butterfly flies out of it. The butterfly flies away to a flowering fence nearby. If you click on the butterfly, you can use it to pollinate the flowers. As it works, the flowers become transformed into fruits, and the fruits will slowly ripen, rot and fall to the ground.

3. South/Water – The Pool – To Bring Together. Two big pools of water rest on a fertile, green, flowering meadow. The pools are made of carved stone and they are connected by a strangely shaped maze. In the first pool, a big orange fish swims around in the clear water. In the other pool is its black counterpart. Your assignment is now to guide either the orange fish through the maze into the pool where the black fish resides or visa versa. When you have brought the two fish together, they will reproduce and the pool will be filled with small orange- and black-spotted fish.

12.4.3 Designing the Demo

In the initial design phase that culminated in a demo of Morgana, we sought to investigate the graphical atmosphere rather than the overall story-line. We wanted to explore specific corners of the Morgana environment and thereby get to the overall visual expression. We explored the interaction and visuals in the three scenarios to get a more precise understanding of the experience. This was done by implementing the puzzles working with a 3D graphic designer and a programmer. This process also brought us closer to understanding the process and communication skills necessary in a full production.

We had three key words for the visual expression in Morgana: complex, organic and textural. The complexity consists of richness of detail, depth and variation. The organic aspect comes from natural elements such as parts of plants, stones, soils, seeds and animals. We wanted Morgana's graphic dimension to be found somewhere between fiction and reality: fictional, in the sense that it could be a landscape found in fairytales or mythological stories; real, in the sense that it refers to familiar landscapes with a high textural intensity. We took great care in choosing the graphic designer who was to help us realise our vision of Morgana. Not only did this person have to master the tools; he or she also needed the aesthetic skills that matched our ambitions.

In order to communicate our ideas to the graphic designer, we spent a lot of time making descriptions, diagrams, sketches and reference images for each of the three scenarios. A website for each scenario/landscape contained all this information organised by content, with themes like animals, surfaces, elements in the landscape, plants and sky (see Figure 12.5). For the Steam Plain Scenario, for instance, there were sections that individually described in pictures the quality of the overall landscape, the soil texture, the lava, the steam plain, the plant life and the animals. We collected a large number of reference images from Internet searches for each element in the landscape. This helped us communicate our ideas to the graphic designer but it also certainly helped us define for ourselves what kind of expression

Figure 12.5 A photo of the Copenhagen Harbour sky was used in the Steam Plain Scenario.

we wanted. Looking through image databases for strange elements and landscapes was very inspiring, and objects and animals appeared which we perhaps couldn't have imagined ourselves, but which seemed just right for our environment.

On the website, one could also find a detailed scenario description including interactive elements and moving parts, a colour chart, a plan drawing of the selected area and sketches of stills through the landscape. Colours were very important and we created colour schemes from our original collages for each of the three scenario environments (see Figure 12.6). We even built a model of a section of the landscape leading up to the Steam Plain Scenario and photographed the journey the user would take in order to examine what kind of spatial experience she would have. We realised, however, that this exercise gave very little information in relation to the actual time it

Figure 12.6 Colour chart for the Steam Plain Scenario in the fire landscape.

Figure 12.7 Photographed flower and leaf for the Pool Scenario in the water landscape.

took to test. We found out that a simple 3D model could quickly be changed and adjusted to the expression desired and was therefore easier to design with.

All the diagrams, images and illustrations on the reference website formed the base material for creating the actual visuals. It was important to find a balance where we could lead the course in getting our vision realised and at the same time leave room for the designer to add his interpretation to the project. We had meetings approximately every second or third workday in order to keep the visual development on the right track.

We made experiments with 3D modelling, but found that the models lacked complexity. We wanted to get closer to that rich textural expression found in actual physical materials in the natural world. With a digital camera we began photographing objects and texture that somehow had a reference to the Morgana landscapes. Now we saw that the organic complexity could be captured, but we still needed depth and perspective in the environments. A simple 3D wire frame model of the landscape matching the Morgana map was built, and photographed objects and textures were added. These were, for instance, plants, skies, and surfaces (see Figure 12.7). Some elements that needed to be turned or moved around were built in 3D with a texture from a picture taken with the digital camera. Other elements were like a stage set in the theatre, cut out and placed as 2D objects in the 3D landscape.

Figure 12.8 Photographs of trees for the Flowering Fence Scenario in the earth landscape.

The forest was created from our own photographs of carefully selected trees (see Figure 12.8). We trimmed and manipulated the images of the trees until they had reached the right expression. The trees were placed into the 3D model with the desired composition. The trees look real or perhaps rather present and convincing. One gets the impression of walking through a forest with both spatial depth and rich detail. It does not look like a photographed forest but it has forest quality, perhaps like a forest one would encounter or imagine in a fairytale.

On the basis of our storyboard, 2D stills of the rendered model were taken. The pictures are strung together and create the structure and a coherent world. This method was chosen because we have given great richness of detail priority over speed and full mobility. We are still exploring these methods, but it seems to give exactly the results we are looking for (see Figures 12.9–12.12).

(a)

(b)

Figure 12.9 (a) View into eastern fire landscape: Volcanoes; (b) The Steam Plain Scenario in the fire landscape.

12.5 Future

Now we have a manuscript, a design document and a demo of Morgana. The project has so far been driven entirely by enthusiasm and personal vision. We have taken the time we needed and we have not been pushed by demands from investors or publishers. But in order to develop the concept into a full product we will, however,

Figure 12.10 (a) View into western earth landscape: Forest; (b) The Flowering Fence Scenario in the earth landscape.

need to partner up with companies that can supply funding, production, marketing and distribution facilities. This will be a huge step, as we will no doubt have to move the development from a personal and intuitive process towards a more structured and managed process.

(a)

(b)

Figure 12.11 (a) View into southern water landscape: Lush gardens; (b) The Pool Scenario in the water landscape.

Figure 12.12 View into the northern air landscape: Cool mountains.

Acknowledgments

We have learned a lot from discussing our ideas with colleagues in the game business and with the people employed to help us investigate our visions. These people are Arthur Steijn, Guus Oosterbaan, Antonin Rustwijk, Pia Skoogemand, Kim Sandholdt and Poul Møller and they each have contributed greatly in making Morgana something unique.

The Morgana project is developed with the support of the MEDIA Programme of the European Union and the Danish Ministry of Cultural Affairs (KUF).

References

American Heritage Dictionary of the English Language (2000) 4th edition, Houghton Mifflin Company, Lexico.com http://www.dictionary.com/search?q=intuition

Brødslev Olsen, J (1991). *Kreativitet i forskning og projektarbejde* [Creativity in Research and Project Work], TNP – serien nr. 18, Aalborg Universitetscenter, Aalborg, Denmark.

Christensen, M and Fischer, LH (2000). *Udvikling af multimedier – en helhedsorienteret metode* [Development of Multimedia, a Holistic Method], Copenhagen: Ingeniøren.

Christensen, S and Kreiner, K (1991). *Projektledelse i løst koblede systemer* [Project Management in Loosely Co-ordinated Systems], Denmark: Jurist- og Økonomiforbundets Forlag.

Crowley, A and Harris, F (1972). *The Crowley Thoth Tarot*, Neuhausen: Urania Verlags AG.

Fleming, J (1998). *Web Navigation: Designing for the User Experience*, Cambridge, MA: O'Reilly Associates.

Karcher, S (1997). *The Illustrated Encyclopedia of Divination: A Practical Guide to the Powers that Shape your Destiny*, USA: Element Books Ltd.

Lopuck, L (1996). *Designing Multimedia*, Berkeley, CA: Peachpit Press.

Mau, B (2000). *Life Style*, London: Phaidon Press.

Olsson, JR and Albæk, P (2001). *Projektets målsætning* [The Aim of the Project], Denmark: Børsen Forum.

Sun Bear and Wabu Wind (1992) *The Medicine Wheel, Earth Astrology*, Lithia Springs, USA: New Leaf Distributors.

Wimberley, D and Samsel, J (1996). *Interactive Writers Handbook*, USA: The Carronade Group.

Ziegler, G (1988). *Mirror of the Soul: Handbook for the Aleister Crowley Tarot*, Boston, MA: Red Wheel/Weiser.

Author Index